BOOKS IN BLOOM

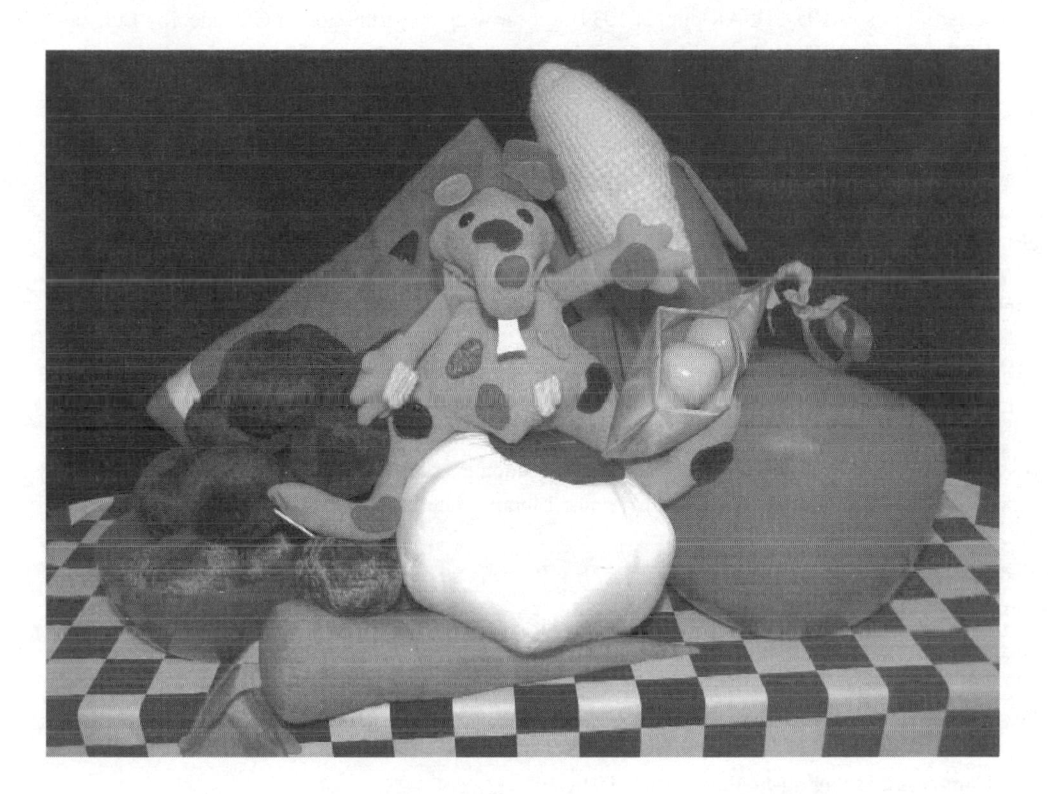

Creative Patterns and Props That Bring Stories to Life

KIMBERLY K. FAUROT

AMERICAN LIBRARY ASSOCIATION

Chicago 2003

The prop patterns contained in this book are intended for personal use by educators. If anyone uses the patterns to create multiple copies of the prop for sale or to present the materials for professional paid shows, they must obtain the primary designer's written permission for use of the pattern, the scriptwriter's written permission for use of the script (if it varies significantly from the original text of the book), and express written permission from the original work's publisher.

Every effort has been made to trace the ownership of all copyrighted material and to secure the necessary permissions to include the material as you see it in this volume. I would like to express apologies for any inadvertent omissions. Grateful acknowledgement is made to the following for permission to reprint the copyrighted material listed below.

The paper used in this publication meets the minimum requirements of American National Standard for Information Sciences—Permanence of Paper for Printed Library Materials, ANSI Z39.48-1992. ♾

Design and composition by ALA Editions in Times New Roman and Tekton using QuarkXPress 5.0 on a PC platform

Printed on 50-pound white offset, a pH-neutral paper, and bound in 10-point cover stock by Victor Graphics

Library of Congress Cataloging-in-Publication Data

Faurot, Kimberly K.

Books in bloom : creative patterns and props that bring stories to life / Kimberly K. Faurot.

p. cm.

Includes bibliographical references.

ISBN 0-8389-0852-7 (alk. paper)

1. Storytelling—United States. 2. Children's libraries—Activity programs—United States. 3. Libraries and puppets—United States. 4. Storytelling—United States—Audio-visual aids. I. Title.

Z718.3.F38 2003

027.62'51—dc21 2003003819

Printed in the United States of America

07 06 05 04 03 5 4 3 2 1

Contents

ACKNOWLEDGMENTS *vii*

1

Introduction 1

This Book Is for You *1*
What Is Included *1*
Reasons for Using Multiple Presentation Formats *2*
  Developmental Characteristics *2*
  Providing Something Special *2*
  Inspiring Young Audiences *2*
Quality Storytelling Props *3*
Practical Issues *4*
  Time, Money, and Ability *4*
  Types of Stories That Can Be Adapted *4*
  Additional Considerations *5*
  Adapting the Text *5*
  Choosing Format and Media *6*
  Copyright Issues *6*
  Accessibility and Storage *8*
Let Your Imagination Take Flight *8*
References *8*

2

Tips and Tools 10

Enlarging the Patterns in This Book *10*
Recommended Tools and Materials for Effective Prop Building *11*
  Glues *11*
  Paints and Brushes *11*
  Fabrics *11*
  Craft and Miscellaneous Supplies *11*
  Scissors *12*
  Hand Tools *12*
  Power Tools *12*
Terms and Techniques *12*
  Visual Storytelling *12*
  Materials *12*
  Sewing *13*
  Knots *14*
  Fusing and Scoring *14*
Sample Permission Form *15*
Sample Storytelling Props Collection List or Database *16*

3

Puppet and Prop Assembly Stories 17

Techniques and Considerations *18*
  Creating *18*
  Presenting *18*
Choosing the Prop Assembly Format *19*
PUPPET AND PROP ASSEMBLY STORIES—
Poppy the Panda by Dick Gackenbach *20*

Script 22
Assembly Instructions (very easy; estimated 2 hours assembly time) 26
Assembly Story Finished Product 27
Storage 29
Summary 29

4

Overhead Projector Stories 30

Techniques and Considerations 30
Creating 30
Presenting 32
Choosing the Overhead Projector Format 32
OVERHEAD PROJECTOR STORIES—
A Color of His Own by Leo Lionni 33
Script 35
Pattern Instructions (easy; estimated 3 hours) 37
Directions 38
How to Make the Transparency Pieces 38
Overhead Projector Story Finished Product 41
Pattern Pieces 43
Storage 53
Summary 54

5

Finger Puppets 55

Techniques and Considerations 55
Creating 55
Presenting 56
Choosing the Finger Puppet Format 56
FINGER PUPPETS—
"Mouse House" 57
Possible Introduction 58
Script 58
Possible Conclusion 60
Other Activities 60
Pattern Instructions (easy; estimated 2 to 4 hours) 61
Directions 62
How to Make the Finger Puppet Mice 62
How to Make the Mouse House 65
Finger Puppets Finished Product 67
Pattern Pieces 68
Storage 71
Summary 71

6

Flannel/Felt Board Stories 72

Techniques and Considerations 73
Creating 73
General Techniques for Creating Flannel/Felt Board Story Pieces 75
Presenting 77
Choosing the Flannel/Felt Board Format 78
FLANNEL/FELT BOARD STORIES—
Fish Is Fish by Leo Lionni 79
Script 81
Pattern Instructions (medium; estimated 6 hours) 84
Directions 85
How to Make the Background Scene 85
How to Make the Story Figures 88
Flannel/Felt Board Story Finished Product 91
Pattern Pieces 93
Storage 105
Summary 106

7

Combination Prop Stories 107

Techniques and Considerations 107
Creating 107
Presenting 108

Choosing the Combination Prop Format *109*
COMBINATION PROP STORIES—
The Most Wonderful Egg in the World by Helme Heine *110*
Script *112*
Other Activities *115*
Pattern Instructions (medium; estimated 10 hours) *116*
Directions *117*
How to Make the Three Adult Chickens *117*
How to Make the Eggs and Baby Chickens *120*
How to Make the Royal Nest *122*
Combination Prop Story Finished Product *122*
Pattern Pieces *123*
Storage *128*
Summary *129*

8
Stick Puppets/ Rod Puppets *130*

Techniques and Considerations *131*
Creating *131*
Presenting *131*
Choosing the Stick Puppet Format *132*
STICK PUPPETS/ROD PUPPETS—
The Nightgown of the Sullen Moon by Nancy Willard *134*
Script *136*
Pattern Instructions (advanced; estimated 20 hours) *140*
Directions *143*
How to Make the Lap/Tabletop Theater and Covering *143*
How to Make the Stick Puppets *144*
How to Make the Nightgowns *147*
How to Make the Miscellaneous Additional Story Pieces *151*
Stick Puppet Story Finished Product *152*
Pattern Pieces *154*
Storage *162*
Summary *163*

9
Hand Puppets *164*

Techniques and Considerations *164*
Creating *164*
Presenting *165*
Choosing the Hand Puppet Format *167*
HAND PUPPETS—
Lunch by Denise Fleming *169*
Possible Introduction *171*
Script *173*
Possible Conclusion *174*
Pattern Instructions (expert; estimated 40 hours) *175*
Directions *179*
How to Make the Mouse Puppet *179*
How to Make the Giant Soft Sculpture Food and Accompanying Food Pieces *186*
Puppet Story Finished Product *199*
Pattern Pieces *200*
Storage *224*
Summary *224*

10
Resources *226*

Favorite Storytime Planners *226*
Bibliography of Storybooks, Stories, and Poems Included or Mentioned in *Books in Bloom* *226*
Books for Further Professional Reading on the Topics and Media Covered in *Books in Bloom* *226*
Internet Resources *228*
Finding Out-of-Print or Used Books *228*
Sound Recordings *228*

Hand Puppets and Finger Puppets *228*
Ready-Made Storytelling Props and Miscellaneous *228*
Book Character Dolls and Toys *229*
Cheap Novelty Items (Crowns and Miscellaneous Cool Stuff) *229*
Craft Supplies *229*
Fabrics and Some Craft Supplies *230*
Colored Acetate/Transparencies *230*
Die-Cut Companies *230*
Flannel Boards and Velcro Boards *230*
General Library Supplies (Colored Corrugated Hinged-Lid Storage Boxes) *231*
Overhead Projectors *231*

Acknowledgments

Special thanks to the following individuals:

Brad Kruse

Cathy Norris and the Children's Department staff, past and present, of the Hedberg Public Library, Janesville, Wisconsin

Beth Murray for *The Most Wonderful Egg in the World* pattern design and script

Kathy Kennedy Tapp for "Mouse House" pattern design

Dr. Shirley Fitzgibbons

Denise Fleming and David Powers

Melissa Brechon, Janet Karius, Brenda Youngdahl, and the staff of the Carver County Library System, Minnesota

All ALA Editions staff who worked on this project, including

Renée Vaillancourt McGrath, consulting editor

Patrick Hogan, editorial director

Jennifer Palmer, editorial assistant

Dianne M. Rooney, design and composition manager

Angela Gwizdala, production editor

Eloise L. Kinney, project editor

Ann Marie Damian, proofreader

1 Introduction

This Book Is for You

Books in Bloom is designed as a practical guide to sharing stories and poetry with children through quality prop, flannel board, and puppet presentations. Many children's librarians, teachers, and day-care workers regularly create flannel board pieces and props to accompany and dramatize picture books and stories. Resources to help us adapt these stories artistically to reflect the original books' aesthetics, however, are rare. This volume contains high-quality patterns that have copyright permissions granted as well as script adaptations, with suggestions for using the pieces to the fullest to truly engage an audience. I believe that anyone who is striving to share literature with children in a manner that will spark their imaginations in new and alternative ways can benefit from the techniques, suggestions, sample scripts, and patterns in this book.

What Is Included

Each chapter in *Books in Bloom* includes a brief discussion of a particular type of physical media into which stories or poetry can be effectively adapted. For each medium, an example of a story or poem that works well in that format is presented along with a pattern and detailed step-by-step instructions for creating it. Each pattern is accompanied by a script for using the flannel or prop story with a group, including suggested setup, presentation, and movement notes. Each pattern also includes estimated difficulty, estimated construction time, estimated cost of materials, recommended age group, possible themes, and presentation running time.

Chapter 10 contains a bibliography of professional works related to the various media represented in *Books in Bloom* as well as resource lists for supplies. I have also listed some of my personal favorite storytime planning helpers and several quick-and-easy storytime pattern books as well as the citations for the picture books, stories, and poems included or mentioned in *Books in Bloom.*

Reasons for Using Multiple Presentation Formats

Throughout history, humans around the world have used realia, masks, puppetry, "magic," drama, storytelling, music, art, and dance to enhance audiences' experiences and to keep their attention for the purposes of religion, entertainment, and education.

Teachers and librarians have long recognized the advantages of employing elements from these diverse art forms in their work with young people. In the United States, the focus on organized preschool education that began in the early 1800s with "infant schools" and that developed into the Kindergarten Movement around 1860 encouraged the use of realia and visuals on a regular basis.

Developmental Characteristics

The defined developmental characteristics of preschool and early elementary age children suggest that the learning processes of this age group are significantly enhanced by intensive visual components. Many children today are avid television watchers and computer users, and as a result they are even more visually oriented than ever. Children's attention spans are likewise discernibly decreasing. Changing societal factors have urged children's group programming to be less restrictive, with the result that groups are often both large and intergenerational. Maintaining the interest and attention of these audiences requires flexibility and at least a little bit of pizzazz. One way of achieving this can be through visual storytelling, where older participants' interest can be maintained orally while younger participants are engaged through the use of visuals.

As we understand more about the diversity of human learning styles, it is clear that individual children will engage differently with different presentation methods. Some children may respond best to the standard-size book that is read; some to a Big Book. Other children may only fully connect with a puppet; some may learn best by acting out a story. Many children need to experience a single story in multiple ways to fully assimilate it. Special needs students in particular often benefit dramatically from being able to touch objects representing the parts of a story. It is therefore extremely important to include a variety of formats in storytelling and teaching.

Providing Something Special

When sharing stories with a group that includes both children and caregivers, we have two important responsibilities as educators and professionals. The first is as models, giving the caregivers ideas of how they might extend stories in a way they can achieve on their own at home or in their classrooms. This may simply be the idea of making animal noises that sound animal-like or using a gruff voice for a large character and a squeaky voice for a tiny character. Second, we need to provide a special element that is not readily achieved elsewhere, so that it provides an extra spark and opportunity for a unique imaginative and even magical experience.

Inspiring Young Audiences

Jane Taylor, a South African librettist, has in lectures described children as interpreters of their own world. She notes the importance of both engaging them and also empowering them to do that interpreting. Children are often submerged in television and films, which do not usually reveal the process through which they achieve their images nor show any actual person putting the piece together. Taylor remarks that when children don't see how things are done and don't see the person doing it, they don't imagine doing or making it for themselves (Taylor, 2001).

It is consequently important for teachers and librarians to engage live performers to present professional storytelling, drama, art, music, and puppetry programs for children at schools and libraries. It is also important for the teachers and librarians to incorporate elements of these exciting, very effective art forms into their own storytelling and programs. Because few if any libraries could possibly afford to hire professional performers for every single library program, the individuals who the children see for the majority of the library's programs are the children's librarians. As part of a child's everyday life, teachers and librarians need to continually try new things and be creative. If our students see us attempting to employ elements of such art forms into our programs and lessons even though we may not be professional performers, they will feel that they can try these things, too.

Along these lines, it is important to occasionally show the children in your audience how you made some of your props, especially if the group is curious. I do not always do this, as I feel it is desirable to retain some elements of magic in the performance; however, it is also good for children to begin imagining that they could make such things, too.

Quality Storytelling Props

Books in Bloom is unique in that the patterns are reflective of the original works in terms of artistic quality and spirit. The storybooks' authors and illustrators spent many months and even years creating the original artwork and text; it is important that if we regularly "replace" a book in storytime with a prop or flannel, it should really do the book justice.

Children do also enjoy the quick-and-easy storytelling pieces for which many patterns and guidelines are readily available. It is fine to make and use those as well. Children recognize and appreciate quality, however, and it is important for us to strive for quality storytelling pieces whenever possible. Although such pieces will necessarily take more time and money to create than something that has no aesthetic integrity, they are well worth the investment.

These prop pieces will be used repeatedly, in a wide variety of ways, for a wide variety of ages, with a wide variety of themes. I have compared the process of constructing the pieces to "building a wardrobe." Clothing consultants suggest that you pay a little bit extra to buy a few top-quality pieces of clothing that are particularly flattering and of good cloth and workmanship, stating that you will wear them again and again with various accessories. Similarly, these story props will be used again and again, "accessorized" differently as parts of different themes, for different age groups, and so forth. Educators need to build quality collections of professional resources and props that they will be able to use repeatedly throughout their careers. It is important to note that the pieces in this book are designed as professional resources, not as playthings.

The patterns included in this book are some that I have found to be essentially "magic." They seem to work every time, with a wide range of ages, and are the kind that can hold an entire room of even very young children spellbound—the kind that you pull out again and again.

Practical Issues

Time, Money, and Ability

Many overworked children's librarians and teachers may not feel that they have the personal time or ability to create some of these patterns. If this is the case, skilled volunteers may be available who would love to create pieces of this sort. The patterns in this book are complete and thorough in their explanations, so a volunteer could create them independently if supplied with the necessary materials.

If you do not have the funds to cover these sorts of expenditures either personally or within your children's department or classroom budget, community service groups as well as library Friends groups love to fund neat stuff of this sort. It also offers an ideal follow-up opportunity to elicit even more funds for other projects when you can take the finished prop to show the funders and demonstrate briefly how you are able to use it with the children.

Try for a goal of creating one or two props each year as you build your collection. Start with some of the easier patterns, such as *Poppy the Panda* by Dick Gackenbach (*see* chapter 3), *A Color of His Own* by Leo Lionni (*see* chapter 4), or "Mouse House" (*see* chapter 5).

Types of Stories That Can Be Adapted

Not all stories and picture books should be adapted into other media, for several reasons. First, some stories simply don't transfer well into alternative formats. Recognizing which stories would and would not transfer well is partly a matter of time and experience, though there are some general guidelines that can help you decide. Professional resources on this topic mostly describe the process in a general sort of way, such as "Choose stories with clear and simple plot structures, cumulative story lines, and repetitive language. Reduce the numbers for stories with too many little pieces" (Cobb, 1996). This is excellent advice. Many resources list picture book titles that would make good flannel or puppet stories, though few include any actual patterns and those that do tend to be quite limited in scope.

When you look at a poem or storybook, several factors can help you determine whether it could (not necessarily should, yet) work well as a prop or flannel story. Ask yourself if it meets the criteria described above: Does it have a straightforward plot? Do the events build on each other? Does it have either one main character doing a series of distinct things, or does it have a succession of unique characters? These are all characteristics of stories that tend to be adaptable to alternative mediums. In your mind's eye, can you figure out fairly easily which pieces of the story you would choose to make? Can you imagine yourself doing the story with them, scene by scene, with all of the necessary manipulations of the pieces? Would you be able to make the pieces large and clear enough so they can be easily seen and enjoyed by a group? If there are many small pieces and minor digressions in the story, would it still make sense or be as effective even if you did not include these pieces visually?

As you begin to make and use story props, you will develop a feel for what type of stories work well with props and which ones do not. Even the process of creating the pieces in this book and comparing the prepared scripts and movement note suggestions to the original text should help you evaluate other stories you are thinking about adapting on your own.

Additional Considerations

Once you decide that a particular story could work as a prop, you need to evaluate whether it will add some important dimension to the story if you present it using props. For example, is the size of the original book too small to share effectively with a group? If so, adapting it into a prop format will enable you to use it when you might otherwise be unable to do so. (Available technology such as document cameras may enable you to share it in its original form; however, such equipment is often bulky and difficult to transport as well as costly.) Similarly, are the illustrations so light or so detailed that a group would be unable to see them very clearly? If so, I would consider making the story into a prop to promote it in that way. Examples in this book of two titles I adapted so I could share them with larger groups are *The Most Wonderful Egg in the World* by Helme Heine (*see* chapter 7) and *The Nightgown of the Sullen Moon* by Nancy Willard, illustrated by David McPhail (*see* chapter 8).

Some books that you think could make a great prop are already ideal for sharing with a group just the way they are. When this is the case, you really don't need to make it into a prop and should probably only do so if it enables you to add a significant dimension that you wouldn't otherwise be able to share. In such an instance, I usually read the book aloud first so that the children can revel in it, then we follow up with the prop as an extending experience. An example in this volume of that type of situation is *Lunch* by Denise Fleming (*see* chapter 9).

One of the main reasons that many teachers and children's librarians share stories using props is that doing so simply enables the storyteller to grab the audience's attention and keep it. The drama of pulling out a new flannel or prop piece often engages a group more effectually than simply turning a page. Ask yourself: Will sharing the story in question as a prop keep the audience's attention much more effectively than sharing it in its original form? If your audience is more likely to actually pay attention to the story if it is presented with props, then consider adapting it! Make certain, however, that you always show your audience the book from which the story came both before and after you share it with the props, and give the author, illustrator, and publication information. An example in this book of a story that intensely engages an audience when it is presented with props is *Poppy the Panda* by Dick Gackenbach (*see* chapter 3). Gackenbach's books do contain clear, visible illustrations that groups can see fairly well; consequently, I would be less inclined to adapt them. *Poppy the Panda,* however, gains an irresistible immediacy for audiences when presented with "real" gathered props.

Adapting the Text

When you are determining exactly how you will retell a story and figuring out how you will manipulate the accompanying props you plan to create, it is important to retain the original story's essential elements. It is desirable to stay as close to the original text as possible; however, you will likely need to reword portions to make it more tellable. Avoid using sentences that will sound stilted when presented orally. Also, you will likely streamline some portions that are too involved and not essential to the forward movement of the story and embellish others for the sake of clarity and interest. For further clarification of this point, compare the script for *The Most Wonderful Egg in the World* by Helme Heine (*see* chapter 7) with the title's original text. You may also make some minor changes to allow for audience participation. For example, in the script for *The Nightgown of the Sullen Moon* by Nancy Willard (*see* chapter 8), I ask the audience to supply places that the moon travels on her way to the nightgown shop. In *Poppy the Panda* by Dick Gackenbach (*see* chapter 3), repeating the refrain "Fussy, fussy, fussy!" allows repeated audience participation. You may also include narration that incorporates elements supplied by the original book's illustrations that were not in the text.

Choosing Format and Media

After you have determined that a particular story would adapt well to being told as a prop story, and also that sharing it in that way would somehow enhance the story experience, you must decide *how* to adapt it—into what medium? Flannel board adaptations are by far the most common; however, it is important to consider both the demands of the story itself as well as the original illustrations when you are deciding what medium might be the most appropriate to the story.

Often, both the type of manipulations required by the story and also the artist's original artwork suggest what media should be used. For example, the flat, bold colors used by Daniel Manus Pinkwater in *The Big Orange Splot* (Hastings, 1977) and also the need to readily manipulate the pieces as the characters change their houses are ideally suited to the flat feeling and easily manipulable nature of flexible colored magnetic sheeting to create a magnet board story. In *Fish Is Fish* (Pantheon, 1970), author-illustrator Leo Lionni's illustrations are soft, without boundary lines. The changes as the tadpole becomes a frog and hops away to see the world require a format that is easily manipulable; the soft fuzzy nature of the illustrations suggests felt as the appropriate medium.

Ask yourself: What activities will be taking place in this story? How can I best accommodate both the demands of that action as well as veracity to the original illustrations?

In Pamela Allen's picture book *Who Sank the Boat?* (Coward-McCann, 1983), the story's focal drama is the tilting of the boat as each animal gets into it and the boat's ultimate upset by the tiny mouse. In contemplating what medium might best showcase this drama, shadow puppetry comes to mind. As a medium, shadow puppetry focuses an audience intently on a fairly small screen. The room is usually darkened, further drawing attention to the one lighted spot in the room and consequently heightening attention to the activity that is transpiring in that space. Also, the shadow medium allows the "boat" to be anchored on a metal brad fastener that allows it to tip wildly forward and back, then balance out again. If you adapted the story as a flannel board, you would have a much harder time demonstrating this.

In each chapter of *Books in Bloom,* I explain why I chose that particular medium for that story or poem. These discussions will help you as you contemplate adapting stories in the future, employing the techniques highlighted in this book as well as whatever you can dream up! I hope that you are able to consider options in a whole new way, on a whole new level.

Copyright Issues

After you have decided that you would like to adapt a particular picture book or story and have ascertained how you plan to do so, you must obtain written permission from the original work's publisher.

When you are requesting permission to adapt a work simply for use within your own library or school, you will typically have fairly positive responses from the publishers (though not always). You may occasionally be asked to pay a small permission fee. Most permissions departments are extremely busy, so actually receiving a reply may take several months. You will need to plan well in advance to have time to both obtain the permission and also create the prop pieces.

Often, trying to figure out who you need to contact to obtain a particular permission is the most frustrating portion of the entire process. Because you will generally be asking for literary permissions, you can at least initially contact the book's publisher's permissions department. Be aware, however, that the publisher may no longer have control of the copyright—it may not have authority over subsidiary rights, or the copyright may have passed to a literary agency that is managing the author's or illustrator's estate. Many publishing houses have also merged; the house that published the story you want to use may no longer be publishing under the name it had then.

Many publishers' Internet websites have detailed guidelines for permission seekers and clearly specify how you should address your request and what information it should include. I recommend starting with these websites when preparing your permission request. If permissions information is not available on the website, you may wish to telephone the publisher to verify that you have the correct address and contact person. You can readily obtain publishers' telephone numbers and operating addresses from several sources, including *Children's Books in Print, Children's Writer's and Illustrator's Market,* or, again, from the publishers' websites. Address your request clearly to the permissions department, and specify that the request is for a juvenile title.

Although it seems like it would be desirable to have the publisher's permissions department verify by telephone that they do indeed control the copyright for the particular work you are asking about, I do not recommend it unless the publisher is a small one. In general, permissions departments are extremely busy and are responsible for a huge number of titles, especially as publishing houses continue to merge. Even if you receive a verbal verification by telephone that the publisher controls the rights to the title you are asking about, you may discover that the information was in error once you have submitted a written request and the permissions manager has had a chance to look over it. If you have an extensive permission request, I recommend sending a preliminary inquiry letter. For a small request simply asking permission to create a flannel board or puppet presentation for use in your library or classroom, you can send it in its entirety because it will only be a page or two. A request must always ultimately be submitted in writing, and you must likewise receive a written permission. Always include a self-addressed stamped envelope (with sufficient return postage) along with your permission request. If you are concerned about verifying that the request arrives and on what date for possible follow-up, you can send the request by certified mail.

A sample permission request form is included in chapter 2.

Because of the difficulties outlined above, it is important to keep a variety of possibilities open as you consider what stories you might like to try adapting. If you request permission to adapt several titles, you will not be at a disadvantage if some replies or permissions are not forthcoming. If one request is delayed or denied, you can simply work on another one!

The patterns and scripts in this book already have permissions granted. Please note that permission has been granted for educational purposes only, however, and that use of the patterns to create multiple copies of the props for sale or to present the materials for professional paid shows is not permitted under the current agreement.

Please see the works covering copyright and permissions that are listed as references at the end of this chapter for an extended discussion of this issue. You may also wish to consult with your school or library's attorney about the distinction of "fair use" for educational purposes. Obeying the law and adhering to copyright standards is important; the props you will subsequently be able to create and use make the process well worth the effort.

Accessibility and Storage

Once you have begun to create some of these storytelling props, it is important to make sure they are and will continue to be available, accessible, and usable. Creating them makes them available in the first place. You must then make sure that they are accessible to those who wish to use them. If props are being created for use by multiple individuals, such as for within a school or a children's department with multiple staff members, they should be entered into an easily findable and updateable tracking list or database (*see* chapter 2, "Sample Storytelling Props Collection List or Database") that describes what they are and how they might be used. If possible, a newly created prop should be demonstrated for fellow staff members who might be able to use it, as they will be more inclined to feel comfortable doing so if they have actually seen it performed. The prop needs to be stored in a place accessible to all of the people who might wish to use it. Furthermore, enough documentation needs to exist so that even if staff members come and go, the prop will still be findable and understandable. These props should be inventoried and included in an institution's assets in case of fire or some other damaging event. Finally, the prop needs to be kept in a usable state of repair through appropriate storage and maintenance. At the end of each chapter, I have included storage considerations and ideas for the props included in *Books in Bloom.* In general, though, props should be stored in a central, accessible place in sturdy, lightweight containers that are clearly labeled. They should be protected from being smashed together or overpacked in any way. Two or more copies of the story script should always be kept with the prop. The original book or story should be kept nearby in a professional "storytelling collection" where it is always available and can be shown when the prop is being presented.

Let Your Imagination Take Flight

The various techniques described in this volume, together with the sample patterns, will enable you to successfully and gradually create some of the storytelling pieces for a professional resource collection that you can use again and again. I hope that through the process of creating them you will ultimately gain confidence and skill in adapting other stories and poems on your own and in actively exploring the rich diversity of media available to you for this process.

References

Alvey, Richard Gerald. "The History of Organized Storytelling to Children in the United States." Ph.D. diss., University of Pennsylvania, 1974.

Baird, Bil. *The Art of the Puppet.* New York: Macmillan, 1965.

Baker, Augusta, and Ellin Greene. *Storytelling: Art and Technique.* 2d ed. New York: Bowker, 1987.

Beatty, Barbara. *Preschool Education in America: The Culture of Young Children from the Colonial Era to the Present.* New Haven, Conn.: Yale Univ. Pr., 1995.

Bruwelheide, Janis H. *The Copyright Primer for Librarians and Educators.* 2d ed. Chicago: American Library Assn., 1995.

Cobb, Jane. *I'm a Little Teapot! Presenting Preschool Storytime.* 2d ed. Vancouver, B.C.: Black Sheep, 1996.

Crews, Kenneth D. *Copyright Essentials for Librarians and Educators.* Chicago: American Library Assn., 2000.

DeGaetano, Gloria. Visual Media and Young Children's Attention Spans [online]. Eugene: University of Oregon, College of Education, Media Literacy Online Project. Available at <http://interact.uoregon.edu/MediaLit/mlr/readings/articles/degaetano/visualmedia.html>.

Huck, Charlotte S. *Children's Literature in the Elementary School.* 7th ed. Dubuque, Iowa: McGraw-Hill, 2001.

Pellowski, Anne. *The World of Storytelling.* Expanded and rev. ed. Bronx, N.Y.: Wilson, 1990.

Roney, R. Craig. *The Story Performance Handbook.* Mahwah, N.J.: Lawrence Erlbaum Associates, 2001.

Ross, Elizabeth Dale. *The Kindergarten Crusade: The Establishment of Preschool Education in the United States.* Athens, Ohio: Ohio Univ. Pr., 1976.

Silveus, Mari. "How to Turn a Story Hour into a Family Outing." In *Kids and Libraries: Selections from Emergency Librarian,* edited by Ken Haycock and Carol-Ann Haycock. Seattle, Wash.: Dyad Services, 1984.

Simpson, Carol. *Copyright for Schools: A Practical Guide.* 3d ed. Worthington, Ohio: Linworth, 2001.

Talab, R. S. *Commonsense Copyright: A Guide for Educators and Librarians.* 2d ed. Jefferson, N.C.: McFarland, 1999.

Taylor, Jane. Librettist for the Handspring Puppet Company's shadow puppetry/live-action adult presentation "Zeno at 4 A.M." from the work *Confessions of Zeno/La coscienza di Zeno* by Italo Svevo, Walker Art Center lecture, Minneapolis, Minn., November 3, 2001.

Wright, Kieth C., and Judith F. Davie. *Library and Information Services for Handicapped Individuals.* 3d ed. Englewood, Colo.: Libraries Unlimited, 1989.

2 Tips and Tools

This chapter contains vital tips, techniques, and explanations of terminology that will help you successfully create the props included in *Books in Bloom* as well as effectively prepare for future projects.

Enlarging the Patterns in This Book

Successful completion of several patterns in this book requires the correct enlargement of the patterns before you begin the project.

Please note the following key points.

Each pattern page in *Books in Bloom* tells you the percentage at which you should copy it on a copy machine. Your patterns will turn out correctly if you follow those instructions exactly. If the pattern page says to copy the page at 125 percent, set your copier to enlarge at 125 percent. If you are unable to enlarge at the size specified on your copier, consider taking *Books in Bloom* to a copy shop that has those capabilities, or enlarge the pieces in stages. For example, if you need to enlarge a pattern to 200 percent but your copier only enlarges up to 150 percent, copy the original at 150 percent and then copy that enlarged image at 133 percent. Your final result will be a 200 percent enlargement. The formula to ascertain how to do this two-part enlarging is as follows:

Example 1

$$\frac{\text{Target percent enlargement (200 percent)}}{\text{Your first enlargement (150 percent)}} = \text{Your second enlargement (133 percent)}$$

Example 2

$$\frac{\text{Target percent enlargement (175 percent)}}{\text{Your first enlargement (140 percent)}} = \text{Your second enlargement (125 percent)}$$

All pattern pieces in *Books in Bloom* that need enlarging state that fact on the pattern piece itself as well as on the pattern page as a whole. Each piece to be enlarged also has a "measure me" verification line that says: "This line should measure exactly 3" when pattern is photocopied correctly." Make use of this feature to double-check that you have enlarged the pattern pieces correctly!

Many of the enlarged pattern pieces will end up much bigger than your copier paper, even if you are able to enlarge them onto 11" × 17" paper. When this is the case, copy the pattern piece in parts and then tape the overlapped parts together to make the final pattern.

Recommended Tools and Materials for Effective Prop Building

I keep the following tools and materials on hand for prop building. Some of these items are used in the patterns included in this book; some are simply materials that I use regularly for other prop projects not included here.

Glues

Aleene's Original "Tacky" Glue (flexible fabric glue, not school glue)

hot glue gun; multiple temperature melt glue sticks

quick-gel superglue

rubber cement

Weldbond

Paints and Brushes

acrylic craft paint (comes in 2-oz. plastic bottles)

fabric paint

puffy paint (comes in squeeze bottles with pointed application tips)

paintbrushes: hair (multiple widths); foam (multiple widths)

Fabrics

fake fur

plush felt

wool felt in many colors

cotton fabrics

trims and laces

Craft and Miscellaneous Supplies

pencil (sharp)

ballpoint pen

Sharpie permanent markers (multiple colors and widths)

lined notebook paper

matte board

large flat cardboard

flexible ruler

sewing, embroidery, and tapestry needles

straight pins and T-pins

crochet hooks

paper clips

spring clothespins

Velcro (multiple colors and widths)

beads (multiple colors and sizes)

sequins

wiggle eyes; solid black eyes (multiple colors and sizes)

buttons

pipe cleaners (multiple colors)

elastic

dowel rods (multiple sizes)

Styrofoam balls

Crafts and Miscellaneous Supplies (Cont'd)

colored pom-poms (multiple colors and sizes)
colored yarns and strings
colored thread
polyester fiberfill
Fray Check
candle and matches/lighter (for fusing fabric edges)

Scissors

small sharp-pointed scissors
fabric shears
pinking shears

Hand Tools

X-acto knife; replacement blades
utility knife; replacement razor blades
hacksaw (mini) and hacksaw (regular)
hammer
needle nose and regular pliers
screwdrivers (multiple sizes, slotted and Phillips)
small wire cutters and heavy-duty wire cutters

Power Tools

lightweight cordless drill
sewing machine
electric fan (for speed-drying projects)
steam iron; ironing board; pressing cloth

Terms and Techniques

Visual Storytelling

Flannel Board

A sturdy board covered in soft, fuzzy flannel or felt onto which felt figures or pieces may be placed to illustrate a story or concept. Flannel/felt boards can be easily made by covering a stiff piece of corrugated cardboard or a piece of plywood with felt; many extremely serviceable commercial boards are also available at fairly reasonable prices.

Props

Derived from the theatrical term *stage property.* Any article, except costumes and scenery, used as part of a dramatic production.

Realia

Real physical items, often three-dimensional, which are touchable and may be manipulated by a child to gain information about his/her world or environment. The items may also be used to represent themselves in a dramatic production or in a play situation.

Materials

Fray Check

Clear viscous liquid that can be applied to fabric edges to keep them from fraying. Dries clear and slightly stiff; may be washed.

"Tacky" Glue

Nontoxic white craft glue that dries clear and flexible. Works well on both nonporous and porous materials (such as felt).

T-pins

Large, sturdy craft pins shaped like a T. They come in several sizes and are particularly useful for attaching large or heavy flannel/felt board pieces to a flannel board during a performance.

Sewing

Blanket Stitch

A popular finishing stitch for edges. The stitch shown is worked from left to right.

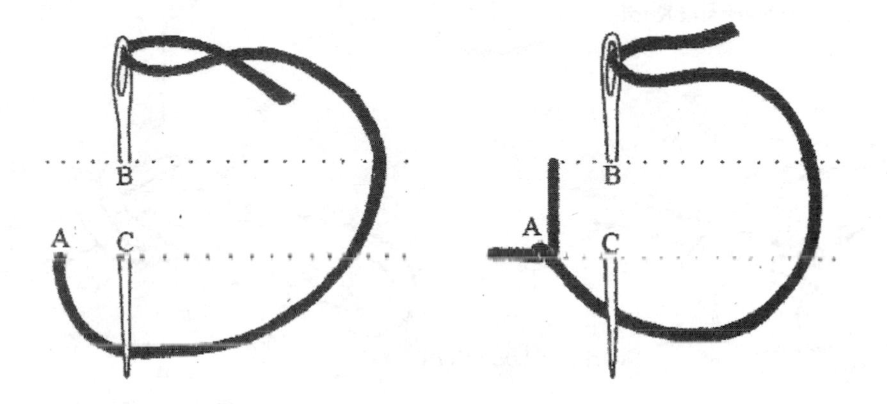

Bring needle through the fabric back to front at point *A*. Insert needle at point *B* and slightly to the right, then exit at point *C,* directly below. Before pulling the needle through, carry the thread under the point of the needle as shown. Go on to the next stitch. Point *C* of the previous stitch is now point *A*. Work the stitch around the entire piece, taking care to keep the height of the stitches fairly even throughout.

Clip

Small V-shaped cuts in a curved seam allowance to enable the curved seam to lay smoothly when turned right side out. Care must be taken to not clip too close to the actual seam's stitching.

Closing Stitch

An effective stitch to bring edges together for closing, evenly worked with stitches alternating to the left and to the right. The stitch shown is typically worked from left to right or top to bottom.

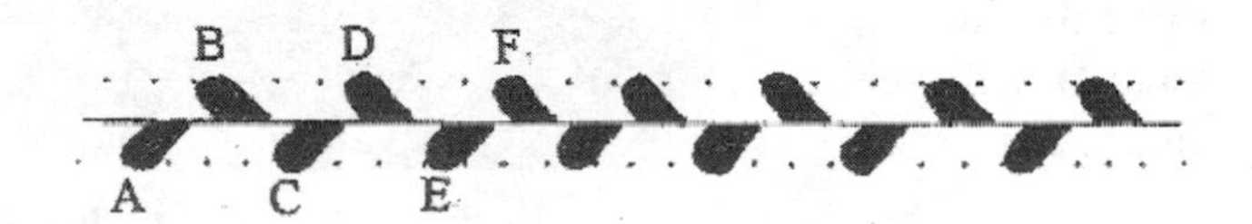

Bring needle through the fabric back to front at point *A*. Insert needle back to front at point *B* and slightly to the right, then back to front at point *C,* and so on along the entire opening. Take care to keep the spacing of the stitches fairly even throughout.

Tack

A small stitch (by hand or machine) to hold two pieces of fabric together.

Topstitch

A seam stitched on the outside, 1/4″ from an edge, seam, or previous stitching, using the presser foot as a guide.

Knots

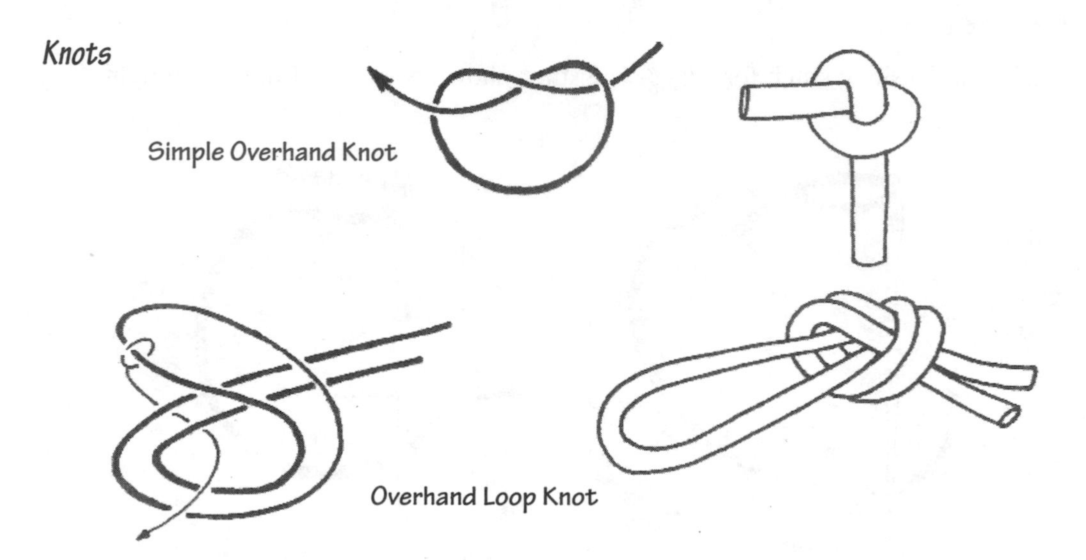

Fusing and Scoring

Heat Fusion

Technique of sealing fabric edges that might fray using heat. The fabric must be of a type that melts when exposed to heat; cotton or other natural fiber fabrics will not work with this method. (Use Fray Check instead for natural fiber fabrics.) Hold the very edge of the fabric to be sealed near a candle flame, just close enough and long enough so that the fibers along the edge melt together, creating a seal. Be careful not to hold the fabric too close to the flame or hold it in one place too long, or it may catch on fire. Move the edge of the fabric along the flame; it will seal as you go along. (*See* figure 2-1.)

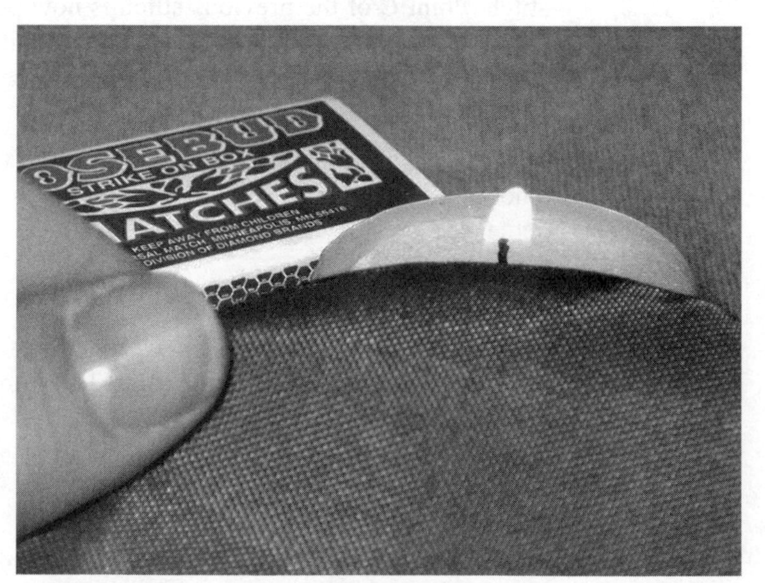

Figure 2-1

Score

To lightly mark a surface with a sharp or pointed object so that the original surface will bend cleanly along the marked line. Also to lightly scrape a surface with a rough or pointed object so that paint or glue will have improved surface adhesion.

REQUEST FOR PERMISSION

To use copyrighted material for nonprofit educational purposes; internal classroom and library use only.

As the educator seeking to facilitate the project proposed below, I am requesting permission to use the following copyrighted material. If you are not authorized to grant such permission, please return this request form or contact me with any information you can provide on reaching the authorized party. This form may be completed and returned if convenient.

My name: ______________________________

Organization's name and address: ______________________________

____

Telephone: ______________________________

E-mail: ______________________________

____

Requested Material:

Source

Full title of work: ______________________________

Author: ______________________________

Illustrator: ______________________________

Publisher, imprint, date: ______________________________

ISBN: ______________________________

Explanation of desired use: ______________________________

Purpose: Nonprofit educational purposes only; internal classroom and library use

Audience: Preschool and early elementary age children and their caregivers

Audience fees: NONE

Rights requested: Nonexclusive rights for nonprofit educational performance by teachers or youth services librarians at schools, libraries, and day cares in the ________________ geographical area.

[Copyright holder or representative: Please use this form for your response if convenient.]

PERMISSION TO USE COPYRIGHTED MATERIAL

Permission is hereby granted for nonexclusive use of the material listed above. Fee, if any: [Permission fees are paid by the school or library.] $________ Payable to: ____________________

______________________________ Due: ____________________

Comments:

Signed: ______________________________ Title: ______________________________

Representing (copyright holder): ______________________________ Date: ______________

[Please return this form to the requestor. SASE is enclosed.]

Sample Storytelling Props Collection List or Database

Hedberg Public Library Story Props
Storytelling Collection (Children's Department)

Title (alphabetical)	*Author*	*Type*	*Format*	*Summary*	*Location*
A Color of His Own	Lionni, Leo	story	transparency	A chameleon is distressed he doesn't have his own color.	Overhead stories box
Fish Is Fish	Lionni, Leo	story	flannel	Fish wants to be like his friend Frog and see the world!	Flannel stories box
Lunch	Fleming, Denise	story	puppet/props	A hungry mouse eats many colorful foods for lunch.	Prop shelves
The Most Wonderful Egg in the World	Heine, Helme	story	comb. prop	The king must choose which hen's egg is the most wonderful.	Prop shelves
"Mouse House"		poem	finger puppets	Three little mice peek out one by one from their little house.	Prop shelves
The Nightgown of the Sullen Moon	Willard, Nancy	story	stick puppets	The moon finally gets what she has really wanted—a nightgown.	Prop shelves
Poppy the Panda	Gackenbach, Dick	story	puppet/props	Katie's toy panda won't go to bed until he has something to wear.	Prop shelves

rev. 06/2003 KKF

Puppet and Prop Assembly Stories

Includes script and pattern for

Poppy the Panda by Dick Gackenbach (Clarion, 1984)

Pattern difficulty level

Very easy

Construction/assembly time estimate

2 hours

Sometimes a story that you want to adapt is particularly well suited to being told with real physical objects. This method of "prop assembly" can be very efficient in comparison to some of the prop creation techniques, and it is often a good choice when many of the primary pieces in a story are real, procurable objects. Puppets, stuffed animals, and the storyteller himself or herself can all be paired with the gathered props to represent living creatures in the story.

This type of gathered prop can lend immediacy to a story's telling, especially if the objects are common ones that audience members would also likely have in their own homes. Many preschool and early elementary age children are learning how to evaluate what is real and what is not. They frequently inquire whether or not puppets, objects, and so forth are real and are delighted when they learn that assembled storytelling pieces really *are* real!

Creating quality representative adaptations of a story's illustrations can take a lot of time. If a story will work well told with three-dimensional real objects, by all means do so. The cost of purchasing the items will almost certainly be less expensive than the cost of your time investment if you make the items yourself. Save your time and your creative energy for making pieces that you can't readily purchase.

Techniques and Considerations

Creating

The art of prop assembly involves dedicated "hunting-and-gathering" techniques and behavior. The best prop gatherers are continually on the lookout for potential story props. Such items may be found at garage sales and secondhand stores, drugstores and craft and discount stores, and in your own attic and basement or that of a friend or fellow staff member. Plan well in advance for your prop assembly stories, so that you will have plenty of time to watch for needed items as you do your regular shopping.

Resist the urge to simply borrow items that you regularly use around the house for a temporary prop assembly story. Although you may want or need to do this on occasion, it is best to invest the time and money up front and create a self-contained prop story that you will be able to use again and again without having to re-create or regather it each time. Having the prop completely assembled will enable you to pull it out at a moment's notice if needed, and it will be a resource that can be readily used by all of your staff for years to come.

Remember that your time is worth money. If you enjoy this type of prop gathering, great. If you do not, then it may be preferable to pay someone who does enjoy it to scrounge prop items for you. My mother was an avid garage saler for years and has also volunteered regularly for several charitable thrift shops. If I am planning in advance, I can let her know specific items I am looking for, and she will watch for them for me! She also keeps an eye out for objects with "prop potential" (such as plastic food, puppets, funny hats), even if they are not things for which I have specifically asked. Some items you can almost guarantee will be useful sooner or later. For example, when my mom found several plastic potato chips and rubber french fries, I didn't have an immediate use for them but added them to my box of miscellaneous prop potential items. When I assembled the prop pieces for Jack Prelutsky's pocket poem "A Frog, a Stick" (in *A Pizza the Size of the Sun: Poems,* Greenwillow, 1996) several years later, I was certainly glad I already had those "Potato chips and soggy fries!"

Presenting

Practice presenting the story with all of the props so you can determine in advance the best way to handle each object, how to have it interact with any accompanying puppets, and so forth. Your movements should be smooth and confident. Learn the story and prop manipulations so you are able to share them with your audience from memory. Remember that the story you are telling is fresh and special for each new audience, even if you feel like you have done it a thousand times. Practice your mannerisms: be dramatic and excited; portray dismay if the story calls for it; act surprised by each new prop that you pull out, as if you don't know what is going to happen next either. Your interaction with and reaction to the story and prop pieces make a big difference for the audience. Be careful that you don't become so wild that you distract from the story itself—just try to give it a little pizzazz. This is important to remember with all types of storytelling.

Keep your props hidden away ahead of time so they don't lose their mystery. You may wish to display one representative element from the story along with the book on the table where you are set up for storytime, but it is best to hide the other pieces away at the outset. Part of the drama and excitement of assembly stories comes in pulling out the next prop item. Any closable box or bin will do for the purpose of hiding the props; however, I like to use the colored cardboard/fiberboard hinged-lid storage boxes available through most library suppliers. You can reach in and pull out an item, and the hinged lid closes back down to hide the rest of the contents from view until you are ready to produce them. After you have told a prop story, it is a good idea to hide any of the fragile or sharp-edged props back in the boxes so that curious children won't hurt themselves or the prop if they try to examine the pieces after storytime.

Choosing the Prop Assembly Format

The script and prop assembly "pattern" and suggestions that follow are for the picture book story *Poppy the Panda* by Dick Gackenbach. As mentioned in my introduction, Gackenbach's illustrations tend to be clearly drawn and visible even for a group; for this reason, I am generally less inclined to adapt them (*see* chapter 1, "Additional Considerations"). In *Poppy the Panda,* however, Poppy's experimentation with all of the different household object "clothing" options that Katie suggests presents an ideal opportunity to share the story with real gathered props. The drama of pulling out the next item that Katie offers is exciting for the audience, and Poppy's appearance in each "outfit" is downright funny.

Adapting the story as a flannel board or into some other format would certainly be achievable; however, a flat representation of the pictures wouldn't really add anything to the story's telling. The motion, emotion, and personality with which you can imbue the puppet or stuffed animal playing the role of Poppy help to bring the character and the story to life. The fact that Poppy is a toy panda trying on real household objects in the story also suggests the appropriateness of simply using a real toy/puppet panda and all of the accompanying real objects when you tell it.

Poppy the Panda

Dick Gackenbach

Summary

Katie can't find the right thing for her toy panda to wear until her mother comes up with the perfect solution.

Possible themes

Bears, Bedtime, Clothes, Pandas, Toys

Approximate running time for prop story

6 minutes

Recommended audience interest level

Preschool (age 3 and older) through grade 2

Please note that the story pieces are designed as professional resources, not as play-things. They do not necessarily conform to child safety play standards, and they could easily become damaged if used in a manner other than that for which they were intended.

Story Pieces

- panda puppet (or plush)
- doll dress
- child's roller skates
- doll umbrella or small child's umbrella
- 1 small child's sandal; 1 small child's shoe
- plastic fruit bowl with plastic apple and banana
- saucepan
- bathroom hand towel
- plastic shower cap
- roll of toilet tissue
- royal blue ribbon
- hand mirror

Use with

table

box to hide the prop pieces

a copy of the book to show the audience both before and after presenting the story

Setup

Make sure you (or whomever will be Katie's mother) have the blue ribbon tied in your hair before the story session begins.

Have all of the pieces hidden in a box where you can easily pull them out one at a time as the story progresses.

Make sure there is a stool or table edge nearby you can use as the "stairs" when Poppy bump-bump-bumps down them.

Presentation

The script calls for you to be four characters: the Narrator, Poppy, Katie, and her mother. The character who is talking is designated by his or her name at the beginning of the text, except for the Narrator.

Story narration is delineated in regular type; movement notes and miscellaneous directions are shown in *[bracketed italics]*.

Learn the story and tell it to your audience from memory, using the prop pieces.

Whenever you are telling Poppy something, hold him out to one side so he is looking at you and you are looking at him. By holding him to the side, the audience will still be able to see him clearly.

When Poppy is talking, move his arms and head so he looks alive.

Movement notes and directions for Poppy assume that he is a puppet; if you have a plush panda instead, please adapt its movements accordingly.

Practice the story before a mirror so that you can work on the puppet's movements and believability.

Slip the puppet on and off your hand as needed if both hands are required to manipulate the other props; if you do take the puppet off your hand during the story, simply hold him on your lap or under your arm.

Although it is not essential to use different character voices when presenting the story, it can truly help maintain the children's interest. Try out different voices to figure out which sounds the best for the different characters. All voices must feel natural for you after practice so that you will be able to use and maintain them successfully during an actual performance.

Repeating the "fussy, fussy, fussy" refrain is intended as an opportunity for audience participation; with just a little encouragement, they will naturally begin to say it with you as you repeat it throughout the story.

Please note: The following script is a slightly adapted story version for telling as a prop and participation story and includes notes for the storyteller on how and when to manipulate the prop pieces. Learn the story and tell it to your audience from memory, using the prop pieces. Please look at the book so that you know what adaptations have been made in this script; you may prefer to tell the story verbatim from its exact original text. Show a copy of the book to your audience both before and after sharing the story with the puppet and props, and give the complete title, author/illustrator, and publication information.

SCRIPT

Poppy the Panda by Dick Gackenbach

Katie O'Keefe *[point to self]* had a toy panda. *[Hold up panda puppet.]* His name was Poppy. Katie took Poppy with her everywhere she went. *[Hug Poppy close.]* She took him to . . . the store. She took him to . . . McDonald's. She took him to . . . the library. *[Let the audience suggest more places.]* And Katie would certainly never think about going to bed unless Poppy came, too.

One night Katie told Poppy, "It's time for bed!"

But Poppy refused to go.

POPPY *(petulant)* "I cannot go to bed. Absolutely not. I can't sleep when I'm unhappy."

[Have Poppy cover his eyes with his hands.]

KATIE *(surprised)* "I didn't know you were unhappy."

POPPY "Well, I am! Everyone has something nice to wear but me. Your doll has a fancy dress. And your soldier has a fine suit and hat. Why, even your cat has a collar. But what do I have to wear? Nothing at all!"

KATIE "Well, Poppy! I didn't know you wanted something to wear. We should be able to do something about that."

POPPY "Good. Otherwise, I doubt if I'll ever want to go to bed."

KATIE "Here's my doll dress! *[Hold up doll dress with hand not wearing Poppy.]* There! *[Take Poppy off your hand and set him on your lap, putting his arms through the dress sleeves; no need to fasten the dress; hold up Poppy so audience can see clearly.]* That looks good on you. Now will you come to bed?"

POPPY *(disgusted and firm)* "I am a boy panda. I will not wear a dress."

KATIE "Fussy, fussy, fussy!"

[Remove dress.]

KATIE "Well, how about these?"

[Hold up roller skates, then set them on your lap; take Poppy off your hand, and put his feet into the skates.]

POPPY "I-I-I'm not sure I approve."

KATIE "Roller skates are fun to wear. You'll see."

Katie gave Poppy a big push.

[Hold the ankles of the skates in your hands and Poppy's legs to hold him into the skates while you weave him around and then bump him down the "stairs."]

Poppy went forward, weaving and bobbing out of Katie's room and into the hallway. He rolled down the hall to the top of the steps and then over.

[Bump-bump-bump the back wheels of the roller skates again and again on the edge of the table or stool to create the sound and idea of bumping down the stairs.]

BUMPITY, BUMPITY, BUMPITY CLOMP! Poppy went all the way down the steps and landed with a thud at the bottom.

[Set skates down on ground and flip Poppy out of them.]

KATIE "Oh, Poppy!" *[Pick up Poppy and hug him close.]* "Are you okay? I'm so sorry. We'll find something else for you to wear."

POPPY "Please make it something without wheels."

KATIE "Let's look in the closet. Here!" *[Hold up umbrella and open it; hold above Poppy's head.]* "Try this on."

POPPY "Nobody wears an umbrella!"

KATIE "Well, fussy, fussy, fussy!"

[Put away umbrella.]

KATIE "Well, here, then. How about these shoes?"

[Hold up shoe and sandal and put one on each of Poppy's feet.]

POPPY "They won't do. They don't even match, and they don't fit right."

[Take off shoes.]

KATIE "You're so hard to please, Poppy! Just fussy, fussy, fussy!"

KATIE "Let's look in the dining room. Here's an idea!"

[Hold up fruit bowl with apple and banana; take the fruit out and put the bowl upside down on Poppy's head.]

POPPY *(disgusted)* "I am your best friend. Not a banana."

KATIE "Fussy, fussy, fussy!"

[Remove fruit bowl.]

KATIE "How about in the kitchen? Here!" *[Hold up saucepan and put it upside down on Poppy's head.]* "It fits fine."

POPPY "It's awful! People will laugh at me."

[Remove saucepan.]

They went upstairs to the bathroom.

KATIE "Here!" *[Hold up towel and wrap it around Poppy's shoulders like a cape.]* "This could be a cape, Poppy!"

POPPY "I am NOT Super-Panda. I do not want to wear a cape."

[Remove towel.]

KATIE "How about this shower cap?"

[Hold up shower cap, and put it on Poppy's head.]

POPPY *(pouting)* "No, I look like a mushroom."

[Remove shower cap.]

Poppy REALLY didn't like it when Katie wrapped him in *[hold up toilet tissue]* toilet tissue.

[Wrap several rounds of tissue around Poppy.]

POPPY *(indignant)* "Absolutely not! Where do you get such ideas? You've made me look like a package."

KATIE "You are the fussiest panda, Poppy! Fussy, fussy, fussy!"

[Remove toilet tissue.]

They went back to Katie's room. They both were tired and sleepy, but Poppy still refused to go to bed.

KATIE "Oh, what will I do with you, you silly panda?"

POPPY "Just find me something sensible to wear. Is that so difficult?"

Just then, Katie's mother appeared at the bedroom door.

[Hold Poppy away from you as if he and Katie are over there together. Look that direction when you are the mother. When you are replying as Katie, hold Poppy close again and look the direction from which the mother was talking to you.]

MOTHER "Katie O'Keefe! Why aren't you in bed?"

KATIE "I'm ready. It's Poppy's fault."

Katie told her mother all about Poppy wanting something to wear.

KATIE "And he's so fussy!"

MOTHER "Poor Poppy. If I *[point to self]* give him something to wear, do you think he'll go to bed?"

[Again, Poppy is held away from you as if he's over with Katie.]

KATIE *[Hold Poppy close.]* "He might. If he likes it."

Katie's mother took the ribbon she was wearing in her hair *[pull ribbon out of your hair]* and tied it in a beautiful BOW around Poppy's neck.

MOTHER "Now, how's that?"

Script adapted by Kimberly K. Faurot, *Books in Bloom: Creative Patterns and Props That Bring Stories to Life* (ALA, 2003).

KATIE "It's perfect!"

But would Poppy like it? Katie picked Poppy up and held him in front of the mirror so he could see his new ribbon.

[Hold Poppy on one hand stretched out in front of you so his back is to the audience. Hold up the mirror so the audience can see both Poppy and themselves. You will need to walk along the group so they can each see. Say "Do you think he'll like it?" to each of the children as they see their own and Poppy's reflections.]

Poppy said:

POPPY *(decided and happy)* "I LOVE my ribbon!"

[Put down mirror.]

KATIE *(wiping brow and rolling eyes in relief)* "He likes it! We're BOTH ready for bed now."

Katie's mother tucked them in, turned out the light, and closed the door.

[Lean your head and upper body sideways, cuddling Poppy, as if the two of you are snuggled up in bed.]

POPPY "I can't wait to show off my ribbon."

KATIE "Tomorrow. But now, good night."

POPPY "Good night."

[Hold up page at end of book where Katie and Poppy are sleeping so audience can see it.]

And they both went right to SLEEP.

[You may want to snore gently at the end.]

THE END

ASSEMBLY INSTRUCTIONS

Prop Assembly Story

Poppy the Panda by Dick Gackenbach

Patterns

Prop assembly suggestions by Kimberly Faurot

Estimated difficulty

Very easy

Estimated assembly time

2 hours

Estimated cost for prop pieces

$75 or less

You Will Need These Items

The following are *Poppy the Panda* story prop pieces with suggestions on where to find them:

- panda puppet (or plush): new puppets available through Folkmanis and Puppet Safari (*see* chapter 10); plush pandas available from toy stores or secondhand stores
- doll dress (infant or child's lacy dress—size depends on your panda; dress placket should open all the way for ease in dressing Poppy): secondhand stores; discount stores
- child's roller skates (boot-style skates or roller blades): secondhand stores; discount stores
- doll umbrella or small child's umbrella: doll umbrellas available at craft stores; child's umbrella available from secondhand stores or discount stores
- 1 small child's sandal; 1 small child's shoe (make sure they look different): secondhand stores; discount stores
- plastic fruit bowl with plastic apple and banana (a clear plastic bowl is nice; bowl size depends on your panda's head size): bowl available from secondhand stores or discount stores; plastic fruit available from craft or toy stores
- saucepan (size depends on your panda's head size): secondhand stores; discount stores
- bathroom hand towel: secondhand stores; discount stores
- plastic shower cap (size depends on your panda's head size): discount stores; drugstores
- roll of toilet tissue
- royal blue ribbon (long enough and wide enough to tie easily in a prominent bow around your panda's neck): fabric stores; craft stores
- fairly large hand mirror: discount stores; drugstores

Assembly Story Finished Product

Figure 3-1

Figure 3-2

Figure 3-3

Figure 3-4

Figure 3-5

Figure 3-6

Figure 3-7

Figure 3-8

Figure 3-9

Figure 3-10

Figure 3-11

Figure 3-12

Storage

You Will Need

1 sturdy, medium-sized box (large enough to easily hold the props without crushing them)

2 copies of *Poppy the Panda* storage label

2 copies of the *Poppy the Panda* presentation notes/script (pages 20–25)

1 copy of prop assembly finished product photos (figures 3-1 through 3-12)

Make two photocopies of the storage label provided for the *Poppy the Panda* prop and fill in the *date* and *name or initials* blanks. Cut out the labels and affix them securely to both ends of your storage container.

Poppy the Panda
Dick Gackenbach (Clarion, 1984)
Prop created ________ by ________________
DATE NAME OR INITIALS
from patterns included in *Books in Bloom* by Kimberly Faurot (ALA, 2003)

Make at least two photocopies of the presentation notes/script (pages 20–25), and include them in the storage container along with the prop pieces. Also include a photocopy of the prop assembly story finished product photos (figures 3-1 through 3-12).

A professional storytelling copy of the original book *Poppy the Panda* by Dick Gackenbach (Clarion, 1984) should either be included in the storage container with the prop or else kept nearby in a professional "storytelling collection" so it may be shown when the prop is being presented. If you are unable to obtain a new copy of the book, investigate purchasing a used copy through one of the resources listed in chapter 10.

Make sure that the prop pieces for *Poppy the Panda* are included on your storytelling props database or list (*see* chapter 2) as well as in your institution's inventory records.

Notify other staff members who might be able to include *Poppy the Panda* in their programming or classrooms that it is ready for use, and demonstrate it for them if at all possible.

Summary

Assembling real, gathered prop pieces to represent a story's main elements can be an enjoyable, quick way to adapt a story for visual storytelling. Always evaluate the original story carefully to determine whether sharing it with gathered props will truly enhance the telling, or if you should simply share it in its original form or use some other adapted format (*see* chapter 1, "Practical Issues"). Prop assembly is generally fairly cost-effective, and audiences enjoy seeing real objects used in storytelling. After seeing this kind of story adaptation, some children are even inspired to gather their own "props" and tell prop assembly stories of their own at home or in the classroom!

4 Overhead Projector Stories

Includes script and pattern for

A Color of His Own by Leo Lionni (Random, 1975)

Pattern difficulty level

Easy

Construction time estimate

3 hours

Overhead transparency machines are a great tool for sharing stories in alternative ways. As group presentations are projected more and more frequently with computer technology, make sure your school or library doesn't get rid of the overhead transparency projector! It is a remarkably versatile piece of equipment: usable on its own to project images directly onto a film screen or a blank wall; able to serve as a light source for traditional shadow puppetry; and capable of producing remarkable special effects when used in tandem with a traditional shadow puppetry screen.

Techniques and Considerations

Creating

One popular storytelling technique using the overhead transparency projector involves placing a transparent baking dish filled with water directly onto the glass surface (projector plate) of the transparency projector. This watery base provides the backdrop for the story's physical "ingredients," which are added to the water in the dish one by one as the story or poem is related. A commonly told example of this type of story is "Witches' Brew," often used as a dramatic finish for Halloween programs. All sorts of supposedly bilious ingredients are added one by one to the "brew," magnified onto the viewing screen or wall so that the audience sees the shadow or image of each as it is added. "Blood" is red food coloring squirted into the water; "spider's web" is a piece of tangled thread; "cat's eye" is a large droplet of cooking oil; and so forth. The final ingredient is a dose of seltzer crystals, which causes the stew to suddenly bubble dramatically and then turn black! Margaret Read MacDonald includes a great version of this story in her book *When the Lights Go Out: Twenty Scary Tales to Tell* (Wilson, 1988).

Another method is performing a "transparency story" or "shadow story" directly on the surface of the projector plate and having it project onto a blank wall or viewing screen. This can either be done using static transparency images or else with small, traditional-type shadow figures on thin wire rods or straws. The technique can be especially effective with large audiences, because the projected images are large and easy to see. This method also enables the storyteller to see and monitor the audience since they are in front of the screen rather than manipulating pieces from behind a shadow screen.

Finally, a projector (or projectors) can be used as both a light source and a second "stage" behind a traditional shadow screen. The storyteller/puppeteer can combine both projected shadow images and traditional "up against the shadow screen" images to produce remarkable interactive and cinematic effects.

The pattern example and script included in this chapter are for a straightforward static transparency image story, because it is one of the most easily achievable techniques and requires the least preparation. I strongly encourage you to investigate some of the more involved options, however; they are extremely interesting to audiences and are relatively cheap and quick to make! By far the best resource on this topic that I have found is *Worlds of Shadow: Teaching with Shadow Puppetry* by David Wisniewski and Donna Wisniewski (Teacher Ideas Pr., 1997).

When you are creating transparency story pieces of this type, you must consider both what type of materials you plan to use as well as presentation issues. Before you begin, measure your machine's projector plate so you are sure to design your pieces to be the right size. Most surface plates are approximately 8" square. For simple pieces like the patterns included here, regular clear transparency sheets and either transparent colored plastic report covers from office supply stores and drugstores or colored artist's acetate from art stores work fine. Using these types of acetate necessitate applying glue to stick layers together. I have used a combination of clear double-stick tape, rubber cement, and craft glue to affix them. You also can use spray adhesive, though it severely darkens and slightly mottles the projected acetate image. Although the spray adhesive seems clear on the acetate pieces themselves, it does not project clear! It can be used to good effect if you want this result, but proceed with caution. The Wisniewskis note this issue of glues showing badly when an image is projected. For this reason, they use a self-adhesive heat-resistant colored acetate-like material (gloss transparent Form-X film, Series 10000; *see* chapter 10) that precludes this problem. It is wonderful if you would like to invest in that material. If you find yourself making lots of overhead transparency props, I would highly recommend purchasing some of the film and trying it. For minimalistic pieces like those I have included here, however, it is fine to use the regular colored acetate or transparencies with household glues and tape to put everything together. Because the pieces are on the overhead for a very short time, the materials do not need to be heat resistant. Knowing that the rubber cement would show somewhat when the pieces were projected, I applied it in a way that would mirror special effects on the pieces being glued, such as in a pattern of leaf veins for the leaves, long brush strokes on the grass blades, and so forth. For this reason, the rubber cement does not distract on these particular pieces.

Another option in creating transparency story pieces involves using colored markers to draw the figure onto a clear transparency backing. This is certainly an option, though you must take care to use markers that won't smudge or evaporate. Also be advised that coloring an image will result in a somewhat blotchy projected image, in contrast to the smooth appearance of acetate cutouts.

Presenting

Make sure to practice presenting your transparency stories so your movements are smooth. With pieces like those for *A Color of His Own,* your hands will necessarily show as you place the story transparency pieces onto and remove them from the projector. This is okay! After placing the sheet onto the projector, however, allow the image to sit there untouched for a moment so that the audience may absorb it fully.

Even when pieces are not "movable," take care to manipulate them by how you place them onto the screen when you have the opportunity to do so. For example, if grass grows, slide your grass panel up into position from the bottom of your projection plate, so it "grows." When the chameleon "walks" out into the grass, have him edge out into position from the side of the projector plate rather than just plunking him down in the middle of the grass. Even with this type of story where you are out in front with the audience, you can use some of the techniques elaborated by the Wisniewskis such as "rain" or "sunshine" effects. For rain, they recommend cutting a thin, transparent plastic vegetable bag from the grocery store into thin strips, still connected at the bottom, and attaching it to a ruler or other flat stick. When it is time for the "rain" to fall, swish the strips back and forth in front of the projector light.

As you can see, overhead transparency projectors may be used for many wonderful purposes that were probably not part of their originally intended functions! The script and patterns that follow will enable you to create and share an effective beginner transparency story in a fairly short amount of time.

Choosing the Overhead Projector Format

In *A Color of His Own,* the chameleon's color changes are paramount. When selecting a format for adapting the story, it is therefore important to consider whether any medium can produce the effect of an instant, fluid color change. The transparency medium enables colors to be combined and separated with ease. Furthermore, colored acetate projects in a vibrant, intense way, ideally capturing the spirit of Lionni's luminous original illustrations. The majority of the acetate pieces are not outlined, reflecting the fact that the book's illustrations have soft edges without outlines. Clear pieces did need outlines, however, so that their shapes would be visible when projected.

The flat projector plate surface also lends itself well to the demands of the story's action as the chameleon visits different venues. Layers can be easily placed on top of one another without threatening to slip apart, and no rods or straws are in the way to make overlapping the pieces difficult.

A Color of His Own

Leo Lionni

(Random, 1975)

Summary

A little chameleon is distressed that he doesn't have his own color like other animals.

Possible themes

Chameleons, Colors, Friends, Seasons—Autumn, Winter, Spring

Presentation time for transparency story

4 minutes

Recommended audience interest level

Preschool (age 3 and older) through grade 2

Please note that the transparency story pieces are designed as professional resources, not as playthings. They do not conform to child safety play standards, and they could easily become damaged if used in a manner other than that for which they were intended.

Transparency Pieces

- clear chameleon 1 (has curly tail)
- parrot page
- goldfish page
- elephant page
- tricolor page
- lemon
- tiger's tail
- yellow leaf page/blue or green leaf overlay
- grey page
- 3 tiny paper snowflakes
- winter (dark) chameleon
- sun
- green grass page
- clear chameleon 2
- red-and-white polka-dot mushroom

Use with

overhead transparency projector

cart or table on which to set overhead projector and lay out story transparency pieces in order

projection screen or large blank white wall

a copy of the book to show the audience both before and after presenting the story

Setup

Stack the large transparency pieces in order so you can access them easily as the story progresses.

Keep the three chameleons and the three paper snowflakes set aside from the larger pages so that they are easy to locate.

Make sure that the transparency pages are stacked so that the glued-on overlays will face *down* onto the projector, leaving the top of the transparency sheet a smooth surface. This way, when the clear chameleons "walk" across the transparencies, they won't catch on the edges of the glued-on overlay pieces.

Paper clip the yellow leaf sheet and blue or green leaf overlay together at the top of the transparency so they won't slip apart before you're ready to remove the blue or green leaves. The yellow leaf sheet goes on the bottom, with the blue or green overlay leaves on top.

Presentation

Before introducing the story, show the audience pictures of real chameleons and talk about the various reasons they really change color.

After you introduce the story by showing the children the book and sharing the publication information, make sure they know what direction to focus their attention for the transparency projection.

Story narration is delineated in regular type; movement notes and miscellaneous directions are shown within the script in *[bracketed italics]*.

Learn the story and tell it to your audience from memory, using the transparency pieces.

The movement notes tell you when to put the transparency sheets *on* the projector. Assume that you remove the sheet before putting the next one on unless the directions tell you otherwise.

Make sure to practice presenting the story so your movements are smooth. Your hands will necessarily show as you put the story transparency sheets on and remove them from the projector. After putting the sheet onto the projector, let the image sit there untouched for a moment so that the audience can absorb it fully.

The script calls for you to be three characters: the Narrator, Chameleon 1, and the older, wiser Chameleon 2. The character who is talking is designated by its name at the beginning of the text, except for the Narrator.

There are only two characters (Chameleon 1 and Chameleon 2) that could employ special character voices in this story, and their lines are very limited. It is not essential to the story to give them distinct voices, but it does provide an extra dimension of interest for the children. Try out different voices to figure out which sounds the best for the different characters. All voices must feel natural for you after practice so that you will be able to use and maintain them successfully during an actual performance.

Words in the text of the script that are shown in CAPITAL letters are good opportunities for the audience to say the word along with you. Pause for them to do so, and encourage the participation.

Please note: The following script is a very slightly adapted story version for telling as a transparency story and includes notes for the storyteller on how and when to manipulate the transparency pieces. Learn the story and tell it to your audience from memory, using the transparency pieces. Please look at the book so that you know what minor adaptations have been made in this script. Show a copy of the book to your audience both before and after sharing the story with the transparency sheets, and give the complete title, author/illustrator, and publication information.

SCRIPT

A Color of His Own by Leo Lionni

Parrots are GREEN *[parrot transparency]*

goldfish are ORANGE *[goldfish transparency; audience will say color with you]*

elephants are GREY. *[elephant transparency; audience will say color with you]*

All animals have a color of their own—*[tricolor transparency]*—except for chameleons.

[Place clear chameleon 1 on top of tricolor transparency.]

They change color wherever they go *["walk" chameleon 1 across tricolor transparency]*.

On lemons they are YELLOW *[place lemon on projector, then chameleon 1 in middle of lemon]*.

And on the tiger's tail they are striped ORANGE and BLACK like tigers *[place tiger's tail at bottom of projector plate's edge, then put chameleon 1 in center of tiger's tail]*.

One day a chameleon who was sitting on a tiger's tail said to himself,

CHAMELEON 1 "I get so tired of changing colors all the time. I wish I had a color of my own. I know! If I remain on a leaf, I shall be green forever, and so I too will have a color of my own."

[Remove tiger tail and chameleon from projector, and place the leaf pages on the projector, extending down from the projector plate's top edge. Make sure that the yellow and blue/green are carefully overlapped so that the leaves are completely green.]

With this thought he cheerfully climbed onto the greenest leaf.

[Place chameleon 1 in the middle of one of the leaves.]

But in autumn the leaf turned yellow—and so did the chameleon.

[Hold the yellow leaf sheet and the chameleon in place with one hand, and quickly but gently pull the blue/green leaf overlay out

from between them with the other hand so that the chameleon is now sitting in the middle of a yellow leaf.]

And then the winter winds blew the leaf from the branch and with it the chameleon.

[Pull yellow leaf sheet and chameleon 1 quickly off the projector plate.]

The days were GREY,

[Place solid light grey sheet on projector.]

and the winter winds came howling, and it began to SNOW *[place the three cut paper snowflakes onto the grey sheet; they will look black].*

The chameleon was black in the long winter night *[place dark chameleon on the grey sheet along with the snowflakes].*

But at last the days began to grow warmer, and the SUN grew brighter *[place sun transparency in center of projector plate],*

And it was spring!

[Hold the green grass sheet below the bottom of the projector plate and move it slowly upward so it looks like the grass is "growing"; then leave the grass on the projector.]

The chameleon walked out into the green grass *[push chameleon 1 out into the grass from one side of the transparency; stop him with his nose in the center].*

And there he met another chameleon *[push clear chameleon 2 out into the grass from the other side; stop him with his nose near the center, facing chameleon 1].*

The first little chameleon told his sad story.

CHAMELEON 1 "Won't we ever have a color of our own?" he asked.

CHAMELEON 2 "I'm afraid not," said the other chameleon, who was older and wiser. "But, I've got a great idea. Why don't we stay together? We will still change color wherever we go, but you and I will always be alike."

And so they remained side by side.
They were green together in the grass,
and purple, and yellow, and many, many colors,

[Remove grass transparency sheet with the two clear chameleons, and place mushroom onto projector plate.]

even red with white polka dots *[place the two clear chameleons on the polka-dot mushroom cap].*

And they lived HAPPILY EVER AFTER.

[The audience can/will likely say this with you.]

[Show audience last page of book, with the two chameleons together on the polka-dot mushroom.]

THE END

Script adapted by Kimberly K. Faurot, *Books in Bloom: Creative Patterns and Props That Bring Stories to Life* (ALA, 2003).

PATTERN INSTRUCTIONS

Overhead Projector Story (Sample Pattern)

A Color of His Own by Leo Lionni

Patterns

Transparency story pieces designed by Kimberly Faurot

Estimated difficulty

Easy

Estimated construction time

3 hours

Estimated cost for supplies

$15–$20

You Will Need These Tools

small sharp-pointed scissors
X-acto knife
piece of cardboard for cutting surface
2 Sharpie permanent black marking pens (1 Fine Point; 1 Ultra Fine Point)
ruler
clear narrow double-stick tape
rubber cement
Aleene's Original "Tacky" Glue (flexible fabric glue)

You Will Need These Supplies

SUPPLIES TO MAKE THE TRANSPARENCY PIECES

8 clear transparency sheets or clear artist's acetate (size 8 1/2" × 11" sheets)

13 colored transparent report cover acetate or artist's acetate (numbers given are for size 8 1/2" × 11" sheets; if you are using artist's acetate, it usually comes in 20" × 25" or 21" × 51" sheets):

- 1 blue (If the blue makes a nice bright green on the projector when overlapped with the yellow, use that for the leaf overlay; otherwise, use green.)
- 4 green
- 2 orange (Orange artist's acetate is often termed "amber.")
- 2 grey
- 3 yellow
- 1 red

1 sheet (8 1/2" × 11") solid color opaque flexible plastic (e.g., from a report cover) or black poster board

1 sheet dark-colored copy paper or wrapping paper

2 paper clips (regular size)

Directions

How to Make the Transparency Pieces

Step 1

Measure the projector plate of the overhead projector that you will be using to tell the story. (Most plates are approximately 8" × 8".) Trim six of your clear transparency/acetate sheets to size 8 1/2" × 8 1/2" and set them aside to be "base" sheets.

Step 2

Photocopy patterns *at sizes specified.* Cut out the photocopied patterns (along the outside of the pattern outline) for the WINTER CHAMELEON and the TIGER TAIL STRIPES only; you do not need to cut out any of the other patterns because you will be tracing them through the colored acetate.

Step 3

Lay the cut-out paper patterns for the dark pieces (TIGER TAIL STRIPES and WINTER CHAMELEON) onto the solid opaque flexible plastic or dark poster board. Trace with your Ultra Fine Point Sharpie marker. Cut out the pieces and set them aside.

Step 4

Lay the colored acetate over their appropriate pattern pieces, taking care to waste as little of the acetate as possible. Trace the cutting lines with your Ultra Fine Point Sharpie marker. Cut out the pieces along the *inside* of the marker lines (so the lines aren't there on the finished pieces) with your scissors, using the X-acto knife for very tight areas such as eyeholes, mushroom dots, and so forth. Lay the pieces on top of cardboard when using the X-acto knife so you don't damage your work surface.

Step 5

Measure and cut out one 8 1/2" × 2 5/8" strip each of yellow, red, and green acetate, and set them aside (these pieces will form the tricolor page).

Step 6

Lay clear acetate over the MUSHROOM pattern, and trace the outline with your Fine Point Sharpie marker. Cut the clear mushroom stem out along the *outside* of the marker lines (so that they *will* show on the finished piece); cut the clear mushroom cap out along the *inside* of the marker lines (so the lines *are not* there on the finished piece).

Step 7

Lay clear acetate over the two clear CHAMELEON patterns, and trace the outlines and facial features with your Fine Point Sharpie marker. Cut out the pieces along the *outside* of the marker lines (so the lines *will* show on the finished pieces) with your scissors. You do not need to cut out between the chameleons' legs or inside chameleon 1's curling tail—just leave the acetate solid at those points.

Cut out a clear acetate eyepiece for the winter chameleon, larger than its eyehole so the piece can be glued around the edge. The eyepiece's outline will not show once it is glued on, so you may cut it out however you wish.

Step 8

Glue the TIGER TAIL STRIPES onto the TIGER TAIL using the tacky glue. Follow the placement shown by the lines on the pattern. Allow glue to dry completely.

Apply a ring of tacky glue around the edge of the winter chameleon's clear eyepiece and place it so the piece covers the eyehole. Allow glue to dry completely.

Step 9

Using rubber cement, glue the parrot's beak and feet onto the parrot, and the tusks onto the elephant. Allow glue to dry completely. If necessary, trim around the beak, feet, and tusks so that the edges of the overlapped colored acetate are even.

Step 10

Using rubber cement, glue the PARROT, the group of GOLDFISH, and the ELEPHANT each to a separate clear base transparency sheet, which you trimmed in step 1. Apply the rubber cement to the colored images in long even strokes. Arrange the goldfish on the transparency like they were on the pattern; place the parrot and the elephant each in the middle of their respective transparency sheets.

Step 11

Using rubber cement, glue the red MUSHROOM CAP over the clear base cap. Glue the mushroom grass tuft at the bottom of the mushroom stem.

Step 12

Hold the yellow and blue or green LEAVES together to make sure their edges will line up exactly when they are overlapped. Trim as necessary so that the edges of the overlapped colored acetate are even.

Step 13

Apply rubber cement to the yellow leaves around the edges and in the middle in a leaf vein pattern. Stick the leaves onto one of the clear base transparency sheets, placing them so the flat edge lines up with the edge of the clear base transparency.

Step 14

Apply rubber cement to one of the tall GRASS blade pieces by brushing it vertically for texture. Lining the grass section up with the bottom edge of one of the clear base transparency sheets for placement, affix it to the base sheet. Flip the second grass section over so that it will be a mirror image of the first section. Apply rubber cement to the section and affix it to the base sheet. Glue the grey GROUND strip across the bottom of the sheet.

Step 15

Brush rubber cement in a circle around the inner edge of the orange SUN'S RAYS. Making sure that the orange and yellow rays are positioned as shown on the pattern, stick the orange sun's rays down onto the yellow SUN.

Step 16

Affix a strip of transparent double-stick tape along both the top and bottom edges of your final clear transparency base sheet. Place the red, yellow, and green colored strips next to each other on top of the clear base sheet, positioning them carefully so the edges line up exactly. Press them down onto the tape so they are fused along the top and bottom, forming the tricolor page.

Step 17

Using your Fine Point Sharpie marker, color in the eyes for the parrot, goldfish, elephant, and winter chameleon. You should have already drawn the clear chameleons' eyes in step 7.

Also make some small dots on the LEMON, following the pattern for placement.

Step 18

Measure your piece of dark copy or wrapping paper into three squares measuring 3" × 3" each.

To make your paper SNOWFLAKES, fold each square in half, then half again, then half again (and once more if possible) so you have three tiny elongated triangles.

Snip small bits out from along the sides of each triangle as well as snipping off the tiny point. Round off the outer edges of the triangles, and then snip out little pieces from along the edge. When you have finished snipping out as many and as varied little bits as you have room for, unfold the paper triangles to reveal your paper snowflakes. Try to vary the finished sizes and styles of your snowflakes as much as possible. (*See* figure 4-1.)

Figure 4-1

Overhead Projector Story Finished Product

Figure 4-2

Figure 4-3

Figure 4-4

Figure 4-5

Figure 4-6

Figure 4-7

Figure 4-8

Figure 4-9

Figure 4-10

Figure 4-11

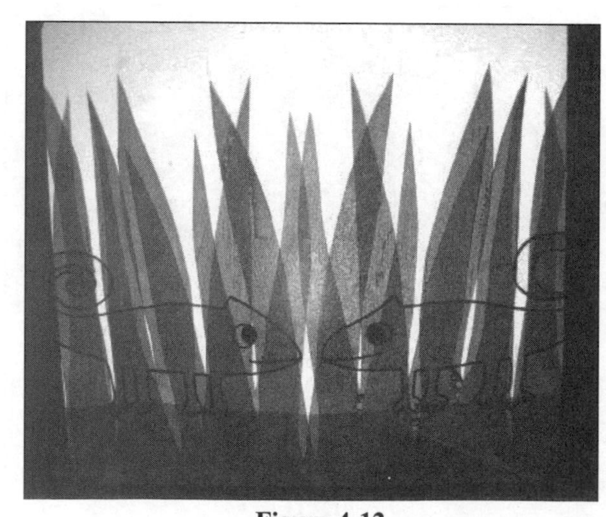

Figure 4-12

Figure 4-13

Photocopy this page at size 100%.

STRIPE 1

STRIPE 2

STRIPE 3

STRIPE 4

STRIPE 5

STRIPE 6

STRIPE 7

STRIPE 8

A Color of His Own
TIGER TAIL STRIPES
Cut stripes from opaque plastic or poster board.

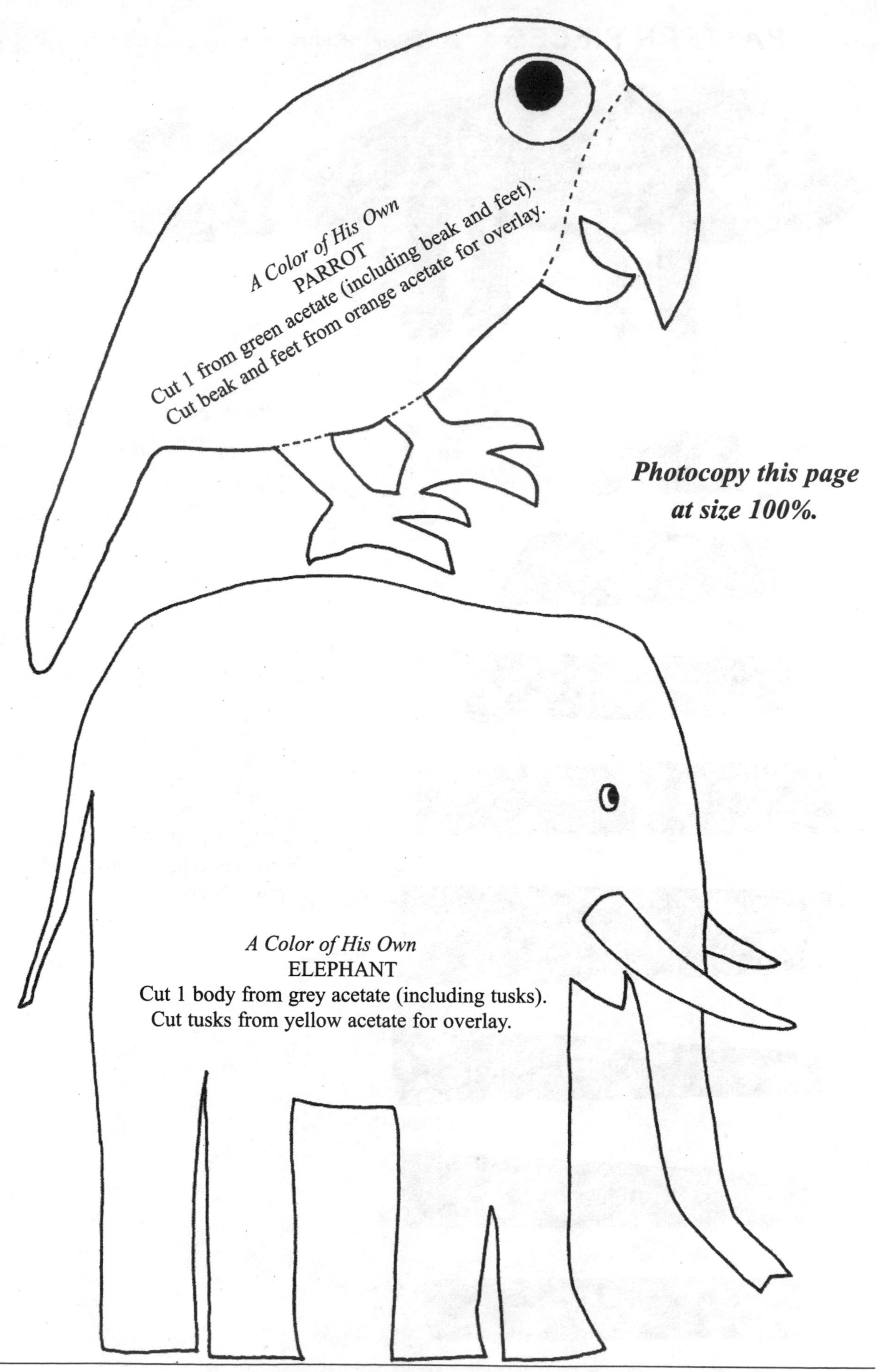

Photocopy this page at size 100%.

Photocopy this page at size 100%.

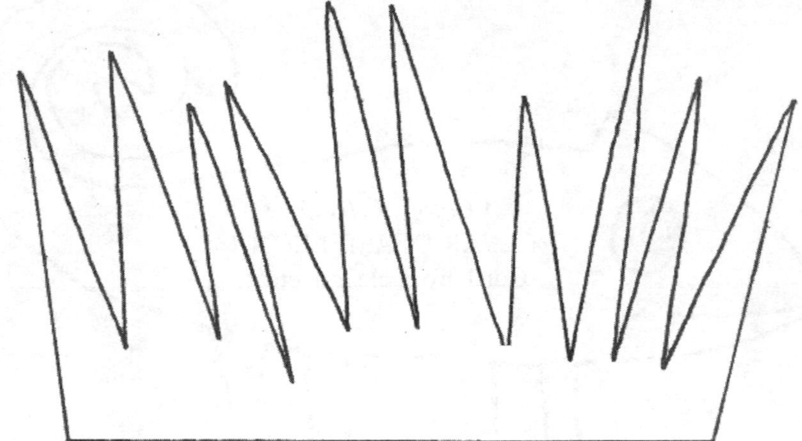

A Color of His Own
MUSHROOM GRASS
Cut 1 from green acetate.

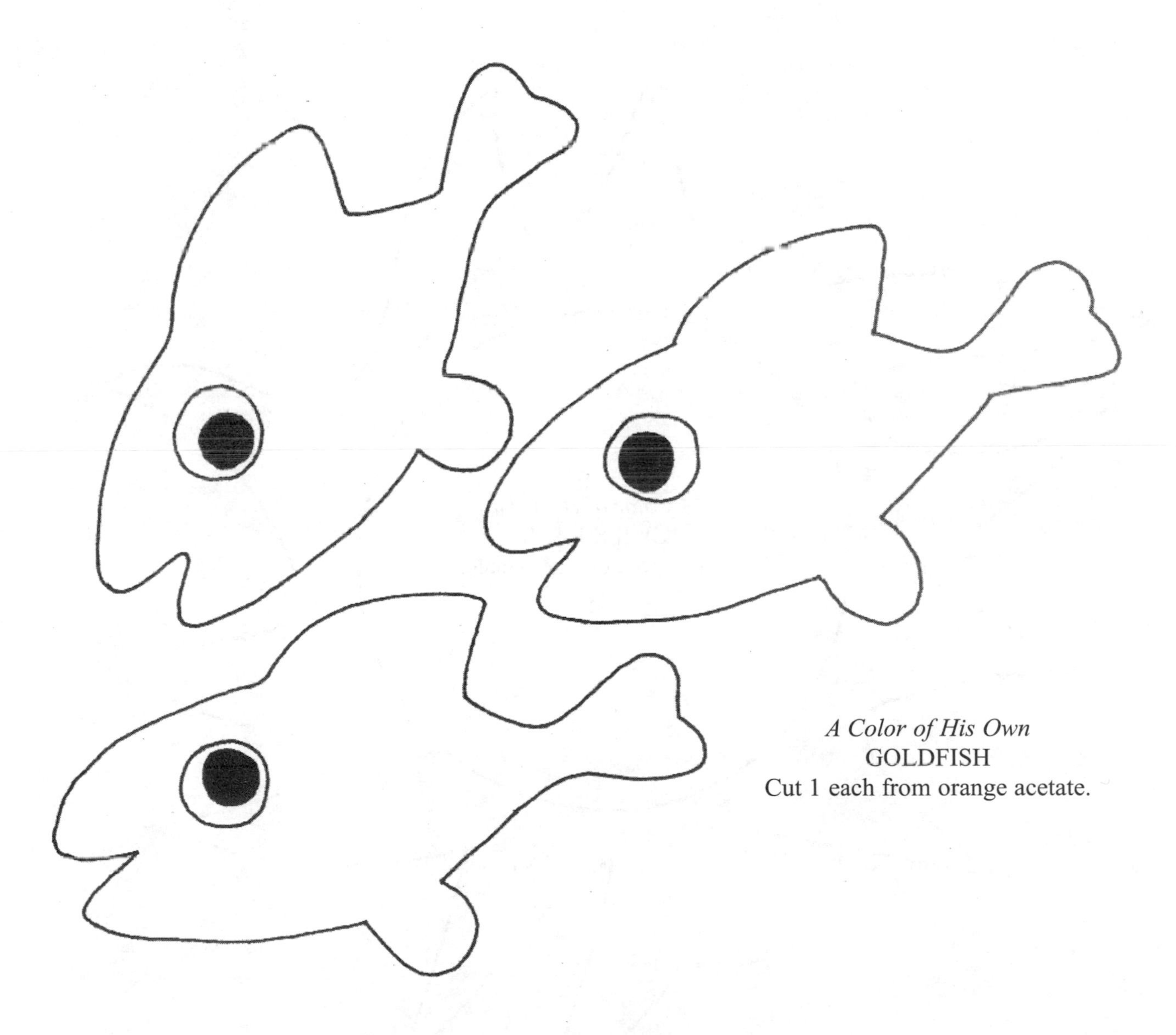

A Color of His Own
GOLDFISH
Cut 1 each from orange acetate.

Photocopy this page at size 100%.

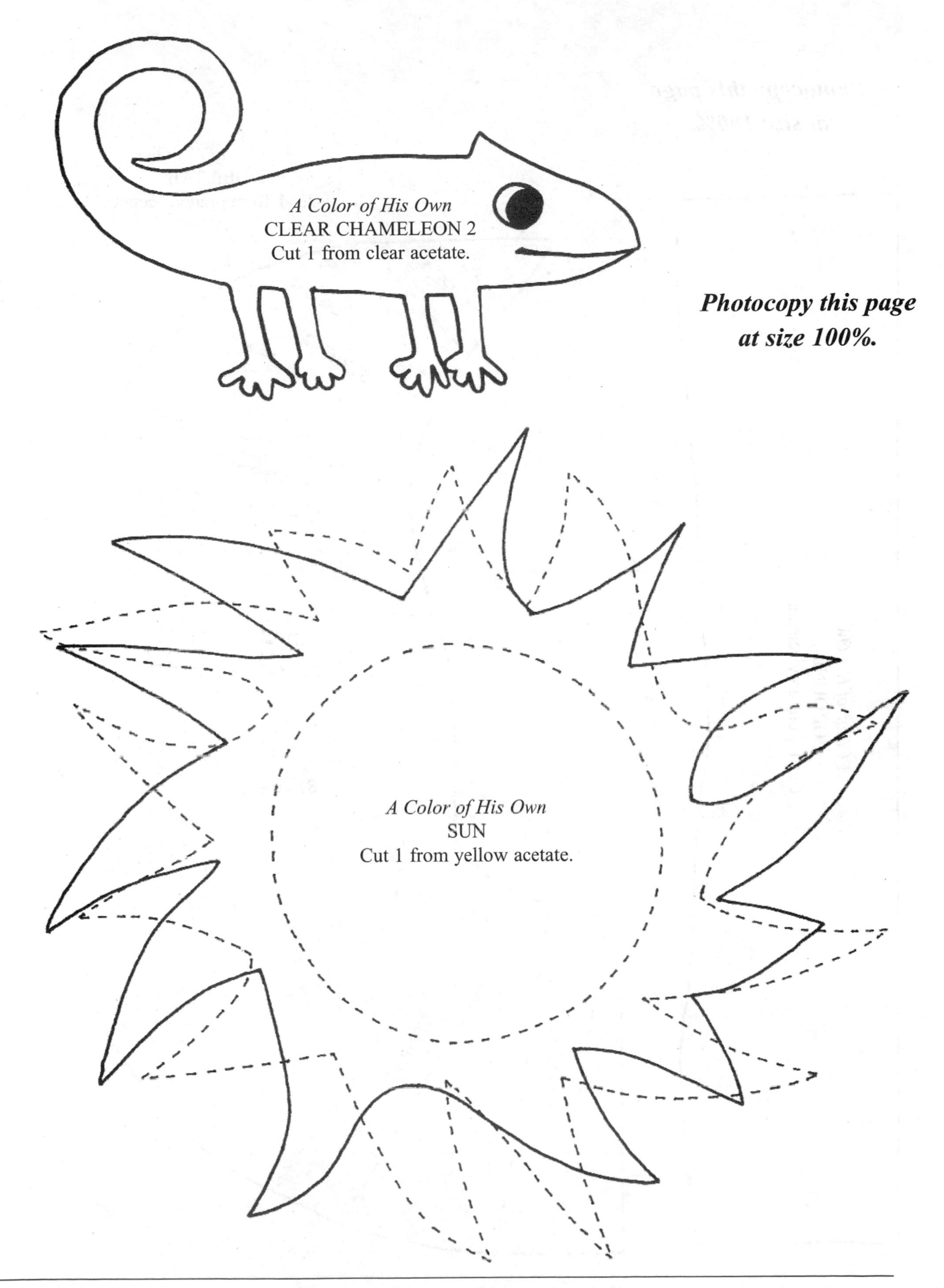

Photocopy this page at size 100%.

Photocopy this page at size 100%.

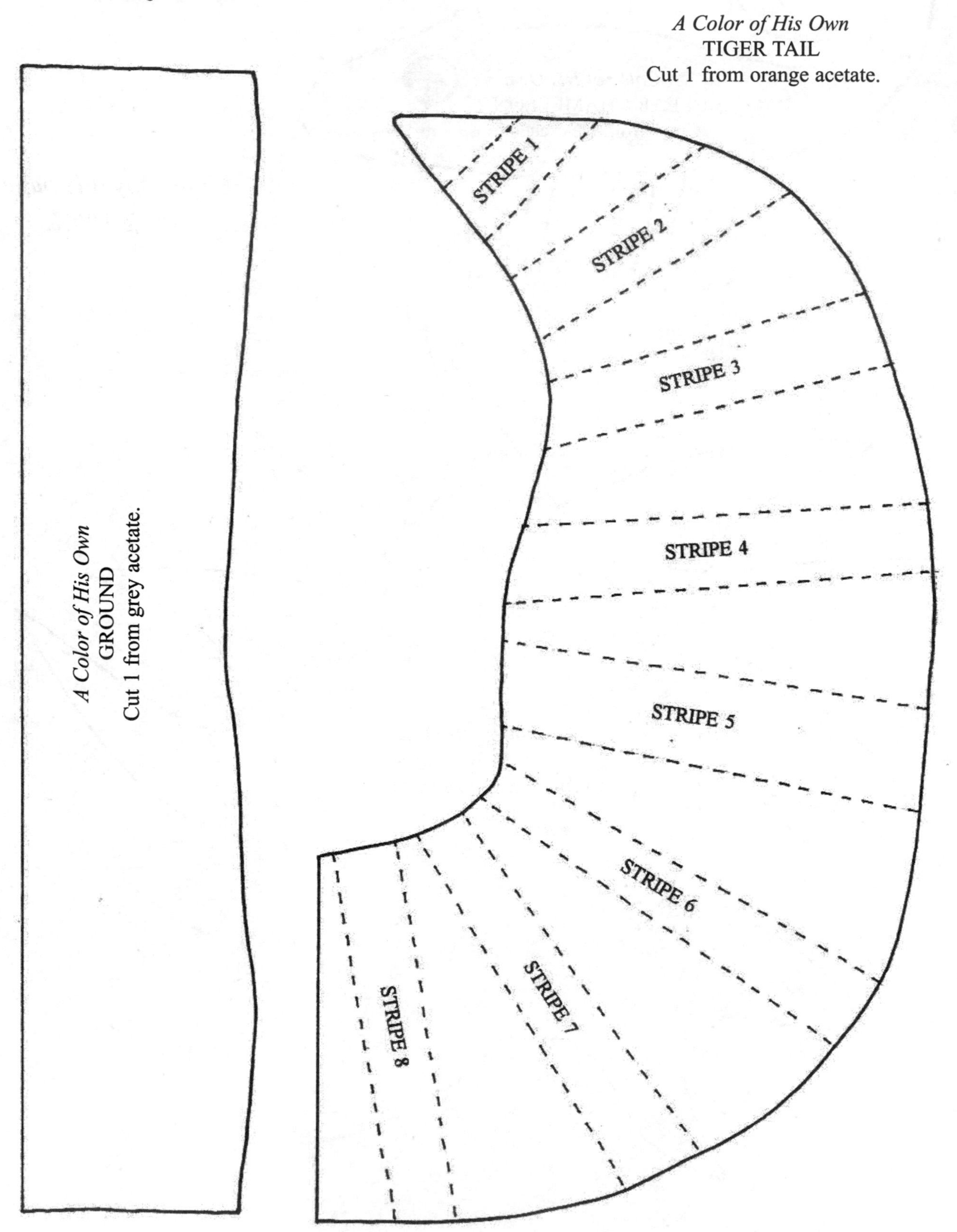

Photocopy this page at size 100%.

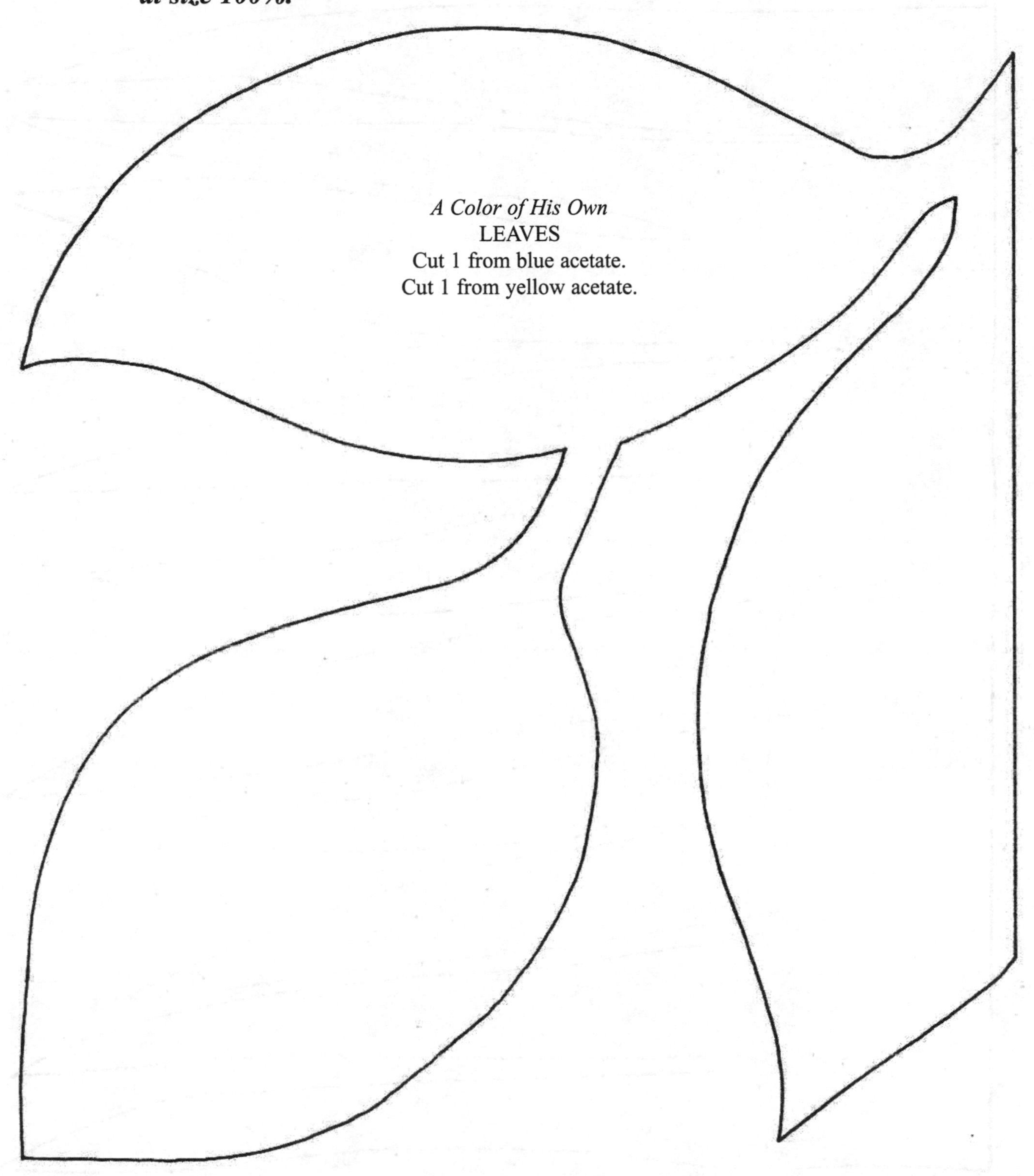

Photocopy this page at size 100%.

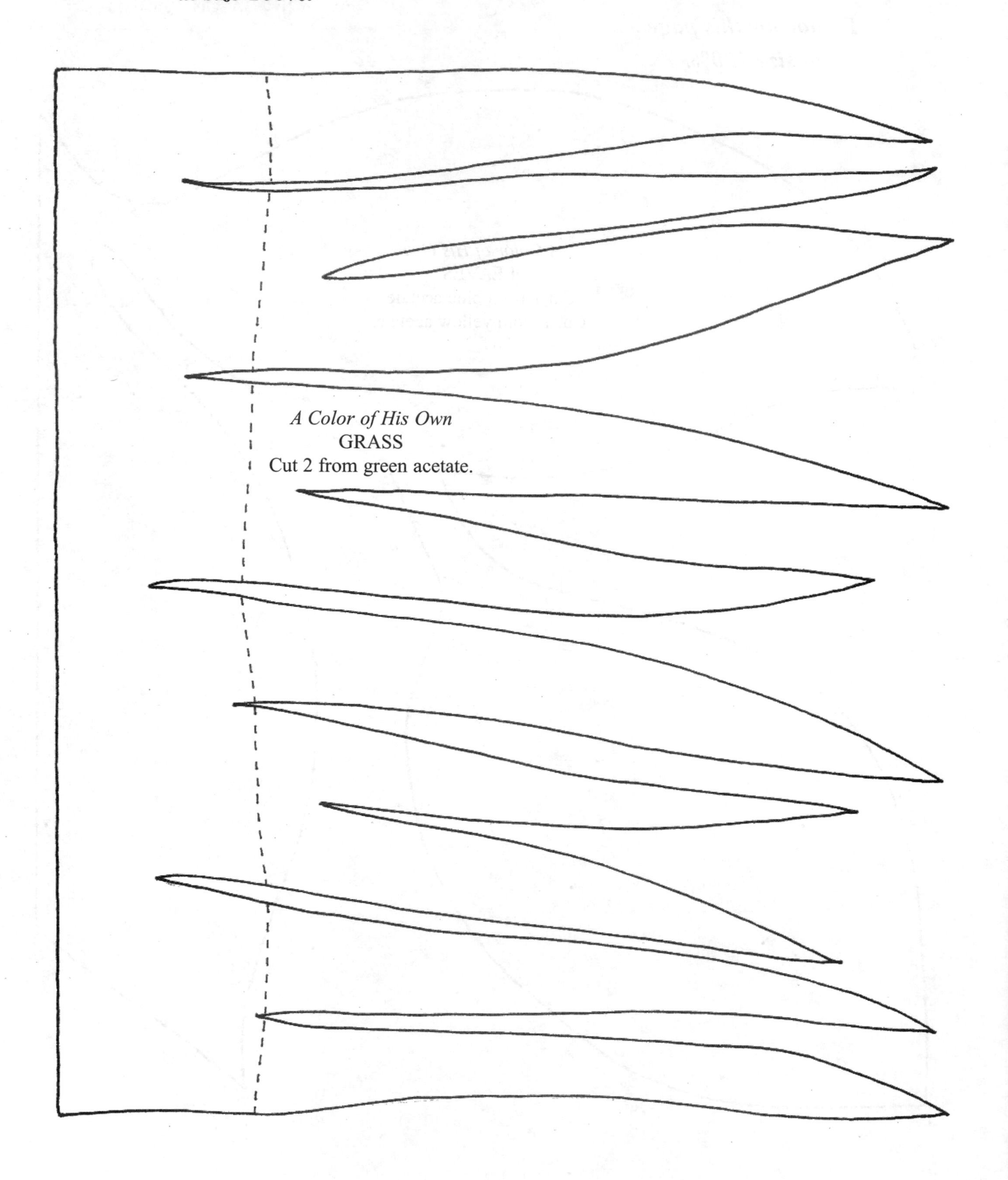

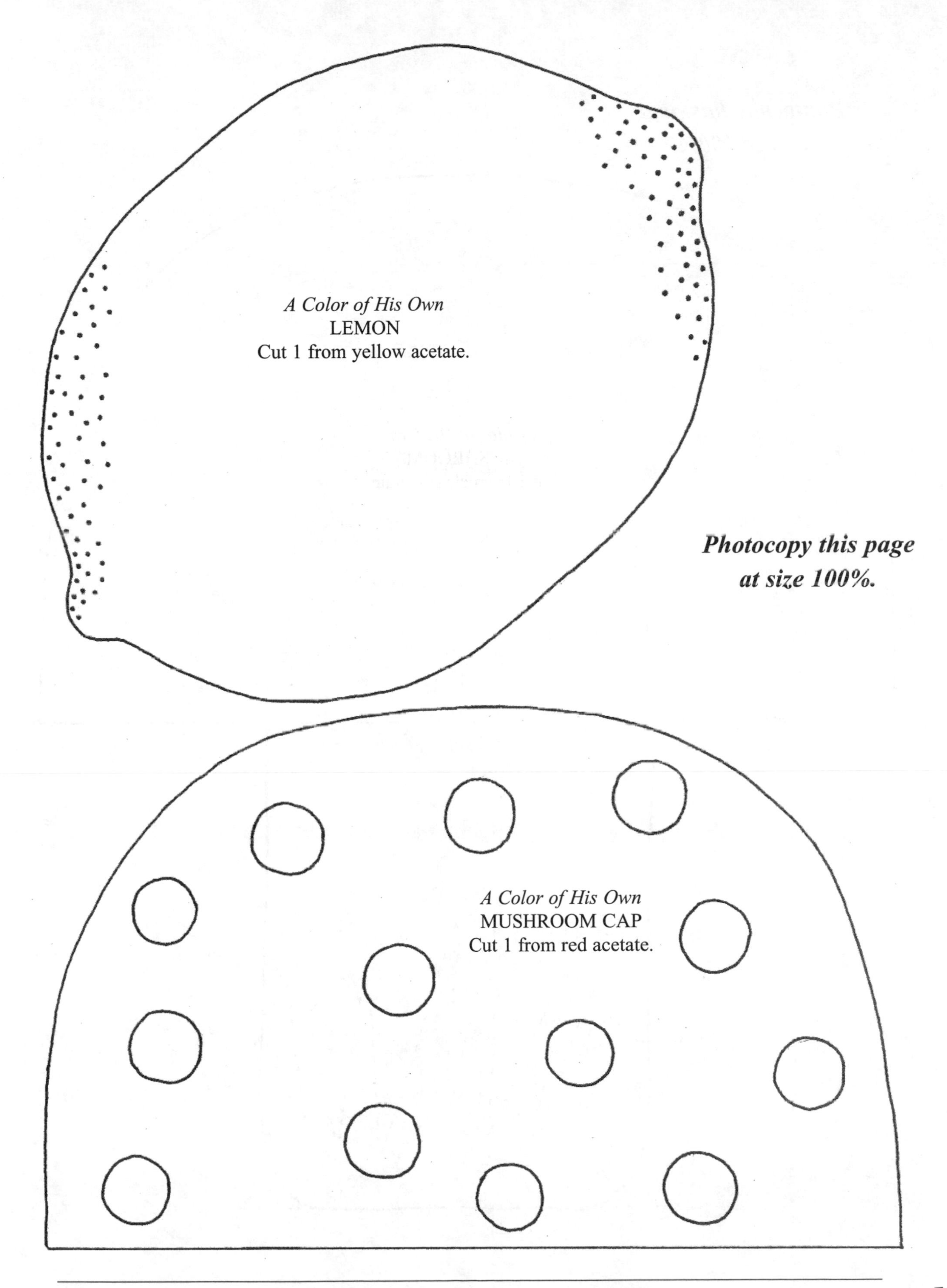

Photocopy this page at size 100%.

Photocopy this page at size 100%.

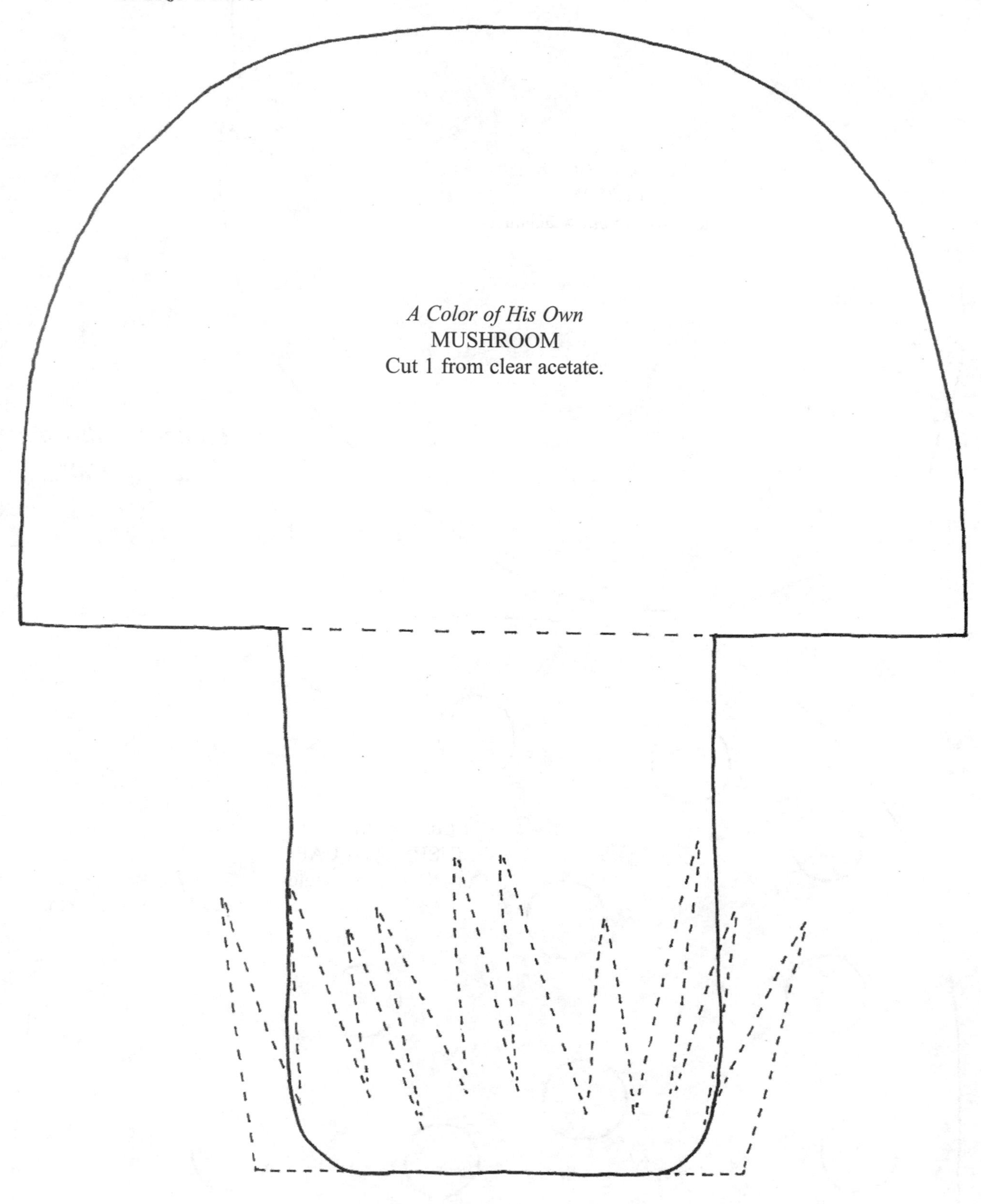

Storage

You Will Need

2 no. 5 1/2 invitation-sized envelopes

1 9" × 12" piece of sturdy cardboard or matte board

1 10" × 13" manila storage envelope

1 sturdy, shallow box, slightly larger than the manila storage envelope (optional)

1–3 copies of *A Color of His Own* storage label

2 copies of the *A Color of His Own* presentation notes/script (pages 33–36)

1 copy of overhead projector story finished product photos (figures 4-2 through 4-13)

Make three photocopies of the label provided for the *A Color of His Own* transparency prop and fill in the *date* and *name or initials* blanks. Cut out the labels. Affix one label to the front of the large storage envelope. If you decide to store the envelope inside its own box, too, affix the other two labels to both ends of the storage box.

A Color of His Own

Leo Lionni (Random, 1975)

Prop created_______ by _________________
DATE NAME OR INITIALS

from patterns included in *Books in Bloom*
by Kimberly Faurot (ALA, 2003)

The transparency pieces for *A Color of His Own* should be stored flat to keep them from bending. Place the three chameleons into one of the no. 5 1/2 invitation-sized envelopes, and label it "CHAMELEONS; transparency pieces for *A Color of His Own* by Leo Lionni." Place the three small paper snowflakes into the second no. 5 1/2 invitation-sized envelope, and label it "SNOWFLAKES; transparency pieces for *A Color of His Own* by Leo Lionni." Separating these small pieces from the larger ones will help keep them from becoming lost or damaged.

Stack the twelve larger-sized transparency pages and pieces in order of appearance in the story. Lay them on top of the piece of 9" × 12" sturdy cardboard or matte board, and slide them all into the manila storage envelope. Including the sturdy cardboard will help keep the transparency pieces from becoming bent or damaged. Put both of the smaller envelopes into the large storage envelope as well.

Depending upon the number of props you have in your collection and the amount of storage space that you have, you may want to store the envelope in a sturdy, shallow box that will further ensure that the pieces don't become damaged. You could begin a box for "Overhead Projector Stories," and store everything you make in that medium in that box. Make sure you label the box extremely well, however, including the titles of all of the stories on the outside of the box.

Make at least two photocopies of the presentation notes/script (pages 33–36), and include them in the storage envelope along with the transparency pieces. Also include a photocopy of the overhead projector story finished product photos (figures 4-2 through 4-13).

A professional storytelling copy of the original book *A Color of His Own* by Leo Lionni (Random, 1975) should either be included in the envelope with the prop (on the other side of the cardboard from the transparency pieces) or should be kept nearby in a professional "storytelling collection" so it may be shown when the prop is being presented. If you are unable to obtain a new copy of the book, investigate purchasing a used copy through one of the resources listed in chapter 10.

Make sure that the transparency storytelling pieces for *A Color of His Own* are included on your storytelling props database or list (*see* chapter 2) as well as in your institution's inventory records.

Notify other staff members who might be able to include *A Color of His Own* in their programming or classrooms that it is ready for use, and demonstrate it for them (along with proper storage caveats) if at all possible.

Summary

Overhead projectors offer exciting alternative techniques for visual storytelling. The materials required are not terribly expensive, and even early elementary age children can learn how to work with the medium. The vivid clarity and exaggerated size of projected images make them ideal for storytelling with large audiences and with a wide range of ages.

Finger Puppets

Includes script and pattern for

"Mouse House" poem

Pattern difficulty level

Easy

Construction time estimate

2–4 hours

Finger puppets may be used very successfully with children, both individually and in a group. These tiny puppets have many advantages: they are easy to make, cheap to purchase, and very nonthreatening because of their small size, even for the shyest child. A finger puppet can be an excellent one-on-one "greeter" or "good-bye" puppet, or an effective segue. It can conveniently live in your pocket and make periodic appearances during formal programming or simply during casual moments.

Techniques and Considerations

Creating

Finger puppets can be created using a wide variety of affordable materials such as paper, felt, cloth, or cardboard tubes. There are many patterns available in craft books as well as on the World Wide Web. Die-cut companies such as Ellison and Accu-Cut (*see* chapter 10) have various finger puppet dies, which enable you to readily punch out large quantities of the figure from heavy paper or from felt. These are flat-shaped figures with two finger holes punched in them for the puppeteer's index and middle fingers to poke through. Three-finger puppets consist of a three-dimensional head that fits on the middle or pointer finger, with the pointer and ring fingers or middle finger and thumb animating two legs or hands for the puppet. Finger puppets may be knitted or crocheted, made from little sewn or glued felt cone bodies with an attached felt head, constructed from toilet paper tubes or other household objects, or shaped from felt or fabric and either glued or sewn.

Even though they are tiny, finger puppets can be imbued with personality through special additions such as feathers, google eyes, or wild fur hair. Try to make your finger puppets visually interesting, with little accessories such as tiny doll hats, glasses, ribbons, and so forth.

Because many types of finger puppets can be made very easily, they can be an ideal craft project for children, either at home or during an organized craft session.

Presenting

There are several important points to remember when manipulating finger puppets. First, they have an extremely limited range of motion by their very nature. Unlike hand puppets, which can at least usually wave their arms about and scratch their heads, finger puppets are restricted to gross forward/back and side-to-side motions. As a result, it is much more difficult to make them seem animated and "alive." Having the puppets pop in and out of various locations as well as turn back and forth as they "look" at the audience can help overcome this problem. Another point to remember is that finger puppets' sounds and voices should be appropriate to their size as well as to their characters.

Finger puppets' success as part of group programming depends largely upon the size of the group. If the group is big, children sitting at the back or sides will be unable to see a finger puppet clearly enough for it to be used in any extended way. Consequently, trying to tell an elaborate story to a large group using small finger puppets would likely result in wandering audience attention. Short poems or activities where the finger puppet's appearance is the goal, however, can often work well. Even if part of the audience is some distance away, they can see the movement of the puppet's sudden appearance. If the segment is short and involves a limited need for extended focused concentration, the entire audience should be able to follow and enjoy the action.

Choosing the Finger Puppet Format

An example of this type of poem/activity where the finger puppets' appearance is of primary importance is "Mouse House." The poem invites audience participation to command each mouse's appearance through the windows of the little mouse house. Although "Mouse House" could certainly be successfully interpreted in other media, such as with a felt board presentation or by a flat poster board house facade with paper stick puppet mice hiding behind it, the three-dimensional house and finger puppets allow a dynamic presentation that feels much more realistic than these other media. The house may be scratched surreptitiously inside as the mice "scamper" and "creep," causing the audience to be quiet and listen attentively for these sounds. When the little mice pop out from behind the window curtains, they have enough range of motion to allow them to turn back and forth to greet the audience, and to nod their heads "yes" and "no."

"Mouse House"

Summary

Three little mice peek out one by one from their little house.

Possible themes

Animals, Babies, Big and Little, Families, Houses, Mice

Approximate running time for poem with props (including introduction and participation)

3–5 minutes

Recommended audience interest level

Preschool (age 1 and older) through grade 1

Please note that the prop pieces are designed as professional resources, not as playthings. They do not conform to child safety play standards, and they could easily become damaged if used in a manner other than that for which they were intended.

Prop Pieces

cardboard box Mouse House with box lid

3 finger puppet mice: 1 boy mouse, 1 girl mouse, 1 baby mouse

Use with

nothing additional needed

Setup

Take the mice out of the plastic storage bag and lay them on the floor of the house.

Keep the lid on the back of the house until it's time for the prop to be used to avoid children peeking around the back.

Presentation

When it is time to use the house, take the lid off and leave it within easy reach so you can replace it when you are done presenting the prop.

Hold the house on your lap if it's a very small group and everyone can see; otherwise, you can hold it up in the air with one hand and "scratch" the floor and manipulate the finger puppets with the other hand.

Depending upon the makeup of a particular audience, your time, and other constraints, you may want to use only part of the mouse family.

Try to encourage as much audience participation as possible. Words in the poem typed in CAPITAL letters are good opportunities for the audience to say the word with you. They will usually say "PEEP!" voluntarily as a group at the end of the poem; if they don't, gesture to them expectantly and say it with them. They will say it on their own the next time.

Story narration is shown in regular type; movement notes and miscellaneous directions are delineated in *[bracketed italics].*

Please note: Below are a brief possible introduction and conclusion for establishing effective audience participation using the story pieces in addition to the poem.

Possible Introduction

HOLD UP THE HOUSE AND ASK THE CHILDREN:

"What kind of an animal puppet do you think might live in this house?" Take guesses.

SAY:

"Look at the size of the house. Do you think a BIG animal could live in there, or is it a SMALL animal?"

Take guesses, saying that all are good guesses. Even if someone guesses "Mouse," keep taking guesses for as long as you like.

TELL THE GROUP:

"This is actually a MOUSE HOUSE. There's a little poem we can say to try and get them to peek out at us, and it goes like this":

SCRIPT

"Mouse House" poem

Inside the little HOUSE,

[Point to the house as you say this to involve group.]

There lives a little MOUSE.

[Encourage audience to say "Mouse" along with you.]

Hear him scamper?

[Scratch with your fingernail inside the cardboard box.]

Script adapted by Kimberly K. Faurot, *Books in Bloom: Creative Patterns and Props That Bring Stories to Life* (ALA, 2003).

Hear him creep?

[Scratch cardboard again, making a different sound.]

He'll look out

[With your hand hidden behind the house facade, slip the boy mouse puppet securely onto your index finger.]

If you say "PEEP!"

[Audience says "PEEP!" Mouse peeks out through one of the upstairs windows.]

"Hi, Mouse!" *[Mouse squeaks "Eeeeeee."]* Have the children squeak "Hi" back to Mouse.

"Mouse, we have a couple of questions for you.

Does anyone else live there in the house with you?" *[Mouse nods head "Yes."]* Ask the children if Mouse is saying yes or no.

"Is it a giraffe?" *[Mouse shakes head "No."]*

"Is it an elephant?" *[Mouse vehemently shakes head "No."]*

"Is it another mouse?" *[Mouse enthusiastically nods "Yes."]*

"Is it a boy?" *[Mouse shakes head "No."]*

"Is it a girl?" *[Mouse nods "Yes."]*

"Do you think she'll look out if we say the poem again?" *[Mouse nods "Yes."]*

"Okay, we'll try it. Thanks for visiting. Tell everybody 'Bye.'"

[Mouse squeaks "Eeeeeee" and disappears behind the house façade again; remove puppet surreptitiously from finger, and hide it again on the floor of the Mouse House.]

Repeat poem again, using *she* instead of *he.* Go through the entire dialogue again, and ask if anyone else lives in the house. *[Girl Mouse nods "Yes."]*

"Is it a big mouse?" *[Girl Mouse emphatically shakes head "No."]*

"Is it a baby mouse?" *[Girl Mouse nods "Yes."]*

"Do you think the baby will look out if we say the little poem again?" *[Girl Mouse nods "Yes."]*

"Okay, thank you! Good-bye!"

[Girl Mouse squeaks "Eeeeeee" and disappears behind the house façade; remove puppet surreptitiously from finger, and hide it again on the floor of the Mouse House.]

TELL THE CHILDREN:

"Okay, we'll try the poem one more time for the baby. Because it's a baby, though, we need to be careful not to frighten it, so we'd better say the poem *very* softly."

Say poem softly.

[Baby Mouse peeks out.]

[Baby squeaks "Eeeeeee" and disappears behind the house façade; remove puppet surreptitiously from finger, and hide it again on the floor of the Mouse House.]

Tell the children it's time for Baby Mouse's nap and for the rest of storytime. Put the lid back onto the Mouse House so the children don't run up to peek behind it.

Possible Conclusion

If the children are very interested in the Mouse House, you may want to repeat the poem once more and have all three mice peek out together at the end of your program. Tell the children that they can make their own Mouse Houses—either as part of a follow-up craft activity or at home. Ask them if they can guess what your Mouse House was made out of: turn it around so they can see the back so they'll see it was a cardboard box. Tell them that the flowers are made of felt, and the curtains are little pieces of material. You may want to include the following craft suggestion on any handouts:

To Make Together at Home:

Try making a little mouse finger puppet from the finger of an old glove.
Glue on eyes and ears, and make him a little shoebox house!
Have a grown-up cut out windows and a little door for the mouse to peek out,
and glue curtains over the windows so the mouse can look out under them!

Other Activities

I often follow up the Mouse House with John Ciardi's poem "I Wouldn't," using the Mouse House and a large stuffed plush cat (*see* chapter 10).

If one or more of the mouse finger puppets will be part of any of your other stories, you can say the "Mouse House" poem and have the mouse actually emerge through the front door of the little house. Help each mouse put on any "costumes" he or she may need for his or her role in the other stories.

PATTERN INSTRUCTIONS

Finger Puppets (Sample Pattern)

"Mouse House" poem

Patterns

Mouse House designed by Kathy Kennedy Tapp

Mouse family finger puppets designed by Kimberly Faurot

Estimated difficulty

Easy

Estimated construction time

2–4 hours (depending on whether you make or purchase the finger puppets)

Estimated cost for supplies

$20

You Will Need These Tools

pencil
fine marking pen
small sharp-pointed scissors
pinking shears
straight pins
hand sewing needle
Aleene's Original "Tacky" Glue
Fray Check
ruler
narrow craft paintbrushes (flat sizes 2, 4, and 6)
X-acto knife or sharp utility knife
electric drill or sharp awl (or can use X-acto knife)
electric fan or hair dryer to speed drying time as needed (optional)

You Will Need These Supplies

SUPPLIES TO MAKE THE FINGER PUPPET MICE

grey plush felt for mouse bodies and ears (can also use other colors; if so, change thread and tail colors accordingly)

thread: grey, black, lavender, white

1/2 yard grey leather lacing for tail (cut into two 7" lengths; one 4" length for baby)

2 black pom-poms (size 7 mm)

1 black pom-pom (size 3 mm)

4 spherical shiny black buttons, approximately 1/8"

2 shiny black seed beads

9 lengths of fishing line, each 10" long (4-lb. test or lighter)

8" length of 1/4" wide lavender grosgrain ribbon

4" length of 1/2" wide white eyelet lace

acrylic craft paint: light pink

SUPPLIES TO MAKE AND DECORATE THE MOUSE HOUSE

corrugated no. 10 bulk envelopes box, approximate size 8 1/2" × 11" × 4" deep (*Please note:* Corrugated works best because it is sturdier; also, the door will hold its position better.)

light blue satin-finish spray paint

9 bright orange pom-poms (size 5 mm)

colored felt squares: white, yellow, orange, red, light green, bright green, true green, dark green (*Please note:* The orange pom-poms and some of the colored felt squares are to make bushes and flowers to decorate the Mouse House—you may prefer to purchase tiny artificial flowers and glue them on the house instead.)

14" green narrow rope trim (Cut into one 8" length and one 6" length.)

fabric for curtains: 3" square piece of white eyelet or woven fabric; two 3" square pieces of red/white gingham; 3" × 5" piece of red, white, and blue calico (When choosing the fabric, select a small print; also, make sure the colors contrast with your mice—if you chose to make white mice, don't make white curtains.)

white, yellow, orange, red, green, and black acrylic craft paint

small 3/8" wooden craft cabinet knob or wooden craft "button" (You can use a felt circle instead.)

copy of "Mouse House" poem template

clear book tape

Directions

How to Make the Finger Puppet Mice

Step 1

Photocopy mice patterns *at sizes specified.* Cut out all of the photocopied patterns along the outside of the pattern outlines.

Step 2

Pin MOUSE BODY and EAR patterns on *wrong* (smooth) side of plush felt. Cut out the fabric pieces as specified on the patterns. Cut a single layer at a time to avoid the plush felt shifting because of its thickness.

Step 3

Mark ear and eye placement lightly on the mouse bodies with pen on *right* (furry) side of fabric.

Step 4

Place a dot of tacky glue on half of each EAR piece. Fold ears over on dotted lines so that each ear is double-layered, and fuzzy on both sides. Allow glue to dry completely.

Step 5

With *right* (fuzzy) side together, fold MOUSE BODIES on dotted line and pin. Stitch along the edge from front to back (by hand or machine). Mouse bodies are inside out.

Along the seam near the body opening, lay one of the tail pieces approximately 1/2" in from the edge of each mouse body. Stitch tail to seam. Dot tied-off knots with Fray Check. (*See* figure 5-1.)

Turn mouse bodies right side out. (*See* figure 5-2.)

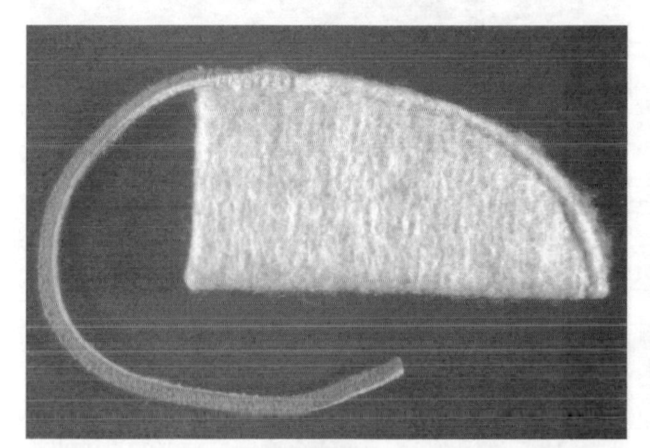

Figure 5-1

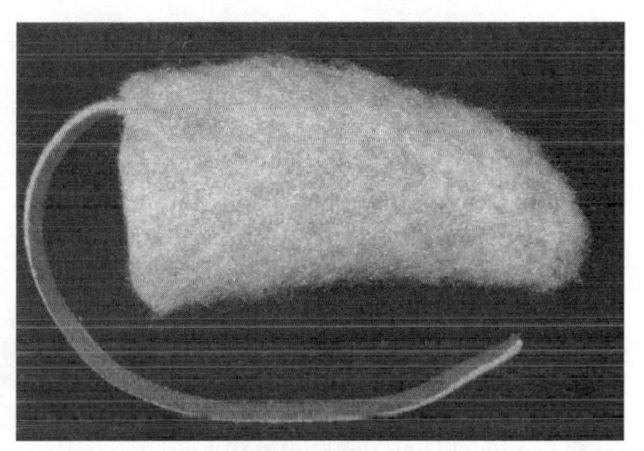

Figure 5-2

Step 6

Position ears according to markings; stitch at a perpendicular angle. For each mouse, use the same piece of thread for both ears. Tie off after stitching second ear; cut thread close. Dot knots with Fray Check. (*See* figure 5-3.)

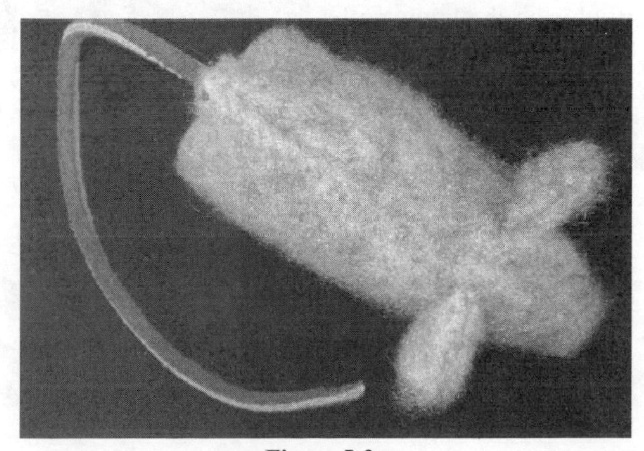

Figure 5-3

Step 7

Knot black thread and insert inside mouse bodies so the needle emerges through the very front tip of the nose. Stitch black pom-pom nose on end of each mouse body. The 7-mm pom-poms are for the larger mice; the 3-mm pom-pom is for the baby mouse.

Knot thread but do not cut. Insert needle outside to inside next to nose, then have it emerge at first eye marking. The spherical buttons are for the larger mice's eyes; the black seed beads are for the baby mouse's eyes. Stitch eyes on, one at a time, knotting the thread after the first eye but not cutting the thread until the nose and both eyes are all firmly attached. To give the mice a little bit more personality, take a couple of stitches from one eye button shank to the opposite one, pulling the eyes in together a little bit so they are indented in the mouse's face. Tie off thread and cut it close. Dot all knots with Fray Check. (*See* figure 5-4.)

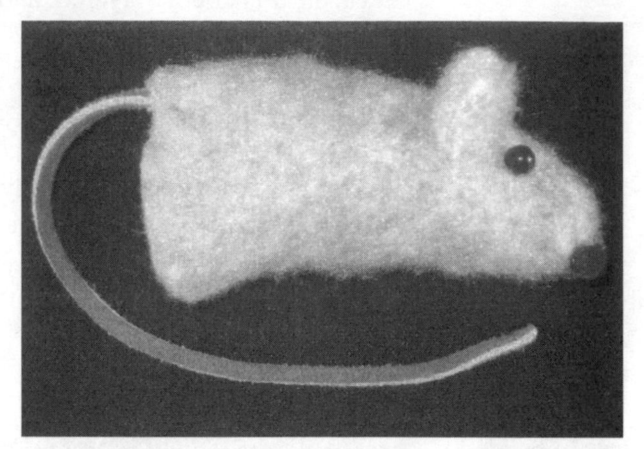

Figure 5-4

Step 8

Thread three 10" lengths of fishing line through a sharp needle with a larger eye. Pull needle through mouse nose just at the base of the pom-pom. Allow the three strands to hang freely off both sides in equal amounts. (*See* figure 5-5.)

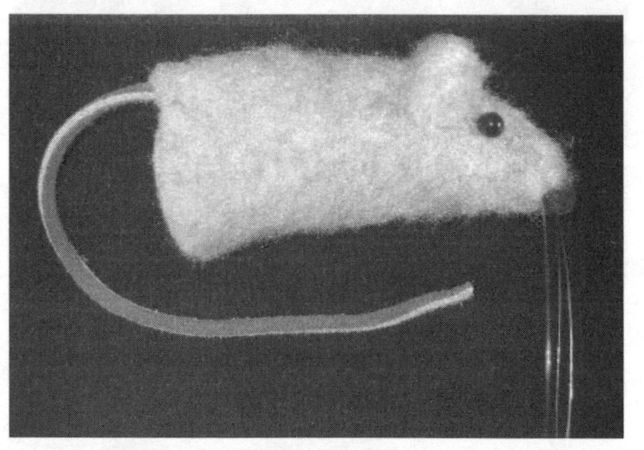

Figure 5-5

First on one side, tie the three strands in a *simple overhand knot* (*see* chapter 2, "Terms and Techniques"). Take care that the direction you tie your knot is the way you want the whiskers to point when you are done. Tie the strands a second time on the same side so the knot will hold.

From the other side of the nose, pull the three strands so the first whisker knot is held tightly against the nose. Tie off the second side of the whiskers. Make sure that you wrap your knots the opposite way so the whiskers will point the same direction as those on the first side. Dot all whisker fishing-line knots with tacky glue so the knots will not work loose.

Trim to approximately 3/4" on each side of the nose for the bigger mice; trim to approximately 1/2" on each side of the nose for the baby mouse. (*See* figure 5-6.)

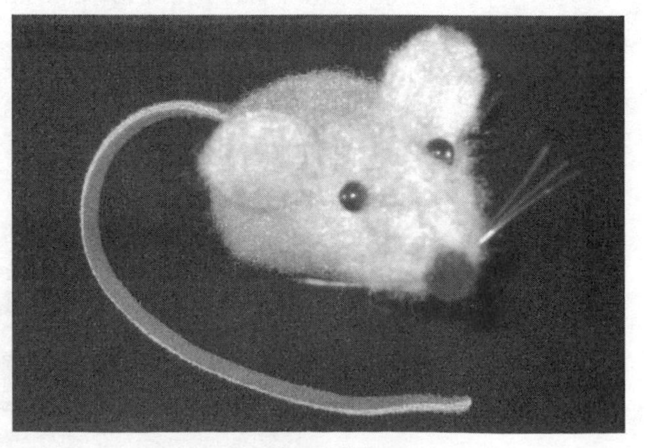

Figure 5-6

Step 9

Lightly paint center fronts of ears pale pink. Allow paint to dry completely.

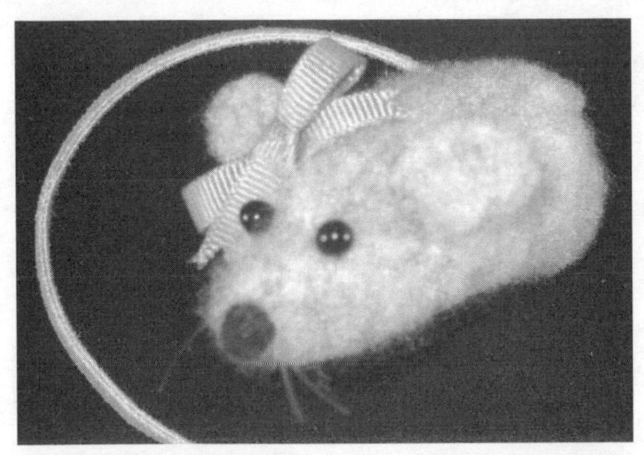

Figure 5-7

Step 10

For GIRL MOUSE only (ribbon):

Tie lavender ribbon into a tiny bow, approx. 1 1/2" long. Trim ends of ribbon in an inverted V as shown. With lavender thread, stitch center of bow so it will not loosen; then stitch to Girl Mouse's ear. (*See* figure 5-7.)

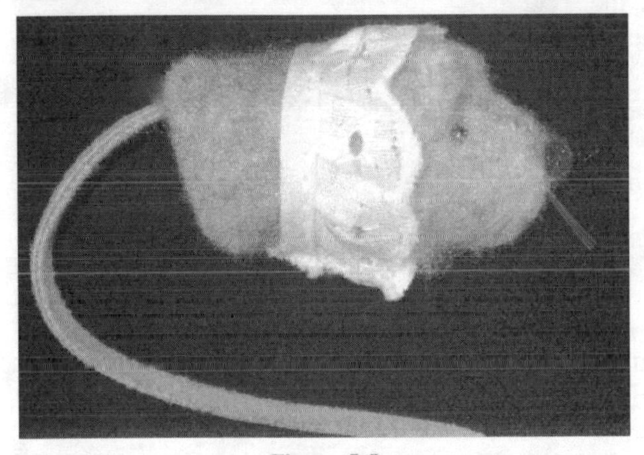

Figure 5-8

Step 11

For BABY MOUSE only (baby bonnet):

Stitch white eyelet together along the cut edges.

Slip eyelet circle over baby's body from the back so it comes up to rest behind her ears. Tack in place with white thread. Dot knots with Fray Check. (*See* figure 5-8.)

How to Make the Mouse House

Step 1

Position the bottom part of the corrugated envelope box so its bottom is face up. Spray paint the bottom and sides of the cardboard box (not the inside). Apply multiple coats of paint as necessary to cover any graphics on the cardboard and for an even appearance. You may spray the lid of the box as well if you like, although it is not necessary because the lid will not be face out to the audience. Allow paint to dry completely.

Step 2

Photocopy Mouse House WINDOW, DOOR, SHUTTER, CURTAIN, FLOWER, STEM, BUSH, and TREE patterns from book *at sizes specified,* and cut them out along the outside of the pattern outlines.

Step 3

Mark the WINDOWS and DOOR on the bottom of the box using the patterns or measuring with a ruler to make sure they are positioned evenly. The downstairs window should be positioned high enough for the tulips to fit beneath it. Cut out the windows with the X-acto or utility knife. To place less stress on the cardboard during the process, try cutting the horizontal window lines first and then going back and cutting the vertical window lines. Cut out the door with the X-acto or utility knife, making sure to leave one side of the door attached. Score the attached side of the door lightly with the knife so it will fold along the bend, being very careful not to score it too deeply. You will need to score it both on the inside of the house and also on the outside of the house, with the outside score being slightly deeper than the inside one. Place ruler along scoring for stability and bend the door gently along it for its first opening. (*See* figure 5-9.)

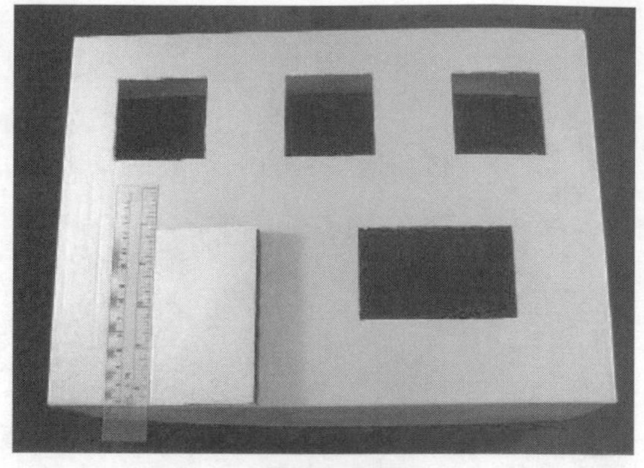

Figure 5-9

Step 4

Paint door and trim around windows. You may certainly use any colors for the trim. Painting the door, downstairs window trim, and center upstairs window trim in the same color (white), then trimming the two edge upstairs windows in another color (yellow), can help avoid ending up with too many disparate colors that could distract from the mice. (*See* figure 5-10.)

Paint the doorknob (yellow) at this point. Wait to affix it until step 9. Allow paint to dry completely.

Figure 5-10

Step 5

Pin the shutter, tree, bush, stem, and flower patterns onto the designated felt colors and cut them out as specified on the patterns to decorate the house. Glue the felt shutters onto the windows, just outside the painted trim. Glue the tree, bushes, stems, and flowers along the bottom and sides of the house. Allow glue to dry completely. (*See* figure 5-11.)

(*Please note:* The patterns and options given here are only one possibility. Be creative! Just make sure that you do not make the house so wild that the mice won't show up clearly when they do emerge.)

Figure 5-11

Step 6

Highlight the tree, bushes, stems, and flowers by brushing them with coordinating craft paint. Even small dabs of paint here and there on the felt will give the pieces much more texture and depth and make them more interesting to look at. Use orange paint on orange felt, green on green, and so forth. You may want to edge some of the flowers or highlight them in another color, but it's not really necessary. If you make the orange lilies, however, do highlight them with black paint as shown on the pattern. Edge the window shutters in a contrasting color. Allow paint to dry completely. (*See* figure 5-12.)

Figure 5-12

Step 7

Glue on the pom-pom flower centers. Allow glue to dry completely.

Step 8

Cut out the Mouse House CURTAINS with pinking shears, according to the patterns provided. Seal all curtain edges with Fray Check; allow to dry completely.

Lay the Mouse House face down and position the curtains inside the windows. They should overlap the window edges generously. Turn the curtains over so you can squeeze a thin row of glue along the very top edge of the *right* (patterned) side of the "top floor" curtains. Position each curtain just above the edge of its window, centering it from side to side, and press it into place.

For the bottom floor window, squeeze tacky glue along the top edge as well as the side edges of the curtain. Position the fabric carefully so that the center of the curtain matches up, and press into place. (If you don't glue the sides of this larger curtain down as suggested, they tend to get stuck outside the window when the mice pop out and in.)

Allow glue to dry completely.

Step 9

Mark the doorknob's placement on the Mouse House's door. If you located an actual craft doorknob, drill or poke a small hole in the cardboard to push the doorknob's screw through. Attach the doorknob to the front of the Mouse House door. If you were unable to procure a little cabinet knob, glue the wooden craft "button" or felt circle onto the front of the door instead. Lay Mouse House with the door facing up while the glue dries. Allow glue to dry completely.

Step 10

Photocopy the "Mouse House" poem template, which follows. Glue or tape the copy inside the Mouse House on the floor as a "cheat sheet" in case you or a colleague forgets the poem while presenting the prop!

"Mouse House"

Inside the little HOUSE,
There lives a little MOUSE.
Hear him scamper?
Hear him creep?
He'll look out if you say "PEEP!"

Finger Puppets Finished Product

Figure 5-13

PATTERN PIECES

"Mouse House" poem

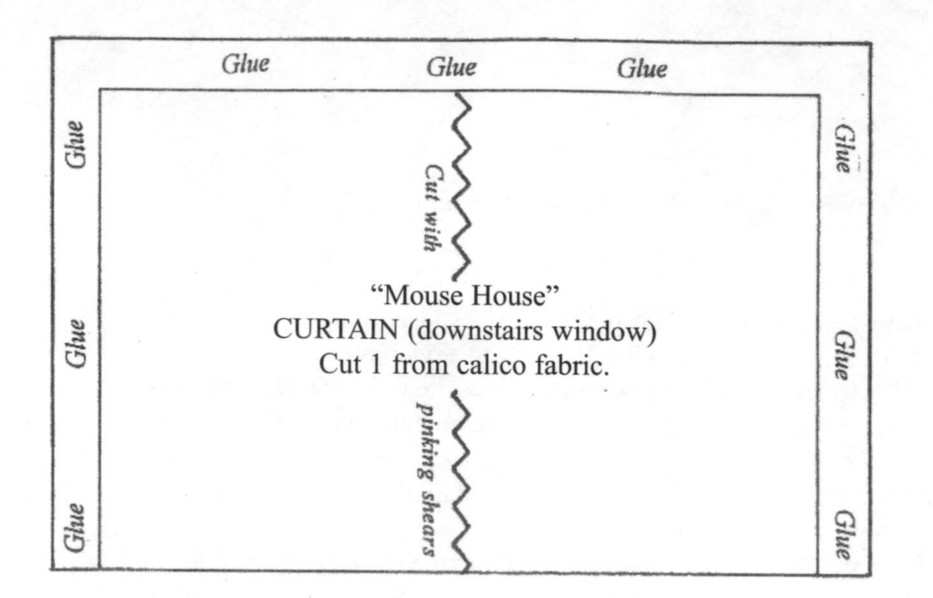

Photocopy this page at size 100%.

Glue Glue Glue

"Mouse House"
CURTAIN (upstairs windows)
Cut 2 from gingham fabric.
Cut 1 from eyelet fabric.

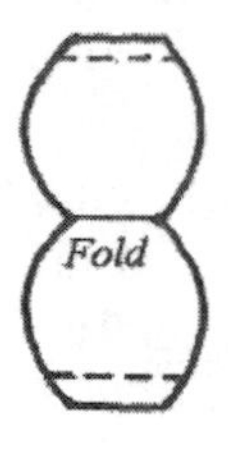

"Mouse House"
Mouse EAR
Cut 4 from grey plush felt.

Fold

"Mouse House"
Mouse EAR
Cut 4 from grey plush felt.

Eye *Eye* *Ear* *Ear* *Fold line*

"Mouse House"
Mouse BODY
Cut 2 from grey plush felt.
Seam allowance 1/8"

Eye *Eye* *Ear* *Ear* *Fold line*

"Mouse House"
Baby Mouse BODY
Cut 1 from grey plush felt.
Seam allowance 1/8"

"Mouse House"
WINDOW (upstairs)
Trace 3 on Mouse House.

Photocopy this page at size 100%.

"Mouse House"
WINDOW (downstairs)
Trace 1 on Mouse House.

"Mouse House"
SHUTTERS (downstairs windows)
Cut 2 from yellow felt.

"Mouse House"
DOOR
Trace 1 on Mouse House.

Doorknob

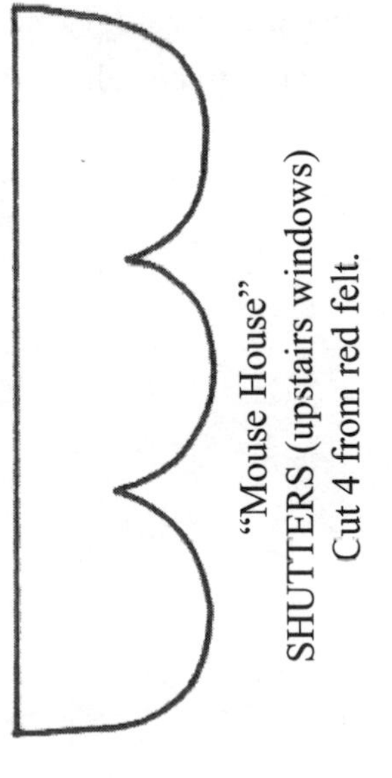

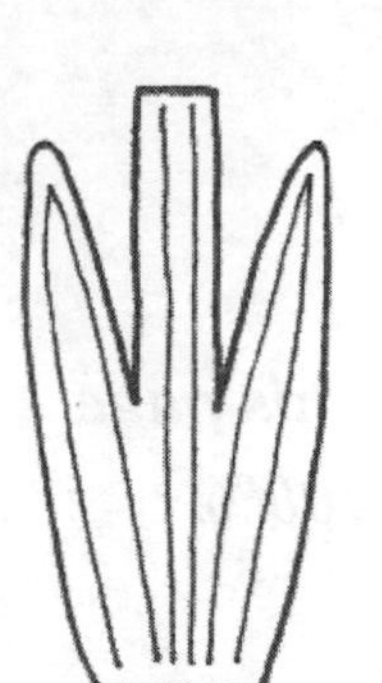

"Mouse House"
TULIP FLOWER
Cut 4 from red felt.
Cut 3 from yellow felt.

Photocopy this page at size 100%.

"Mouse House"
TULIP STEM
Cut 7 from light green felt.

"Mouse House"
FLOWER
Cut 9 from white felt.

"Mouse House"
LEAF
Cut 12 from bright green felt.

"Mouse House"
LILY FLOWER
Cut 5 from orange felt.

"Mouse House"
TREE
Cut 1 from dark green felt.

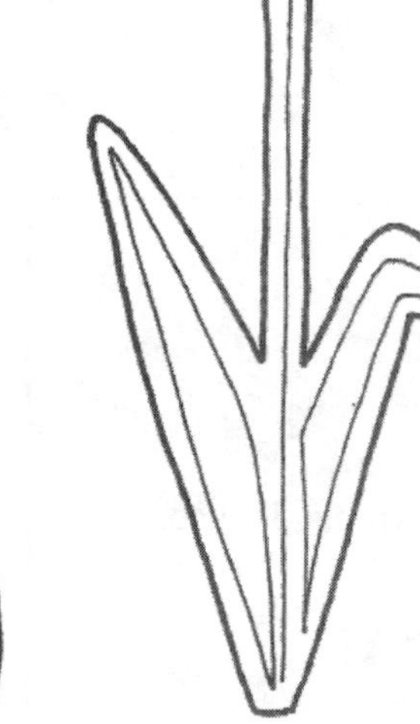

"Mouse House"
LILY STEM
Cut 5 from dark green felt.

"Mouse House"
BUSH
Cut 3 from true green felt.

Storage

You Will Need

1 sturdy, shallow box slightly bigger than your Mouse House box
1 plastic sandwich bag
2 copies of "Mouse House" storage label
2 copies of the "Mouse House" presentation notes/script (pages 57–60)
1 copy of finger puppets finished product photo (figure 5-13)

Make two photocopies of the label provided for the "Mouse House" prop and fill in the *date* and *name or initials* blanks. Cut out the labels and affix them securely to both ends of your storage container.

"Mouse House" ***poem***

Prop created_______ by _________________
DATE NAME OR INITIALS

from patterns included in *Books in Bloom*
by Kimberly Faurot (ALA, 2003)

Your "Mouse House" and its occupants should be stored in a sturdy box that is slightly bigger and deeper than the Mouse House itself. You may wish to keep the three mice in a plastic sandwich bag, which can then be stored inside the Mouse House. Store the house face down in its storage box so its curtains lay flat against the windows and don't curl in.

Include at least two photocopies of the presentation notes/script (pages 57–60) in the box with the prop. Also include a photocopy of the finger puppets finished product photo (figure 5-13).

Make sure that the "Mouse House" prop is included on your storytelling props database or list (*see* chapter 2) as well as in your institution's inventory records.

Notify other staff members who might be able to include "Mouse House" in their programming or classrooms that it is ready for use, and demonstrate it for them (along with proper storage caveats) if at all possible.

Summary

Finger puppets can supply a delightful storytime component. Although they are too small to be used extensively with a very large group, occasional appearances where the finger puppet's movement is central can be highly successful. Children in particular enjoy seeing creatures that are much smaller than themselves. Because finger puppets are fairly easy to make and also cheap to purchase, you can expand your collection quite readily. Try incorporating finger puppets into your welcome or your ending time, to signal what the day's lesson will be about, or just for fun.

6 Flannel/Felt Board Stories

Includes script and pattern for

Fish Is Fish by Leo Lionni (Random, 1970)

Pattern difficulty level

Medium

Construction time estimate

6 hours

Traditionally, one of the most popular physical mediums for storytelling adaptations has been flannel/felt board stories. Although three-dimensional "prop" stories as well as Velcro board storytelling (which can support heavier objects) are becoming more common among teachers and librarians, flannel boards are still used extensively. Reasons for this popularity include the fact that felt stories are relatively inexpensive to make, are very portable and easy to store, and are part of a long tradition in the elementary school and library worlds.

Flannel/felt board stories are presented using oral storytelling techniques, as are all of the scripts in this book—the story is learned and told to the audience rather than read. As the story unfolds, the storyteller places the representational story figures onto the board one at a time to highlight the tale. Children are curious to see what will appear next, so the method can help maintain young audiences' attention. Distinct advantages of the flannel/felt board medium include the fact that the stories are usually contained within and presented on the board. It is possible to entirely transform or create a world on the flannel/felt board by applying background scenery and embellishments. The characters and pieces can easily be made so they are reversible, enabling them to face different directions as needed in the story for maximum flexibility.

Flannel/felt board storytelling can be useful for presenters who are just beginning to explore the art of oral storytelling, because having the story figures at hand in order of their appearance can help prompt a nervous or flagging memory. As with most oral storytelling, the flannel/felt board technique enables the presenter to enjoy an intimate, direct contact with the audience. Because you are not holding a book or trying to read text, you are able to look at your audience and speak directly to them. You can readily see their reactions and adjust your pacing or drama as appropriate. Flannel/felt board storytelling is sometimes presented in traditional storytelling literature as a "means to an end," referring to its role in helping fledgling storytellers become more comfortable with the oral tradition. Flannel/felt board storytelling is also a wonderful end in itself, however, offering many of the advantages of oral storytelling while still maintaining concrete visual sparks for young imaginations.

Techniques and Considerations

Creating

The terms *flannel board* and *felt board* are used somewhat interchangeably, though they are technically different and have some unique characteristics. Flannel boards are covered with soft, fuzzy flannel, while felt boards are covered in felt. Many of the available commercial boards are still covered with flannel, usually black in color. Felt sticks directly to these flannel boards, as do other pieces of flannel and Pellon stabilizer (a white translucent material that is normally used as a fabric stiffener). Sandpaper will stick to flannel, though Velcro does not. All of these materials will also adhere to felt, including the hook side of the Velcro. Historically, flannel/felt board figures have been made from felt; paper with sandpaper, flannel, or felt backing; and Pellon. Felt pieces are often outlined or highlighted with markers or paints; Pellon pieces may be colored with crayons, colored pencils, and paints.

You can easily make your own felt board by covering a stiff piece of corrugated cardboard or a piece of plywood with felt. Many books describe methods for making flannel/felt boards. If you are interested in making your own board and would like specific detailed directions for how to do so, please refer to the resources listed in chapter 10. There are also many extremely serviceable commercial boards available at fairly reasonable prices (*see* chapter 10).

Both flannel and felt boards "wear out" when their fuzzy surfaces, to which the story figures adhere, become bald from steady use. The boards can have many renewed lives, however, if you cover them with felt pieces cut to the size of the board. Simply pin the felt coverings over the flannel board with T-pins (available in craft and fabric stores) all around the edges. This technique is actually desirable whether or not your flannel board is worn out. As mentioned, many standard commercial flannel boards are black, which is not necessarily the best color for sharing all felt stories. If the felt story that you are sharing is adapted from a picture book, look at the background colors in the book's original illustrations. If the story pieces will show up clearly on that color, try to replicate it. If the pieces would not show up well, choose another color that still retains the spirit of the original book. Keep an array of felt coverings for your flannel board that are cut to the right size. You will need to purchase the felt that is available on bolts for this purpose, not the small felt squares. I use light blue, white, and green felt the most frequently for backgrounds.

As noted, hook Velcro will stick to these felt coverings; it does not stick to the commercial black flannel board itself, so the covering enables you to use the Velcro. Although pulling the Velcro off the felt covering pulls at the weave of the felt and it wears out after a while, felt is quite cheap, and it is well worth just replacing your stock of felt coverings every few years.

Because flannel/felt board storytelling has some history in the library and education world, many professional titles discuss the format and give suggestions for creating felt story pieces. Although the books vary in thoroughness and practicality, it is interesting to note that they contain a great deal of conflicting advice. For example, one book cautions the reader to first cut out a paper pattern and pin it to the felt pieces before cutting them; another dictates that you should cut the paper pattern and the felt all at once. One title suggests using only felt from large bolts for your story figures, averring that the sizing in the smaller squares keeps them from sticking securely to the flannel/felt board; the next book recommends using the squares instead of the bolts because the felt from the squares will stay crisp and stiff whereas the figures made from "bolt felt" become wrinkled and lose their shape. One author suggests that it is easier to color the figures *before* cutting them out; another encourages you to color the pieces *after* cutting them out. The lesson from all of this conflicting advice seems to be that you should experiment as much as possible, and find out what technique works best for you! I will detail my own preferences here and within the pattern construction portion of this chapter, but I encourage you to read other professional titles from the list of resources in chapter 10 as well as to experiment on your own.

Experimenting and finding your own style is also important when considering what stories to try adapting into the flannel/felt board medium. Many professional resources list titles recommended for flannel/felt board adaptations. Candidates should have clear plot structures, and they must be simple enough that you can easily add and subtract the story figures from the board as the story progresses. Make sure that the story pieces are all large enough to be seen by your entire group. If the story line requires many little pieces, either reduce the numbers (if you can do so and still remain true to the spirit of the original) or else choose a different story! Otherwise the putting up and taking down of the figures begins to dominate the story and becomes a distraction for the audience rather than an enhancement.

If any of your story figures promise to be really saggy or delicate and they are pieces that you must add to and remove from the board, it may be necessary to strengthen them. You can either make the figures as double-layer puffy pieces (slightly stuffed) or else stiffen them by gluing pipe cleaners onto their backs for added support. Double-layer puffy pieces are also nice for suggesting a three-dimensional look and feel.

Felt pieces may also be created that extend beyond the frame of your flannel/felt board (such as the tree in this chapter's patterns for *Fish Is Fish*) or that spring forward to create a three-dimensional look (like the *Fish Is Fish* flannel/felt board story's butterfly). Be creative and do not be limited by the seemingly two-dimensional nature of the flannel/felt board medium.

Following is a general summary of how I create flannel/felt board story figures, including the whole range of styles (flat, multi-layered, double-layer puffy). The sample pattern and instructions that are included later in this chapter incorporate a few of these techniques but certainly not all. I have included the complete information simply for your consideration and interest as you contemplate further experimentation with the medium.

General Techniques for Creating Flannel/Felt Board Story Pieces

Step 1

Determine what characters and pieces of scenery you need to make as felt pieces to successfully relate the story to an audience.

Step 2

If you are adapting an existing picture book and have obtained the requisite copyright permission to adapt it as a flannel/felt board story (see chapter 1, "Copyright Issues"), go through the original book and mark the pages that show the characters and scenery pieces that are essential for your adaptation. Choose pictures that show the characters in poses that will work throughout the entire flannel/felt board presentation if at all possible. Photocopy the pictures, adjusting them for size so that the final pieces are all in relative proportion to each other. Also make sure that the pieces are all as large as they can possibly be and still fit on your board along with the other figures from the various scenes in which they will appear. Keep in mind, however, that the size of the pieces may also be restricted by other story elements that you are integrating.

If you are creating completely original figures, you may wish to refer to images with copyright permissions already granted, such as those in various teacher support publications.

Step 3

When making photocopy patterns from pictures that only partially show the character or figure being copied, you must sketch in the rest of the figure on the photocopy as best you can. For example, a picture that you feel represents the best general pose for a particular character may show only the character's head, body, and one leg. To create a pattern for the complete character, you must sketch in the missing leg on the paper pattern freehand or make another copy of the existing leg and tape it onto the pattern to provide a base from which to work.

Step 4

Cut out the figures from the photocopies.

Step 5

Pin the photocopies onto the felt or other fabric you will be using to make your story piece with sewing straight pins. Cut out the felt/fabric. If you are making a double-layer puffy piece, you can cut both layers of the felt at once.

Please note: I use both felt squares and felt from the bolts for my storytelling pieces, depending on what colors and sizes I need. If you make the figures sturdy at the outset, arrange for them to stick to your board with supplementary Velcro or pins if needed, and store the pieces properly, the type of felt and fabric you use doesn't really matter. Just consider whether the material accurately reflects the spirit of the story you are telling, and make sure it is relatively easy to handle!

Step 6

If you are making a multi-layered decorated piece, such as putting a real patterned fabric dress on a felt pig, cut the photocopy pattern apart to the next level so that you can cut out the piece for the dress separately from the body of the character. If there are smaller pieces layered on top of that, such as a collar or pocket that you want to add in a different color, cut the pattern apart further to achieve that level, and so on.

Step 7

To make a double-layer puffy piece, squeeze a line of tacky glue (flexible fabric glue) all around the edge of the bottom layer, leaving a small section open from which to stuff the piece. (To reinforce a narrow part that needs extra support, glue a piece of pipe cleaner between the layers.) If it is also a multi-layered decorated piece, glue all of the layers on to the base with tacky glue at this point and allow to dry completely. If you are unsure exactly where to place the smaller top-layer pieces, lay the paper pattern with the cut-out pieces back on top of the original layer, then glue the top layer piece within the hole from which its piece was cut.

Step 8

After the figure is assembled, you are ready to paint any outlines and highlights onto the figure. Although many people use Sharpie markers and highlighters to outline and color felt figures, I find that acrylic craft paint goes on more quickly and is easier to use, is more flexible in the variety it allows, and is crisper in appearance. If you are unsure where to draw the outlines that are within the body of the figure, cut along the line on your original paper pattern and lay the pattern on top of the figure. Bend back a portion of the pattern along the line so you can follow it for outlining purposes. Outline the figures to match the style and colors of the original illustrations: if they are outlined in black in the original, do the same with your felt story figures; if they have no outlines, do not outline them, or else make very soft outlines. If the original illustrations are done in a painterly style so the figures have color variations, paint those colors onto your figure with colored acrylic craft paints. Allow the painted pieces to dry completely.

Step 9

If you are making a double-layer puffy piece, lightly stuff between the layers with polyester fiberfill and glue the opening shut. Hold the opening together with clip clothespins until the glue dries completely.

Step 10

If you have made a puffy piece, consider whether it would be enhanced by taking a few "tucks" here and there. For example, perhaps a small stitch through all of the layers of your pig near the arm or in the stomach area would give him additional three-dimensionality. Using matching thread, hand stitch a small stitch through the layers; then knot the two ends of your thread so that it pulls the fabric layers together and puckers just a little bit. Take multiple tucks if you like.

Step 11

Add any final details that could enhance the piece such as bead or button eyes, feathers, fur, trim, and so forth.

Presenting

A problem often experienced with flannel/felt board story presentations is that larger figures may droop because of their weight and unwieldiness and frequently fall off the board. Although young audiences are usually delighted when this type of mishap occurs, it definitely detracts from the story as well as from the storyteller's concentration! These problems are easily solved by making sure that you have plenty of pins on hand. I typically use T-pins (available from craft or fabric stores), but straight sewing pins will also work. Pin all background scenery that will remain on the board for the whole story firmly onto the board. Pieces that will be taken on and off the board and that exhibit any likelihood of buckling or falling off should also be pinned. You can simply position a pin in the top of the figure before beginning the story, and then press the pin quickly into the board when you place the piece in view. With just a little bit of practice, you will find that using pins in this way isn't difficult, and it is definitely preferable to having pieces dropping off the board! Always keep some extra pins stuck into the back of the board where they are hidden but accessible if you should need them unexpectedly.

Learn the story and tell it to your audience from memory, using the felt pieces. Practice the story in private with the felt figures before you present it for an audience, even if you think you know the story well and have presented it dozens of times in the past. You should always run through the story with the prop pieces at least twice (twice if you already know it well and have previously shared it many times—far more than twice if it is new for you!) before you present it for your class or group. Practice telling the story out loud while manipulating the story pieces; this will ensure that your movements are smooth and that you remember how and when to manipulate the figures.

Each time you place new story pieces onto the board, allow the scene to sit there untouched for a moment so that the audience may absorb it fully. It is also generally a good idea not to move the figures around on the board while you are talking. Doing so tends to take the audience's focus away from what you are saying; furthermore, if you are turned toward the board while speaking, your voice will not carry as well and it will likely be difficult for your audience to hear you. It does work well to hold up a new piece while you are talking and have the audience name it, but then pause as you put it on the board—either in the middle of your sentence or at the end.

Once again conflicting advice is often given about the flannel/felt board figures—in this case regarding how to present them. One storyteller directs you to "Move the figures as little as possible . . . they are illustrations of the story events, not puppets" (Sierra, 1987). Another suggests that you can make the pieces move by "walking" them across the board, moving them to match the action of the story. Again, determine what works best for you and your own audiences.

Although some stories and poems are best shared as pure listening experiences, others readily invite audience participation. It is generally desirable to encourage the children to name characters and pieces along with you when possible, and to join in any repetitive phrases. This can help retrieve wandering attention while reinforcing vocabulary and concepts. Children also especially love to help apply the flannel/felt board story figures. Pieces used for this purpose must be reasonably sturdy, and they should not be decorated with any sharp accoutrements. You must also make sure you have enough pieces so that everyone can participate and that the pieces will stick effectively to the board on their own without the help of pins. Tell the children that you will need their help telling the next story, and hand out the figures. Assure them that you will let them know when it is their turn to bring up their pieces. Flannel/felt board stories that are clearly sequential and cumulative work best for this type of audience participation. Keep these factors in mind when planning as well as presenting your flannel/felt board creations.

Choosing the Flannel/Felt Board Format

The story of *Fish Is Fish* requires several manipulations as the tadpole becomes a frog and as he describes the land creatures he has seen to his friend the fish. The changes require an adapted format that is flexible and easily manipulable. Although this requirement could suggest several different options, it is clear upon an examination of the original illustrations that a flannel/felt board version is particularly appropriate to the story. Leo Lionni's scenes are soft and muted, adapting readily to an interpretation in soft, fuzzy felt.

Few of the felt pieces are outlined, reflecting the fact that the book's colored pencil illustrations have soft edges without outlines. Some pieces that need outlining to show up or to differentiate between segments are outlined with a soft complementary color so that they retain the gentle spirit of the originals.

The felt medium and use of the flannel/felt board allows the creation of an entire landscape background for the story. The depictions of the fish's dreamy, imagined visions of the land creatures described by the frog imposed against the familiar backdrop of the fish's home in the pond enhance the sense of secure reassurance that underlies the entire story.

Finally, the original book is cozy and classic, familiar to many children and their families. Flannel/felt board storytelling is likewise cozy and classic, and it is an ideal format for sharing the traditional story with audiences in a new way.

Fish Is Fish

Leo Lionni

(Random, 1970)

Summary

When a frog tells his friend the fish about the world outside the pond, the fish dreams about it and determines to see it for himself.

Possible themes

Fish, Friends, Frogs, Metamorphosis, Ponds, Swimming, Trips

Approximate running time for felt story

5 minutes

Recommended audience interest level

Preschool (age 4 and older) through grade 2

Please note that the felt story pieces are designed as professional resources, not as playthings. They do not conform to child safety play standards, and they could easily become damaged if used in a manner other than that for which they were intended.

Felt Story Pieces

- white felt background
- blue felt pond
- embankment
- pond rocks (attached to embankment)
- tree (clip-on) with butterfly
- water lily
- tadpole 1
- tadpole 2 (with legs)
- hopping frog (two-sided)
- sitting frog (two-sided)
- fish (two-sided)
- Pellon bird-fish
- Pellon cow-fish
- Pellon people-fish

Use with

24" × 36" flannel board
easel to hold flannel board

table or cart on which to lay out story pieces

a copy of the book to show the audience both before and after presenting the story

Setup

Have the white felt background, light blue felt pond, water lily, and embankment pinned to the flannel board before you begin. The flannel board will be on your left as you are looking at the audience. Clip the tree over the edge of the flannel board at the end closest to you and pin the trunk to the flannel board. Hide the hopping frog behind the felt pond layer, right at the top and opposite the water lily.

Lay out all of the pieces in order behind or next to the flannel board so that you can access them easily as the story progresses but so that the audience does not see them ahead of time.

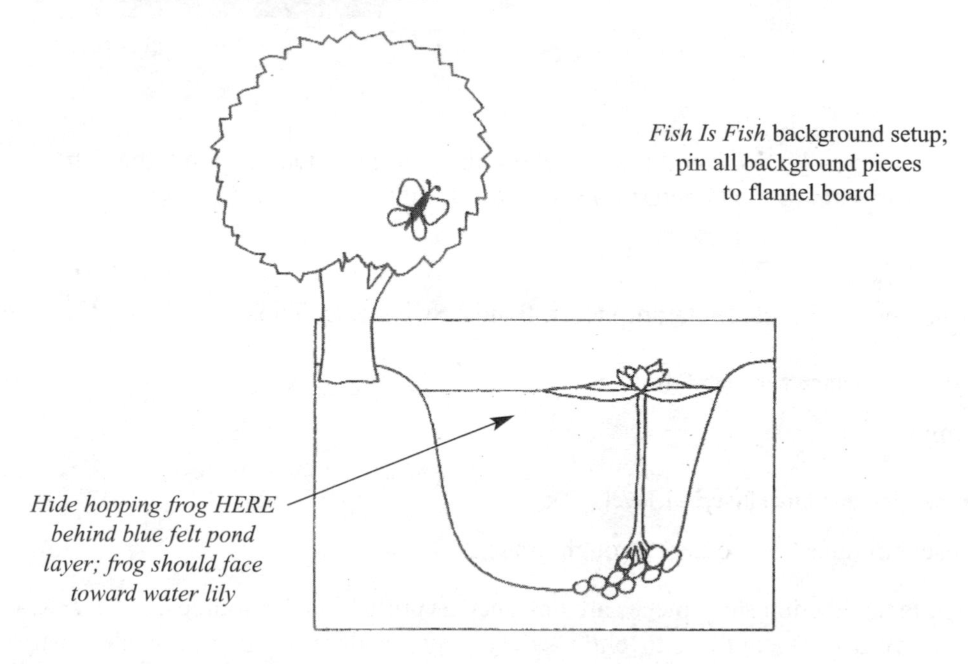

Fish Is Fish background setup; pin all background pieces to flannel board

Presentation

Before introducing the story, show the audience pictures of real tadpoles turning into frogs; also explain what *gills* are and how fish breathe.

Story narration is delineated in regular type; movement notes and miscellaneous directions are shown in *[bracketed italics]*.

Learn the story and tell it to your audience from memory, using the felt pieces.

The script calls for you to be three characters: the Narrator, the tadpole/frog, and the fish. The character who is talking is designated by its name at the beginning of the text, except for the Narrator.

Although it is not essential to use different character voices when presenting the story, it can truly help maintain the children's interest as well as help them distinguish which character is talking. Try out different voices to figure out which sounds best for the different characters. All voices must feel natural for you after practice so that you will be able to use and maintain them successfully during an actual performance.

The story pieces require several careful manipulations (such as the tadpole turning into a frog), so be sure that you are well rehearsed and can smoothly manipulate the pieces at an appropriate pace.

Make sure that you pause slightly between scenes so that the audience can see and enjoy each change and vignette.

Please note: The following script is a very slightly adapted story version for telling as a flannel/felt board story and includes notes for the storyteller on how and when to manipulate the felt story pieces. Learn the story and tell it to your audience from memory, using the felt pieces. Please look at the book so that you know what minor adaptations have been made in this script. Show a copy of the book to your audience both before and after sharing the story with the felt story pieces, and give the complete title, author/illustrator, and publication information.

SCRIPT

Fish Is Fish by Leo Lionni

At the edge of the woods *[point to tree]* there was a pond *[gesture to pond]*, and there a minnow *[place fish in pond, facing you]* and a tadpole *[place tadpole 1 layered over tadpole 2 in pond, facing the fish]* swam among the weeds. They were inseparable friends.

One morning the tadpole discovered that during the night he had grown two little legs.

[Remove tadpole 1 carefully from board, making sure to leave tadpole 2.]

TADPOLE/FROG "Look!" he said triumphantly. "Look, I am a frog!"

FISH "Nonsense," said the minnow. *[Point to fish.]* "How could you be a frog if only last night you were a little fish, just like me!"

They argued about it until finally the tadpole said,

TADPOLE/FROG "Frogs are frogs and fish is fish and that's that!"

In the weeks that followed, the tadpole grew front legs and his tail got smaller and smaller as his back legs got longer and longer.

[Remove tadpole 2 from board and pull out hopping frog from behind the water; place frog in pond where the tadpole had been, facing the fish.]

And then one fine day, a real frog now, he climbed out of the water and onto the grassy bank, in search of adventure.

[Hop frog onto lily pad and then embankment furthest from you, then hop him around out of sight behind the flannel board; hide him behind the board.]

The minnow too had grown and had become a full-fledged fish. *[Point to fish in pond.]* He often wondered where his four-footed friend the frog had gone *[flip fish over so he is looking in the direction where the frog left; position him at the bottom of the pond for when the frog comes back]* and what adventures he might be having. Days and weeks went by.

Then one day, with a happy SPLASH! the frog jumped into the pond.

[Hop sitting frog back in sight from the same side the hopping frog had exited and down to the bottom of the pond to sit on the rocks.]

FISH "Where have you been?" the fish asked, very excited.

FROG "I have been about the world—hopping here and there," said the frog, "and I have seen extraordinary things!"

FISH "Like what?" asked the fish.

FROG "Birds," said the frog mysteriously. "Birds!" *[Hold up Pellon bird-fish figure for audience to see.]* And he told the fish about the birds, who had wings, and two legs, and many, many colors.

As the frog talked *[place bird-fish figure on the board above the fish and frog, partially on the embankment closest to you]*, his friend saw the birds fly through his mind like large feathered fish.

FISH "What else did you see?" asked the fish.

FROG "Cows," said the frog. *[Hold up Pellon cow-fish figure for audience to see.]* "Cows! They have four legs, horns, eat grass, and carry pink bags of milk."

[Add the cow-fish figure to the board above the fish and frog, next to the bird-fish.]

FISH "What else did you see?" asked the fish.

FROG "People!" said the frog. *[Hold up Pellon people-fish figure for audience to see.]* "Men, women, and children!"

[Add the people-fish figures to the board above the pond, next to the cow-fish.]

The frog talked and talked, telling the fish about all of his adventures until it was dark in the pond.

The pictures in the fish's mind from the stories the frog had told him were full of lights *[point to the bird-fish figure]* and colors *[point to cow-fish figure]* and marvelous things *[point to people-fish figures]*, and he couldn't sleep.

FISH *(wistfully)* "Oh!" thought the fish. "If only I could jump about like my friend the frog, and see that wonderful world for myself!"

Script adapted by Kimberly K. Faurot, *Books in Bloom: Creative Patterns and Props That Bring Stories to Life* (ALA, 2003).

The days went by. The frog was off *[remove sitting frog from board and hide him behind it where you can retrieve him quickly]* busy about his business, and the fish lay dreaming about birds in flight *[remove bird-fish figure from board, hold it up for audience to see again, then "fly" it behind the flannel board]*, grazing cows *[remove cow-fish figure from board, hold it up for audience to see again, then hide it behind the flannel board]*, and those strange animals, all dressed up *[remove people-fish figures from board, hold them up for audience to see again, then hide them behind the flannel board]*, that his friend the frog called people.

His dreams made him so curious that at last he finally decided that come what may, he too must see that wonderful world about which the frog had told him!

FISH — "I just can't stand it any more! I simply must see those wonderful creatures for myself!"

And so, with a mighty thwack of his tail, he jumped clear out of the water and onto the bank!

[Flip fish up onto embankment closest to you, under the tree.]

He landed in the dry, warm grass. Could he breathe? No! He lay gasping for air, unable to breathe or to move!

FISH — "Help!" groaned the fish.

Luckily his friend the frog *[hold up sitting frog]*, who had been hunting butterflies nearby, saw him and with all his strength pushed him back into the pond.

[Move frog so he pushes fish toward the pond, then place the fish into the pond facing the water lily and the frog on the water lily leaf facing the fish.]

The fish floated about for an instant. Then he breathed deeply, letting the clean cool water of the pond run through his gills. Now he felt weightless again and with an ever-so-slight motion of his tail he could move to and fro, up and down, just like before.

The sun shone down into the pond, and it made beautiful colors in the water. Surely this world was the most beautiful of all worlds, thought the fish. He smiled at his friend the frog, who sat watching him a little bit anxiously from a lily leaf.

FISH — "You were right," the fish said. *[Point to fish.]* "FISH IS FISH."

[Show audience last two double-page spreads of the book: first the frog pushing the fish back in the pond and then the frog and fish together in the very last double-page spread.]

THE END

PATTERN INSTRUCTIONS

Flannel/Felt Board Story (Sample Pattern)

Fish Is Fish by Leo Lionni

Patterns

Felt story pieces designed by Kimberly Faurot

Estimated difficulty

Medium

Estimated construction time

6 hours

Estimated cost for supplies

$30

You Will Need These Tools

- Sharpie permanent black marking pen (Fine Point)
- small-sharp-pointed scissors
- straight pins
- Aleene's Original "Tacky" Glue
- craft paintbrushes (round sizes 10/0 and 0; flat sizes 6 and 10)
- wire cutters
- needle nose pliers
- colored pencils (such as Prismacolor 36 Color Art Pencil Set)

You Will Need These Supplies

SUPPLIES TO MAKE THE BACKGROUND SCENE

- colored felt from bolts: white background (24" × 36"); light blue pond (16" × 36"); brown ground backing (19" × 36"); brown tree trunk and foliage backing (20" × 24"); moss green foliage backing (18" × 20"); apple green water lily root (5" × 14")
- colored felt squares (1 each unless otherwise noted): pale pink, peach pink, rose pink, lavender, apple green (3), moss green (2), sage green, kelly green (2), denim blue, harvest gold (4), cinnamon brown, rust brown, walnut brown (2), cocoa brown, charcoal grey, glitter black
- acrylic craft paint: pale pink, peach pink, rose pink, lavender, apple green, true green, moss green, golden brown, chocolate brown
- polyester fiberfill stuffing
- 2 standard-sized wooden spring clothespins
- 1 wooden ruler, 12" or 15" length (or a wood slat of comparable size)
- 1 black "bump chenille stem"/pipe cleaner (has four wider "bumps" on the chenille stem)
- 6" length of 24-gauge hobby wire

SUPPLIES TO MAKE THE STORY FIGURES

colored felt squares (1 each unless otherwise noted): white, harvest gold, maroon, glitter green (2)

acrylic craft paint: white, light pink, rose pink, true green, lavender, beige, medium brown, dark brown, grey, black

Pellon stabilizer (12" × 22" piece)—either "Pellon stabilizer midweight for medium weight fabrics" or "Pellon stabilizer heavyweight for heavyweight fabrics." Make sure to purchase Pellon stabilizer, not Pellon interfacing.

Please note: *This pattern is designed for a 24" × 36" flannel/felt board. If you have a larger board and would like to make the pieces larger, enlarge them uniformly on the copy machine.*

Directions

General Step 1

Photocopy patterns *at sizes specified.* (*See* chapter 2, "Enlarging the Patterns in This Book.") Cut out all of the photocopied patterns along the outside of the pattern outlines.

General Step 2

Lay the cut-out paper patterns onto the designated colors of felt or Pellon and pin. Cut out the felt and Pellon pieces, as specified on the patterns. *Make sure to cut out the glitter green felt with right sides together when cutting out two or more pieces so they will be mirror images of each other.*

How to Make the Background Scene

BACKGROUND

Cut the white background felt to measure 24" × 36" (or size to completely cover the front of your flannel board).

POND

Cut the light blue pond felt to measure 16" × 36."

GROUND/EMBANKMENT

Step 1

Position the individual soil sections on the GROUND BACKING piece and affix them in place with tacky glue.

Step 2

Lightly brush some of the soil sections with coordinating craft paint to give them additional depth and texture.

Step 3

Glue the POND ROCKS along the bottom right-hand scoop of the ground piece, as shown in the photographs. Overlap the rocks and vary the colors to create a natural look.

TREE

Step 1

Apply a solid layer of tacky glue to the *tree trunk* portion of the brown bottom TREE base piece, and affix the matching tree base piece to it.

Step 2

Apply a thin line of tacky glue just around the *edge* of the foliage portion of the brown TREE base piece, leaving a section about 4" long without glue along the very top of the piece. You will eventually stuff the top part of the tree through this opening. Press the rest of the matching brown tree base piece down along this glue outline.

Step 3

Apply a solid layer of tacky glue to the moss green foliage backing piece and affix it to the brown tree trunk and foliage unit. Glue the individual leaves onto the foliage backing piece with tacky glue. Lightly brush some of the leaves and the tree trunk with coordinating craft paint to give them additional depth and texture. Allow glue and paint to dry completely.

Step 4

Position the wooden ruler on the back of the TREE, along the trunk as well as up into the foliage. Glue the ruler in place with a generous amount of tacky glue. Allow glue to dry completely.

Step 5

Lightly stuff the tree with acrylic stuffing. It should be puffy without being overstuffed. Glue the top opening shut, holding it shut with spring clothespins while it dries. Allow glue to dry completely.

Step 6

Hold the TREE up to the flannel board so you can see where it should be positioned to clip over the edge of the board. Make sure the base of the trunk reaches all the way down to the embankment! One of the spring clothespins will be affixed to the ruler to provide the main stability, and the second clothespin will be glued directly onto the back of the felt foliage for additional support. Hold the clothespins up to the back of the tree and mark their placement with your marking pen. The two clothespins should line up horizontally. Apply glue to the clothespins and affix them as shown in figure 6-1. Allow glue to dry completely.

Figure 6-1

Figure 6-2

BUTTERFLY

Step 1

Paint the BUTTERFLY *on both sides* in the design shown on the pattern. Use the following colors: apply light pink to outline around the edges and to divide it into sections; paint the wings' sections with lavender paint; apply rose pink paint over the lavender near the butterfly's body; and use peach pink paint over the lavender along the wings' outer edges. (*See* figure 6-2.)

Allow paint to dry completely.

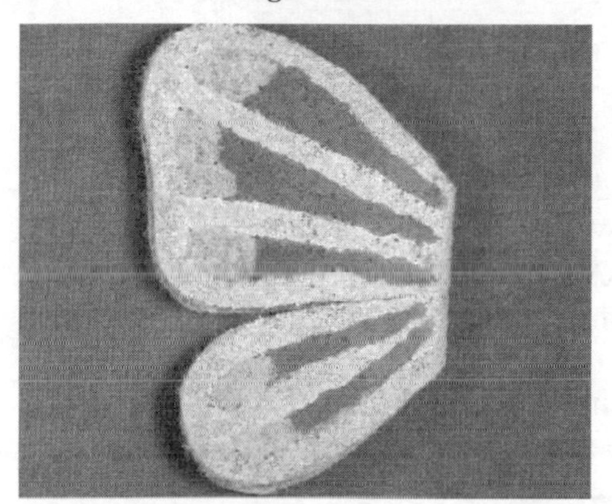

Figure 6-3

Step 2

Apply a thin line of glue along the center of the butterfly. Fold butterfly in half and allow glue to dry completely. (*See* figure 6-3.)

Step 3

Cut a two-bump section from your black "bump chenille stem"/pipe cleaner, making sure to retain the skinny lengths on the ends. Fold the pipe cleaner in half so that the two bump sections match up to each other. Apply a thin line of glue on the front of the butterfly along the fold, and another line of glue along its back in between the wings. Position the pipe cleaner bumps so one is along the butterfly's front and the other is along its back. Hold the pipe cleaner in place with spring clothespins while the glue dries. Allow glue to dry completely.

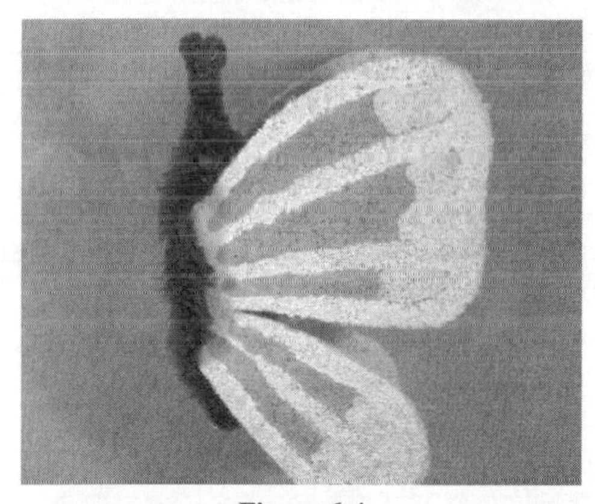

Figure 6-4

Step 4

Twist the pipe cleaner together at the top; then spread each end out to make antennae. Twist under the very ends of the antennae to make them slightly "clubbed." Twist the folded pipe cleaner at the bottom of the butterfly together and then twist under as well. (*See* figure 6-4.)

Figure 6-5

Step 5

Insert the length of hobby wire around the chenille stem that is along the butterfly's stomach *and also through the felt.* Twist the end of the wire around to secure it. (If you wrap the wire just around the chenille stem without also going through the felt, the butterfly will flop around too much.) (*See* figure 6-5.)

Stick the other end of the hobby wire through the felt of the tree so that it comes through the back right next to the spring part of the clothespin that is glued directly onto the felt. Wrap the hobby wire through the spring part of the clothespin, and around and around to secure it. (*See* figure 6-6.)

Figure 6-6

WATER LILY

Step 1

Glue the water lily flower petals together. The petals should all layer on top of the peach pink water lily flower backing. The large peach pink water lily flower is the bottom layer, the lavender and peach pink flower petals are the middle layer, and the rose pink flower petal is the top layer. Lightly brush the petals with coordinating craft paint to give them additional depth and texture. Allow paint to dry completely.

Step 2

Glue the LILY PAD LEAVES onto the WATER LILY FLOWER, overlapping the flower as shown on the pattern. Glue the LILY PAD STEM/ROOT to the back of the water lily flower and lily pad leaves unit, overlapping the stem/root as shown on the pattern. Allow glue to dry completely.

Lightly brush the lily pad leaves with coordinating craft paint to define the leaves, as shown on the pattern. Brush the lily pad stem/root with the same color of paint to give it additional depth and texture. Allow paint to dry completely.

How to Make the Story Figures

Step 1

Glue the multi-color or multi-layer story figure pieces together. The patterns for the multi-layer "underneath" pieces have dotted lines to designate how the top piece should be overlapped onto it. Because the "reversible" pieces for this story are made from single-sided glitter felt, they must be made from two pieces glued together so they will be glittery on both sides.

Glue pieces as follows:

TADPOLE 1—glue EYE onto BODY and then onto BASE LAYER

TADPOLE 2—glue EYE and LEG onto BODY and then onto BASE LAYER

HOPPING FROG—glue two body pieces together so frog is glittery on both sides; glue EYELIDS onto both sides; glue EYE 1 and EYE 2 onto both sides

SITTING FROG—glue two body pieces together so frog is glittery on both sides; glue EYELID onto both sides; glue EYE onto both sides

FISH—glue FISH FIN & TAIL between two FISH BODY layers; FISH BODY pieces should be glued together so fish is glittery on both sides; glue FISH GILL FINS onto both sides; glue FISH EYES onto both sides

Allow glue to dry completely.

Step 2

Paint the felt pieces with craft paint in the manner indicated on the pattern pieces and with the colors described here:

Figure 6-7

Figure 6-8

Figure 6-9

TADPOLE 1—lightly outline body with golden brown paint, and then soften by outlining over that with soft white paint; paint highlights along tail with kelly green paint as shown on pattern, and paint between kelly green splotches with golden brown paint; paint black pupil in eye; rim eye with rust brown paint (paint around the edge of the eye, on the green body). (*See* figure 6-7.)

TADPOLE 2—lightly outline body with golden brown paint, and then soften by outlining over that with soft white paint; paint highlights along tail with kelly green paint as shown on pattern, and paint between kelly green splotches with golden brown paint; highlight leg with apple green paint, outline with golden brown paint, and then outline with soft white paint; paint black pupil in eye; rim eye with rust brown paint (paint around the edge of the eye, on the green body). (*See* figure 6-7.)

HOPPING FROG—highlight legs, arms, body edges, and eyelids with apple green paint; outline body, eyelids, arms, and legs with soft white paint; paint light black spots along the back and upper leg; paint black pupils in eyes. (*See* figure 6-8.)

SITTING FROG—highlight legs, arms, body edges, and eyelids with apple green paint; outline body, eyelids, arms, and legs with soft white paint; paint light black spots along the back; paint black pupil in eye; paint black smiling mouth; lightly underline black mouth with soft white paint. (*See* figure 6-8.)

FISH—highlight upper body with maroon paint; paint black smiling mouth and black gill line; paint black pupil in eye; paint black stripes on gill fin, dorsal fin, and tail; paint maroon stripes between black stripes on fins and tail; paint white stripes among black and maroon stripes on fins and tail; lightly outline body with soft white paint; lightly underline black mouth with soft white paint; lightly edge in front of the black gill line with soft white paint; rim eye with rust brown paint (paint the edge of the white eye). (*See* figure 6-9.)

Allow paint to dry completely.

Paint the reverse sides of the HOPPING FROG, SITTING FROG, and FISH so they are completely reversible. Allow paint to dry completely.

Step 3

Color the Pellon pieces with colored pencils to match the pictures in the original book. You should be able to see through the Pellon clearly enough to follow the pattern lines. After finishing with the colored pencils, paint the highlights with white craft paint as detailed below:

BIRD-FISH—follow outlines provided on pattern and color with colored pencils to match the pictures in the original book; highlight the feathers and other white outlining with white acrylic craft paint. (*See* figure 6-10.)

COW-FISH—follow outlines provided on pattern and color with colored pencils to match the pictures in the original book; highlight the fins and tail and other white outlining with white acrylic craft paint. (*See* figure 6-11.)

PEOPLE-FISH—follow outlines provided on pattern and color with colored pencils to match the pictures in the original book; highlight the fins and tails and other white outlining with white acrylic craft paint. (*See* figure 6-12.)

Figure 6-10

Figure 6-12

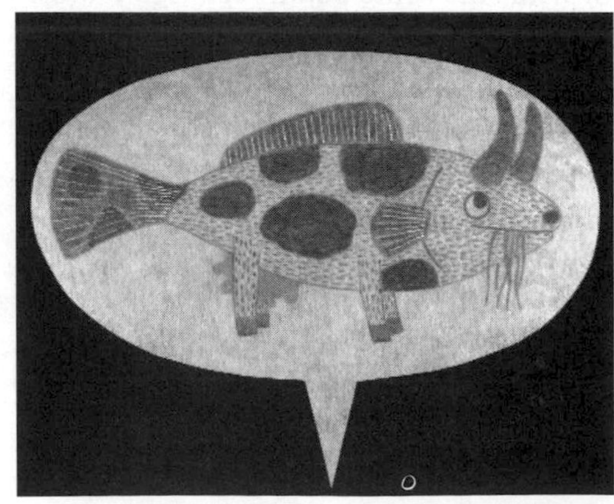

Figure 6-11

Flannel/Felt Board Story Finished Product

Figure 6-13

Figure 6-14

Figure 6-15

Figure 6-16

Figure 6-17

Figure 6-18

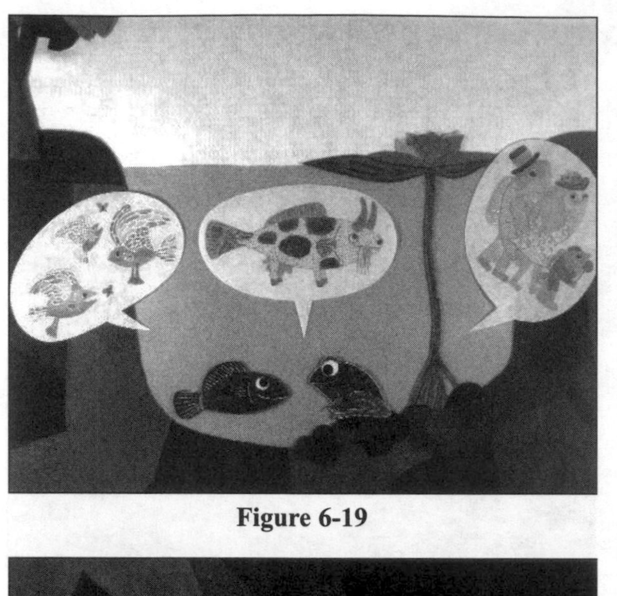

Figure 6-19

Figure 6-20

Figure 6-21

Figure 6-22

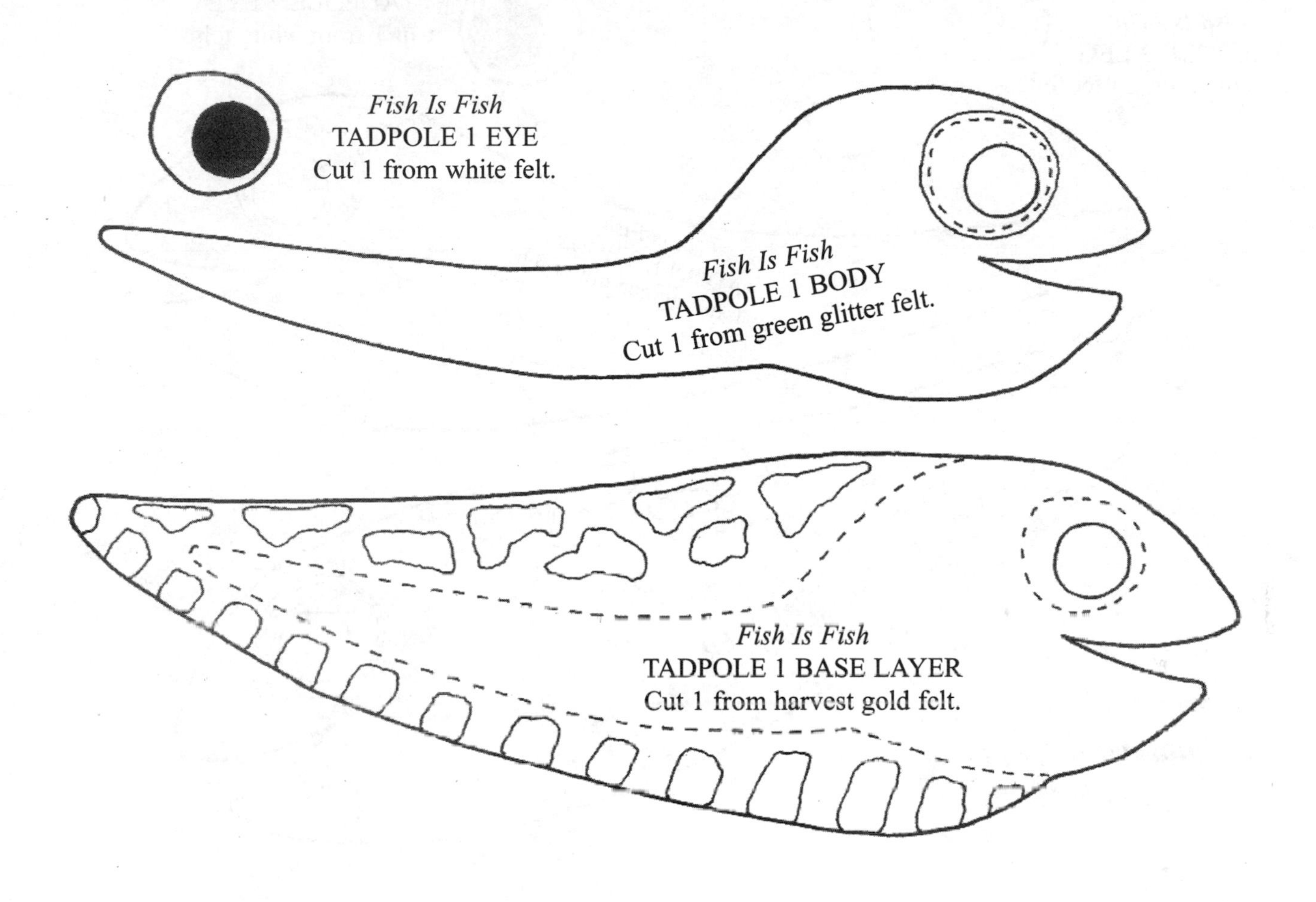

Photocopy this page at size 100%.

Fish Is Fish
SITTING FROG EYELID
Cut 2 from green glitter felt.

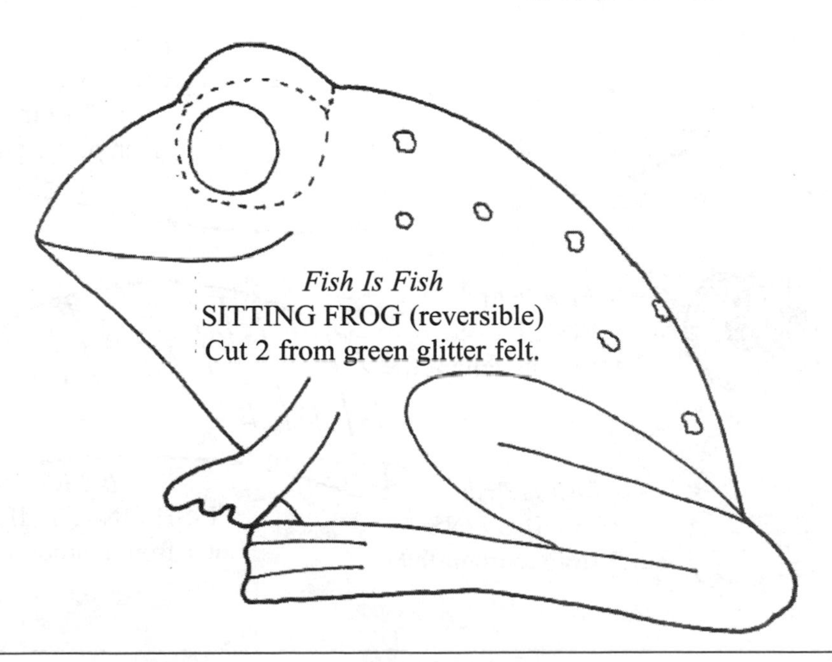

Fish Is Fish
SITTING FROG EYE
Cut 2 from white felt.

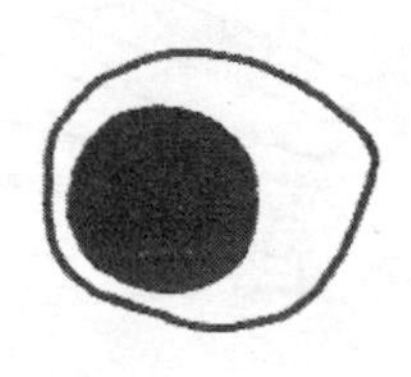

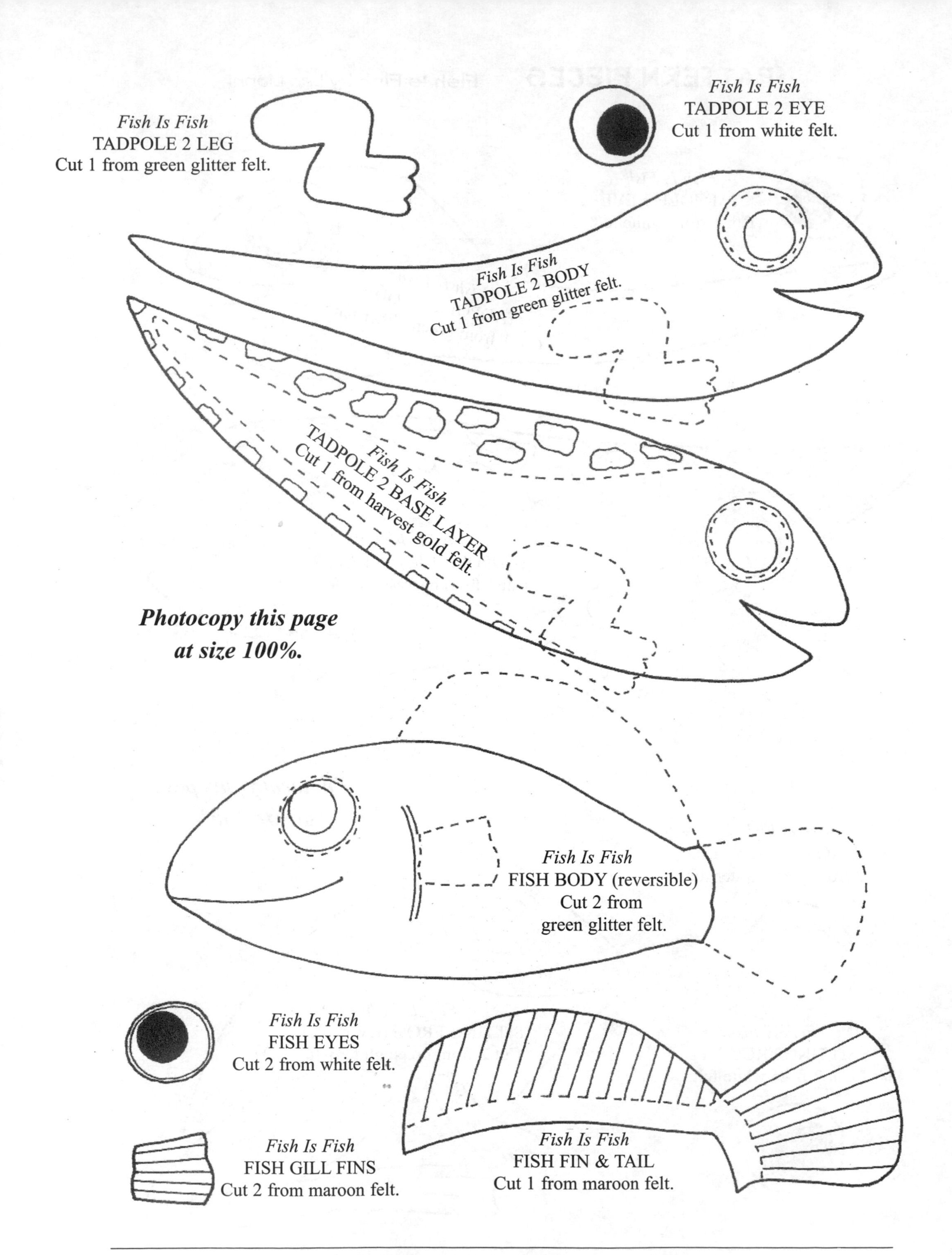

Photocopy this page at size 100%.

Photocopy this page at size 100%.

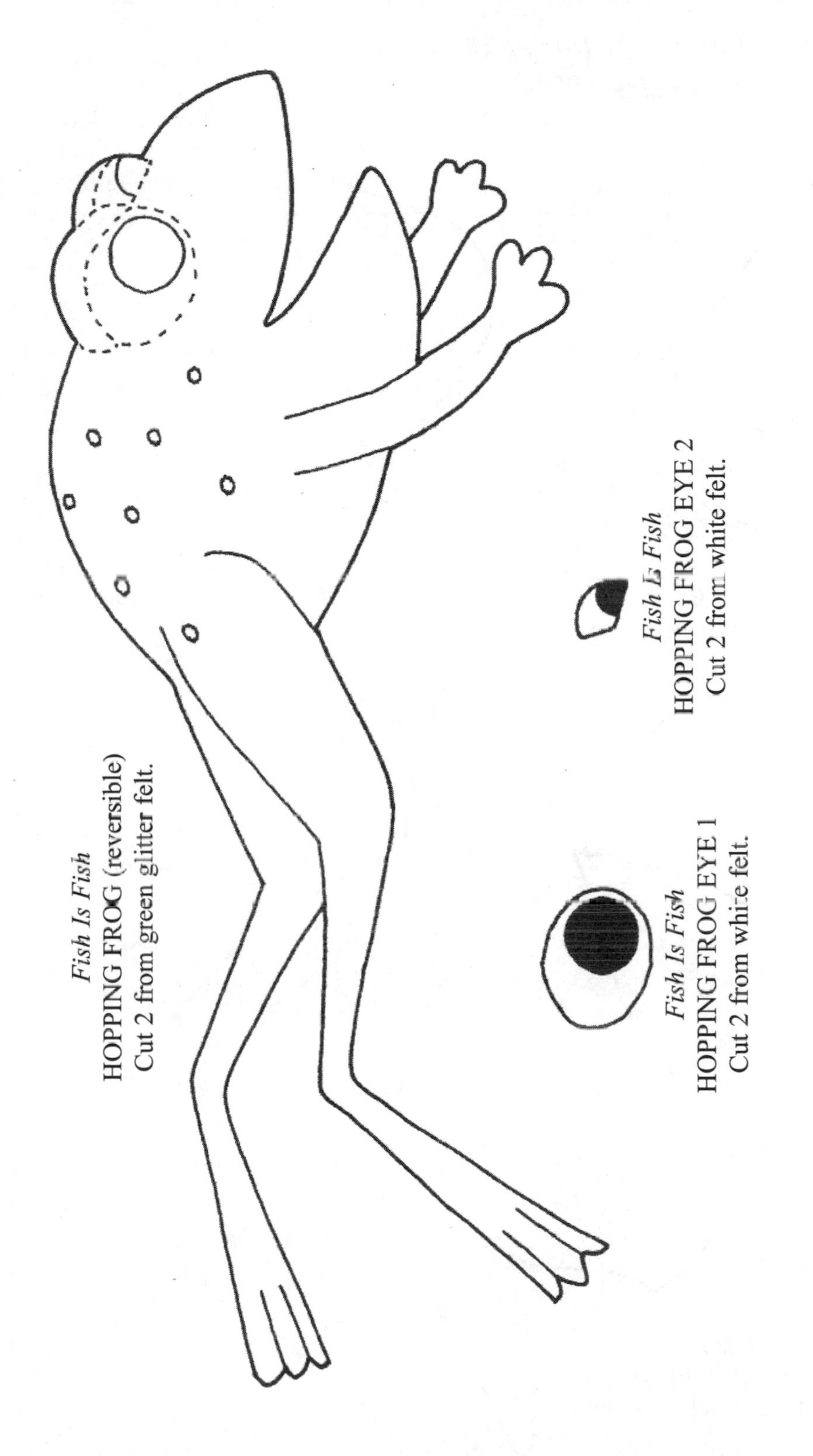

Fish Is Fish
HOPPING FROG (reversible)
Cut 2 from green glitter felt.

Fish Is Fish
HOPPING FROG EYE 2
Cut 2 from white felt.

Fish Is Fish
HOPPING FROG EYE 1
Cut 2 from white felt.

Fish Is Fish
HOPPING FROG EYELIDS
Cut 2 from green glitter felt.

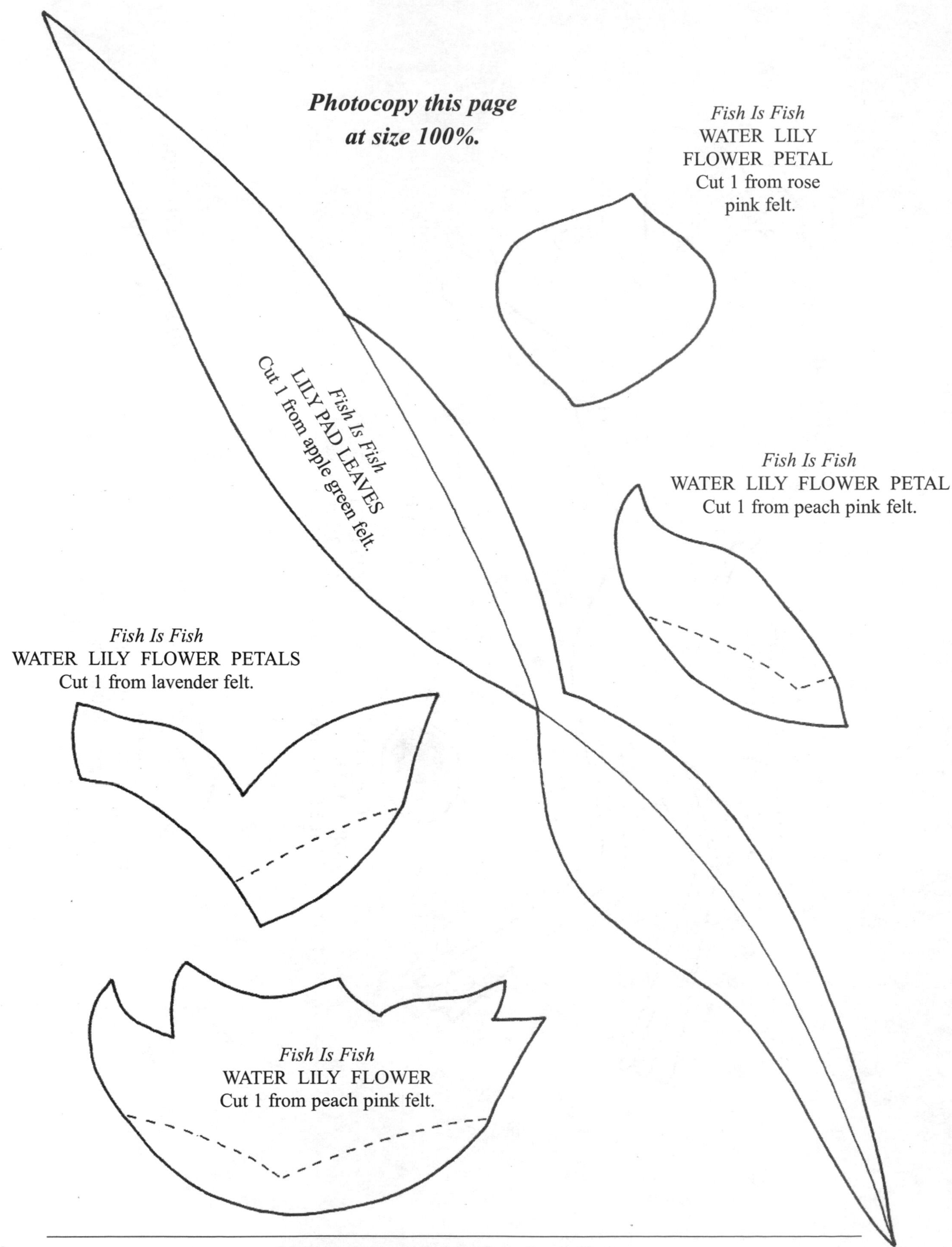
Photocopy this page
at size 100%.
Fish Is Fish
WATER LILY
FLOWER PETAL
Cut 1 from rose
pink felt.
Fish Is Fish
LILY PAD LEAVES
Cut 1 from apple green felt.
Fish Is Fish
WATER LILY FLOWER PETAL
Cut 1 from peach pink felt.
Fish Is Fish
WATER LILY FLOWER PETALS
Cut 1 from lavender felt.
Fish Is Fish
WATER LILY FLOWER
Cut 1 from peach pink felt.

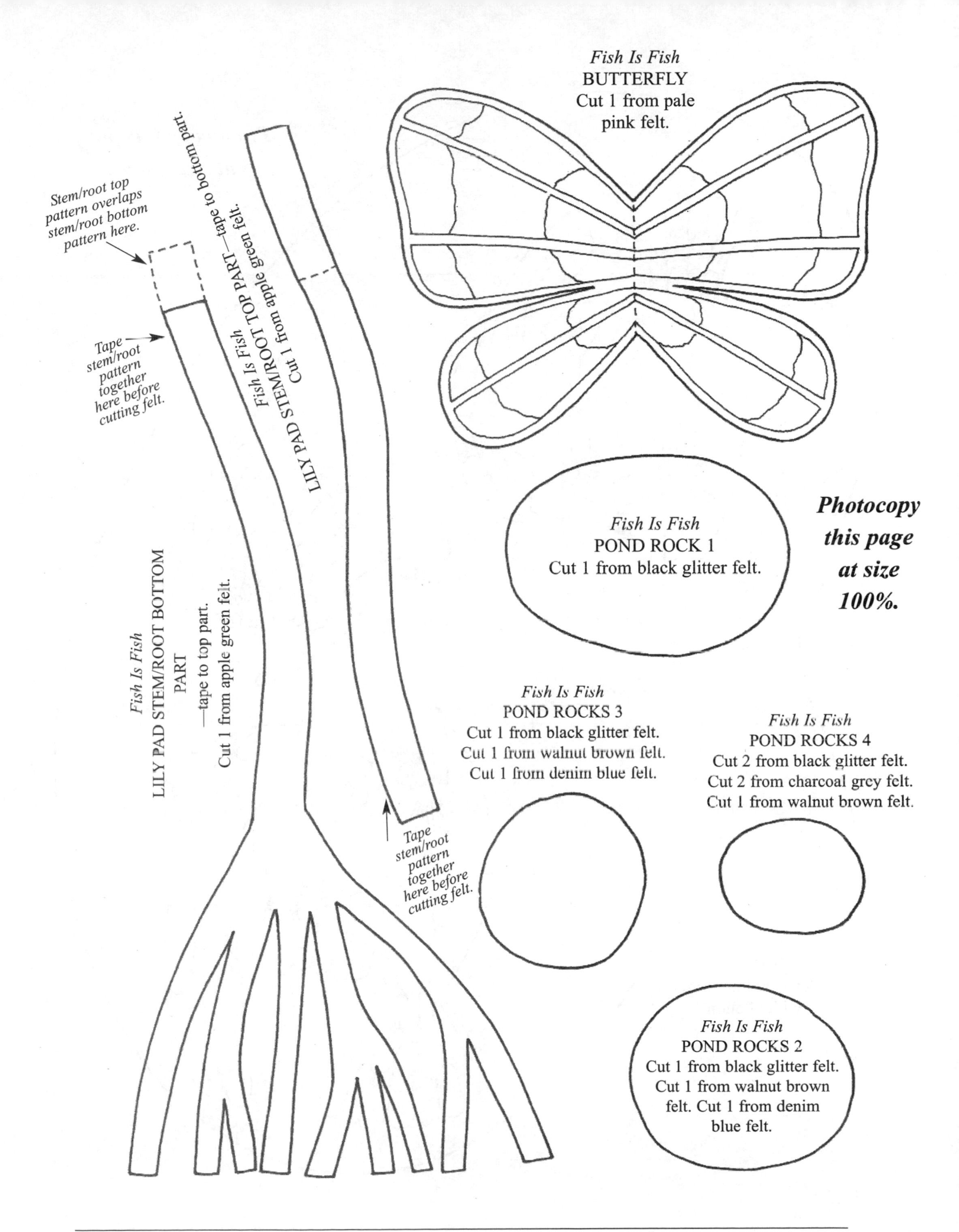

Fish Is Fish
BUTTERFLY
Cut 1 from pale pink felt.
Stem/root top pattern overlaps stem/root bottom pattern here.
tape to bottom part.
Fish Is Fish
LILY PAD STEM/ROOT TOP PART—tape to bottom part.
Cut 1 from apple green felt.
Tape stem/root pattern together here before cutting felt.
Fish Is Fish
LILY PAD STEM/ROOT BOTTOM PART
—tape to top part.
Cut 1 from apple green felt.
Tape stem/root pattern together here before cutting felt.
Fish Is Fish
POND ROCK 1
Cut 1 from black glitter felt.
Photocopy this page at size 100%.
Fish Is Fish
POND ROCKS 3
Cut 1 from black glitter felt.
Cut 1 from walnut brown felt.
Cut 1 from denim blue felt.
Fish Is Fish
POND ROCKS 4
Cut 2 from black glitter felt.
Cut 2 from charcoal grey felt.
Cut 1 from walnut brown felt.
Fish Is Fish
POND ROCKS 2
Cut 1 from black glitter felt.
Cut 1 from walnut brown felt. Cut 1 from denim blue felt.

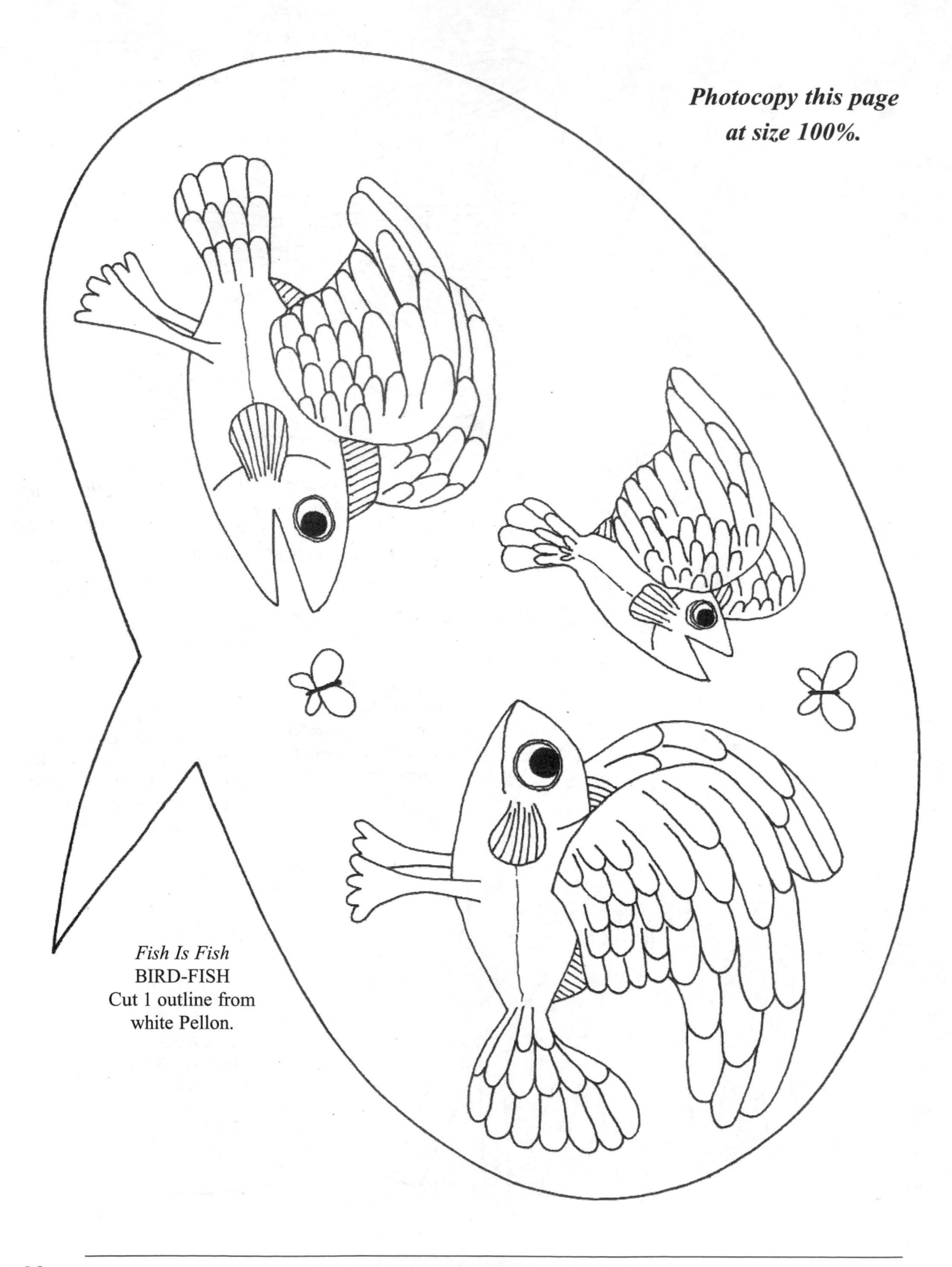
Photocopy this page at size 100%.
Fish Is Fish
BIRD-FISH
Cut 1 outline from white Pellon.

Photocopy this page at size 100%.

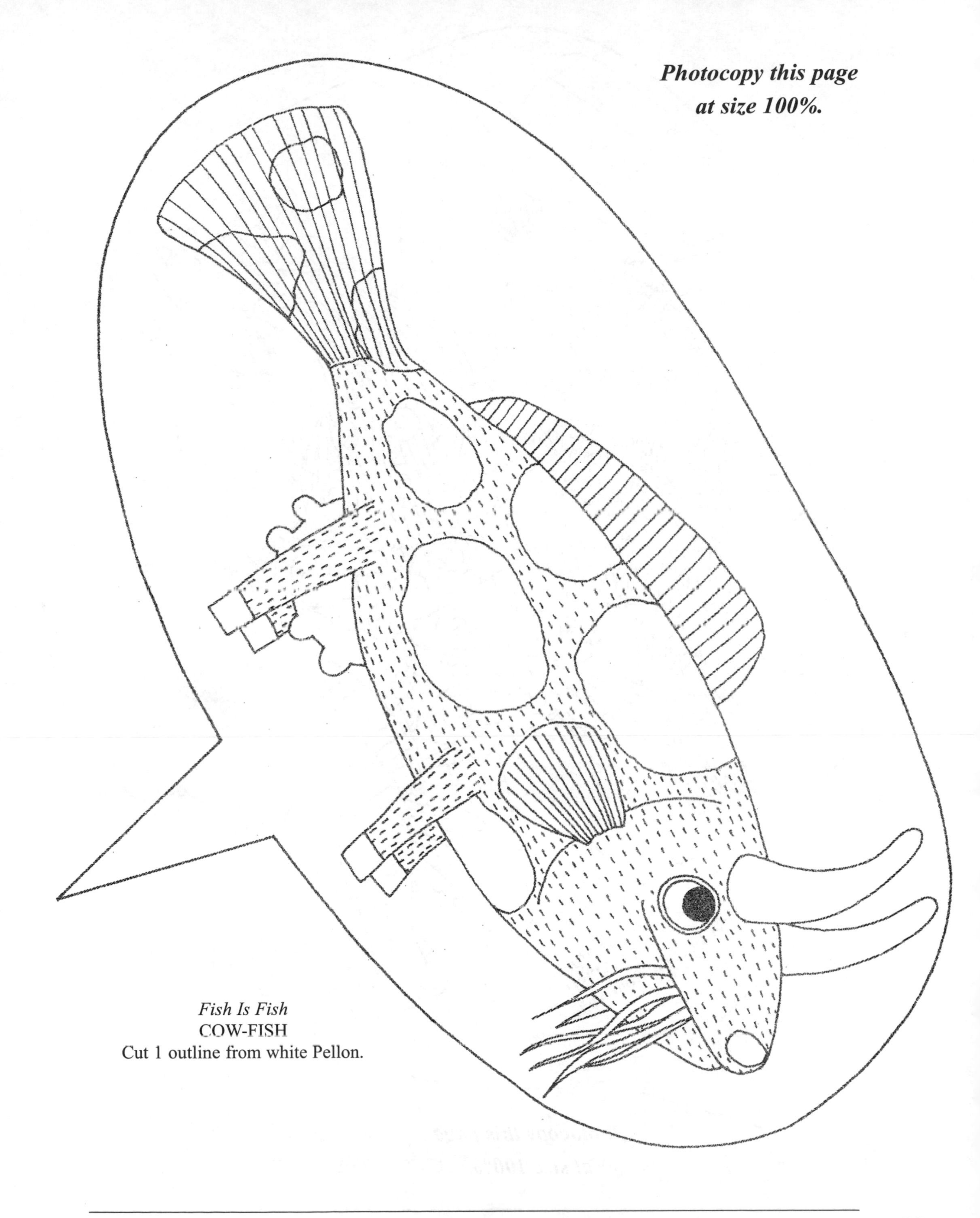

Fish Is Fish
COW-FISH
Cut 1 outline from white Pellon.

Photocopy this page at size 100%.

Photocopy this page at size 200%.

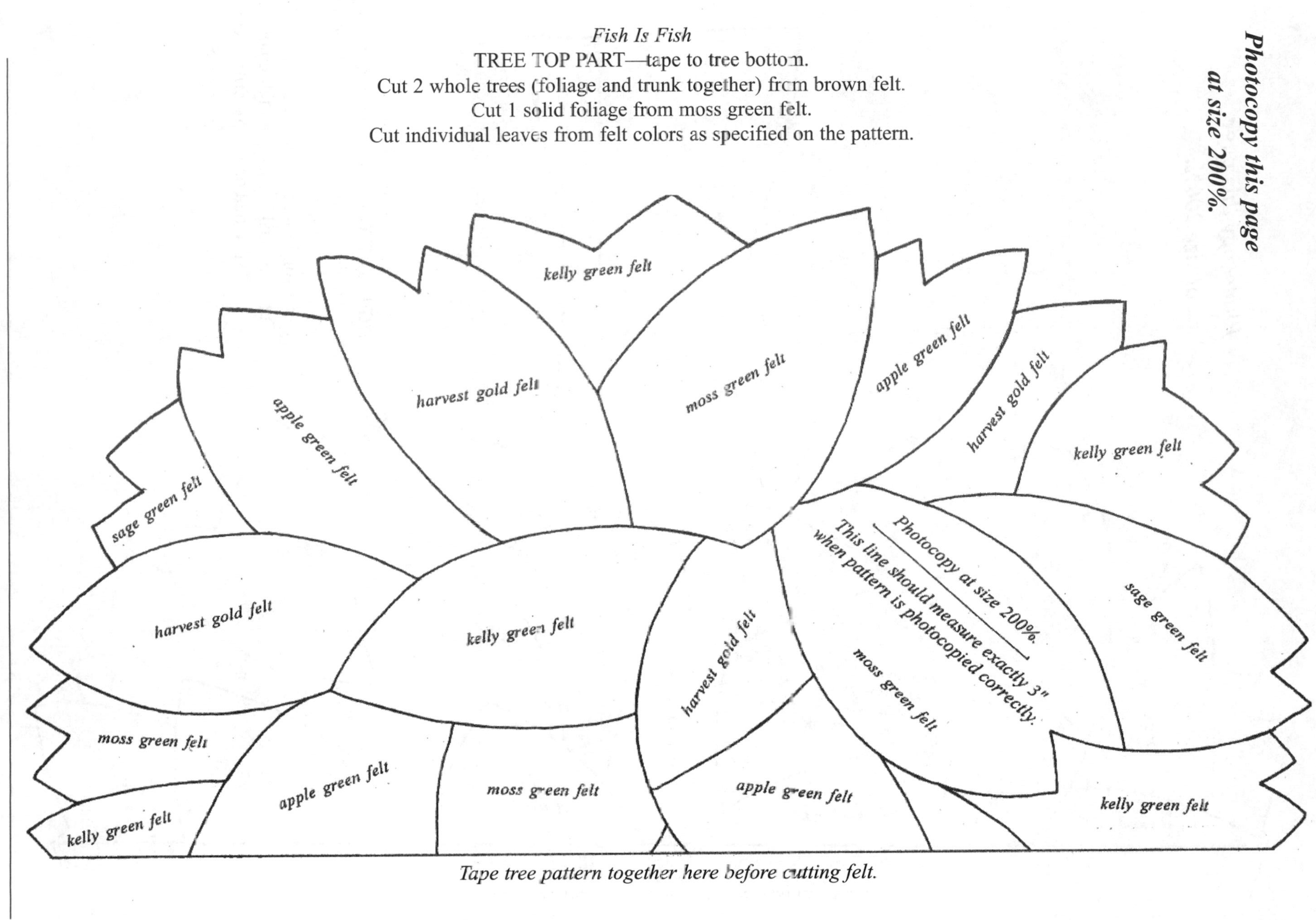

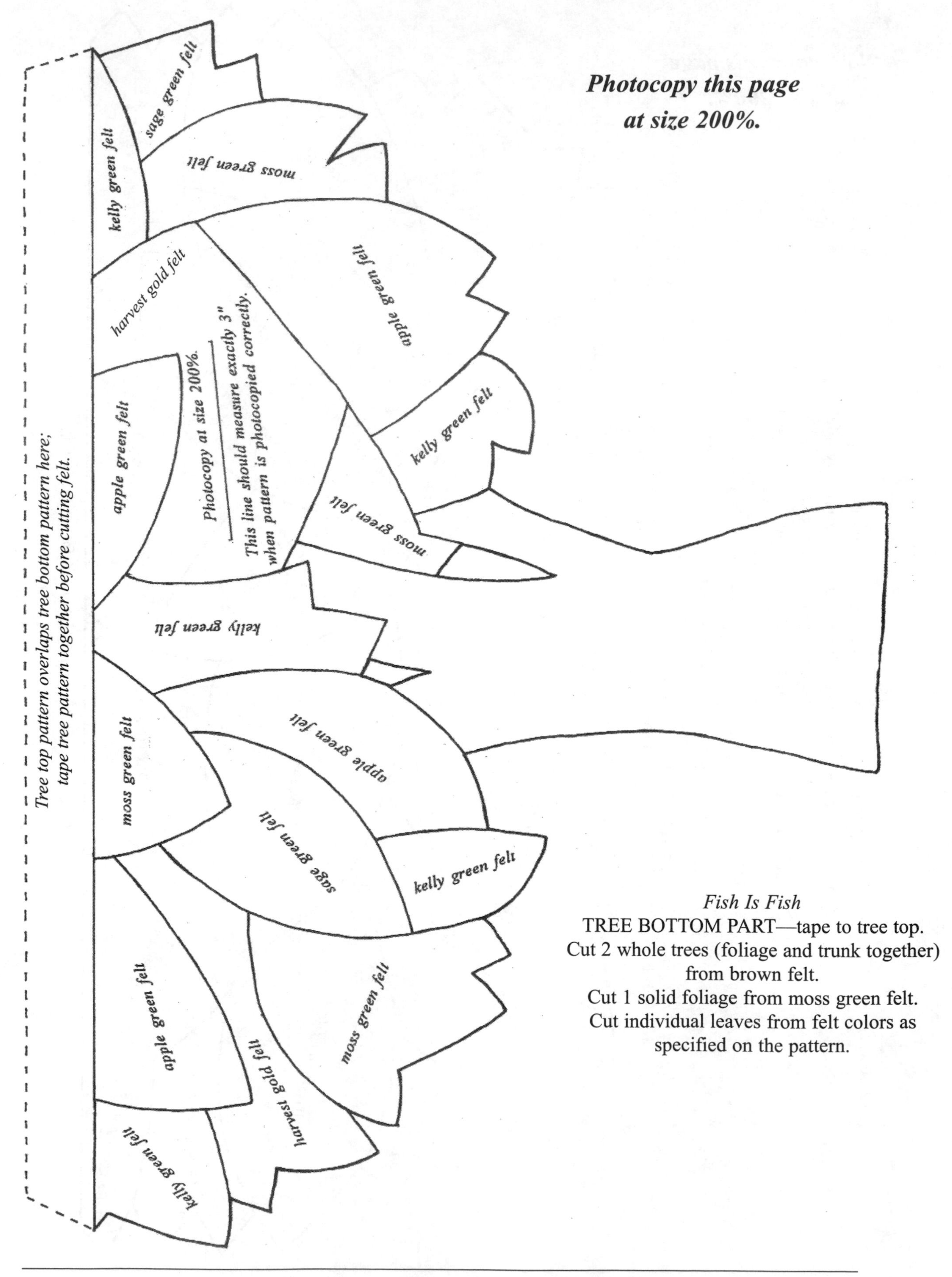

Photocopy this page at size 200%.

Fish Is Fish

TREE BOTTOM PART—tape to tree top.

Cut 2 whole trees (foliage and trunk together) from brown felt.

Cut 1 solid foliage from moss green felt.

Cut individual leaves from felt colors as specified on the pattern.

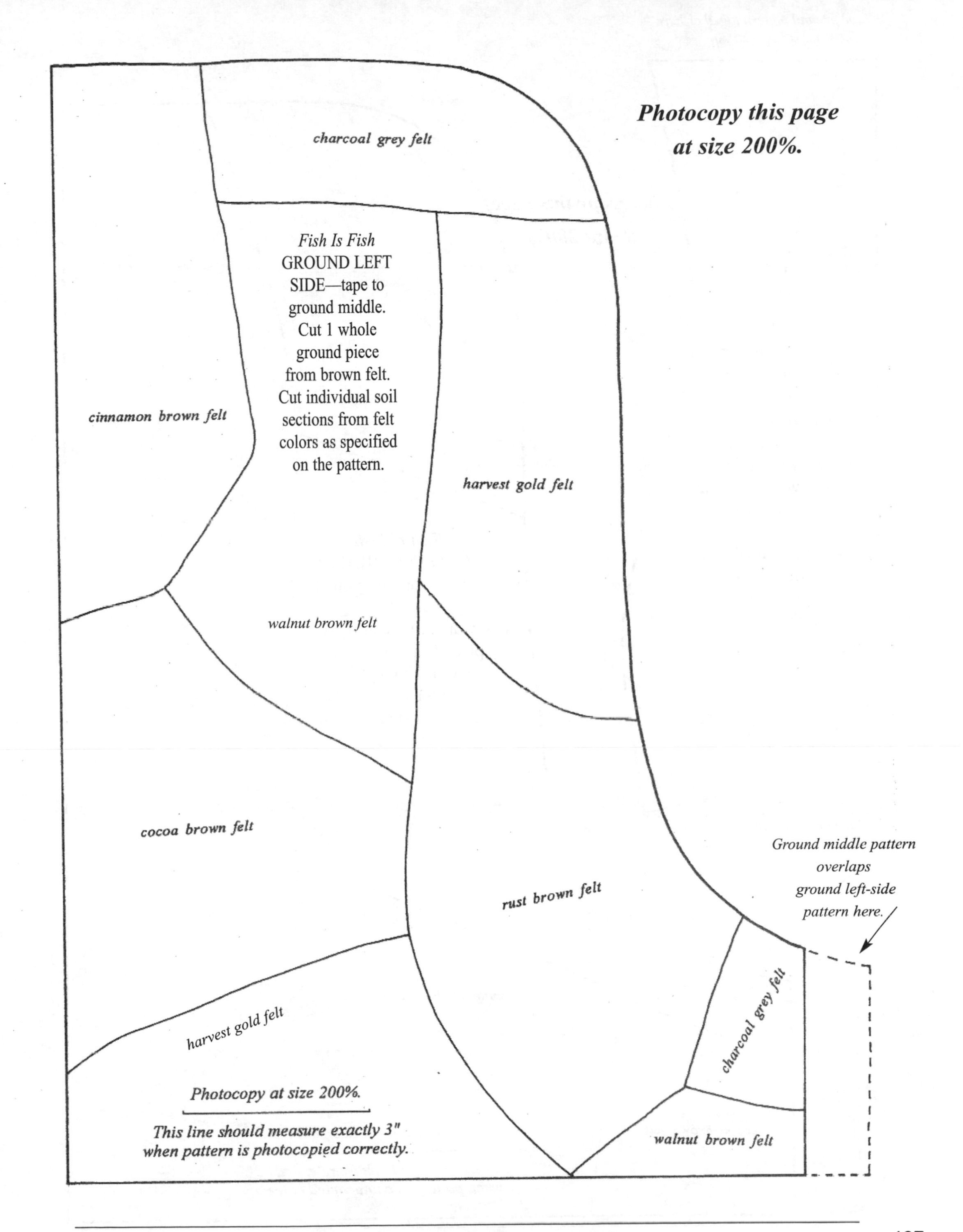
Photocopy this page
at size 200%.
charcoal grey felt
Fish Is Fish
GROUND LEFT
SIDE—tape to
ground middle.
Cut 1 whole
ground piece
from brown felt.
Cut individual soil
sections from felt
colors as specified
on the pattern.
cinnamon brown felt
harvest gold felt
walnut brown felt
cocoa brown felt
rust brown felt
Ground middle pattern
overlaps
ground left-side
pattern here.
charcoal grey felt
harvest gold felt
Photocopy at size 200%.
This line should measure exactly 3"
when pattern is photocopied correctly.
walnut brown felt

Tape ground pattern together here before cutting felt.

walnut brown felt

charcoal grey felt

Photocopy this page at size 200%.

Fish Is Fish
GROUND MIDDLE—tape to ground left and right sides.
Cut 1 whole ground piece from brown felt.
Cut individual soil sections from felt colors as specified on the pattern.

cocoa brown felt

harvest gold felt

Tape ground pattern together here before cutting felt.

rust brown felt

cocoa brown felt

harvest gold felt

Fish Is Fish
GROUND RIGHT SIDE—tape to ground middle.
Cut 1 whole ground piece from brown felt.
Cut individual soil sections from felt colors as specified on the pattern.

walnut brown felt

charcoal grey felt

Ground middle pattern overlaps ground right-side pattern here.

cinnamon brown felt

cocoa brown felt

Photocopy at size 200%.

This line should measure exactly 3" when pattern is photocopied correctly.

Storage

You Will Need

1 large (10" × 13") envelope

1 piece sturdy cardboard or matte board, size 9" × 12"

1 sturdy box approximately size 20" × 26" × 8" deep

3 copies of *Fish Is Fish* storage label

2 copies of *Fish Is Fish* presentation notes/script (pages 79–83)

1 copy of flannel/felt board story finished product photos (figures 6-13 through 6-22)

Make three photocopies of the label provided below for the *Fish Is Fish* flannel/felt board story pieces and fill in the *date* and *name or initials* blanks. Cut out the labels. Affix one label securely to the front of the large envelope and the other two to both ends of your storage container.

> ***Fish Is Fish***
>
> Leo Lionni (Random, 1970)
>
> Prop created _______ by ________________
> DATE NAME OR INITIALS
>
> from patterns included in *Books in Bloom*
> by Kimberly Faurot (ALA, 2003)

The felt and Pellon pieces for *Fish Is Fish* should be stored flat to keep them from creasing or stretching. You will probably need to fold over the embankment, pond, and white background pieces, but everything else should be kept completely flat and unfolded. To protect the smaller story figures (tadpoles, frogs, fish, and Pellon pieces), store them in the envelope and then inside the larger storage box. Lay the figures on top of the piece of sturdy cardboard or matte board, and slide them all into the storage envelope. All of the *Fish Is Fish* pieces can then be kept together within the storage box.

Felt story pieces may often be stored just in large envelopes with a sturdy cardboard or matte board backing to give the packaging support and to keep the pieces flat. (The story figures for *Fish Is Fish* need a box because of the three-dimensional butterfly addition.) Depending upon the number of props you have in your collection and the amount of storage space that you have, you may want to store all of your felt stories in individual sturdy, shallow boxes to further ensure that the pieces don't become damaged. You could also begin a larger box for "Flannel/Felt Board Stories," and keep everything you make in that medium in that box. Make sure you label such a box extremely well, however, including the titles of all of the stories on the outside of the box.

Make at least two photocopies of the presentation notes/script (pages 79–83), and include them in the storage container along with the felt story pieces. Also include a photocopy of the flannel/felt board story finished product photos (figures 6-13 through 6-22).

A professional storytelling copy of the original book *Fish Is Fish* by Leo Lionni (Random, 1970) should either be included in the storage container with the prop or else should be kept nearby in a professional "storytelling collection" so it may be shown when the prop is being presented. If you are unable to obtain a new copy of the book, investigate purchasing a used copy through one of the resources listed in chapter 10.

Make sure that the flannel board storytelling pieces for *Fish Is Fish* are included on your storytelling props database or list (*see* chapter 2) as well as in your institution's inventory records.

Notify other staff members who might be able to include *Fish Is Fish* in their programming or classrooms that it is ready for use, and demonstrate it for them (along with proper storage caveats) if at all possible.

Summary

Many teachers and librarians are already familiar with basic flannel/felt board figure creation and storytelling techniques and use the format regularly in their classrooms and programs. Flannel board pieces have traditionally been flat, with minimal adornment so they can adhere to the board on their own. Using Velcro or pins to stick figures to the board enables you to add considerable pizzazz to your felt pieces. "Puffy" figures can be created for a three-dimensional look; paint can provide texture and detail; accoutrements such as feathers, yarn, glass or google eyes, beads, fabric, tiny straw baskets, jewelry, and so forth may be added for interest and enable the creator to more fully capture the spirit of a story's original artwork. Because felt is relatively inexpensive and easy to work with, students can create their own storytelling pieces for literary units in the classroom, and they can use the figures to tell stories to younger students. The possibilities are endless!

Combination Prop Stories

Includes script and pattern for

The Most Wonderful Egg in the World
by Helme Heine (Atheneum, 1983)

Pattern difficulty level

Medium

Construction time estimate

10 hours

"Combination props" utilize multiple types of media and presentation techniques to tell a single story. This approach enables you to share the best of many worlds with your audience. A story that seems tied to a flannel or Velcro board "stage," for example, can suddenly come alive in a new way as the flannel board pieces begin to interact with three-dimensional objects or even puppets. Pieces can be very large and dramatic, and the overall assembly can be less time-consuming because you don't have to create all of the parts from scratch.

Techniques and Considerations

Creating

The choice and combination of media depend upon the type of manipulations needed by the story as well as considerations of what would enable the most dramatic and realistic presentation for the audience. It must all be easy to use, so that manipulating the pieces doesn't detract from or disrupt the story in any way.

When creating combination prop story pieces, make sure that your choices of media can be integrated successfully. If flannel/felt board pieces will be removed from the board to interact with three-dimensional pieces at any point, the flannel/felt board pieces must be sturdy enough to hold their shape on their own. You can achieve this by making the pieces as lightly stuffed double-layer pieces or by strengthening them with pipe cleaner inserts, among other techniques (*see* chapter 6, "Flannel/Felt Board Stories," for specific directions). Additionally, any two-dimensional pieces should be "snazzed up" and given a little bit of body so that they match with the three-dimensional pieces a little bit better.

Both two- and three-dimensional story pieces can be stuck to a flannel or Velcro board in several ways. You can glue or stitch a strip of Velcro hooks to the piece (hook Velcro will stick to felt or to a Velcro board), or you can use T-pins and simply pin the story piece to the board. Just one T-pin is usually enough to firmly secure an item. Velcro and T-pins are especially essential for heavier story pieces like those included in this chapter.

As suggested in chapter 6, experiment with various colors of background felt for your flannel board. Keep an array of felt coverings for the board that are cut to the right size. You will need to purchase the felt that is available on bolts for this purpose, not the small felt squares. Light blue, white, and green felt often work particularly well as backgrounds. Pin the felt coverings over the flannel board with T-pins all around the edge.

When determining what color background covering to use, examine the background colors in the book's original illustrations. If your story pieces will show up clearly on that color, try to replicate it. If the pieces would not show up well, choose another color that still retains the spirit of the original book. For example, the illustrations' background color in *The Most Wonderful Egg in the World* is predominantly white. The white prop chickens wouldn't show up well if they were displayed against a white background. The book's original cover, however, displays the chickens against a rich light blue, so I chose that as the background color for telling the flannel/felt board portion of the prop story.

Presenting

Hide prop pieces from view until time for their story appearance. You can either hide them on a cart behind the board you are using or in a closable box or bin. Make sure the pieces will be easily accessible (in the correct order!) when you are telling the story. If some pieces are three-dimensional and will be displayed on a table "stage" or other surface as part of the story, try making the surface appear special by draping it with a piece of colored fabric (functioning like a tablecloth). Keep a variety of fabric pieces on hand to complement your various prop stories. I have royal blue, grass green, and bright red fabric pieces that I use regularly for this purpose.

Make sure to practice presenting the story so your movements are smooth and so that you are able to integrate the different formats you have combined in a seamless manner. Practice out loud using any special voices you may have developed for the characters. Present the story pieces as if they are vibrant and alive. For example, have two-dimensional characters that you are holding talk directly to the audience like a three-dimensional puppet; stretch their legs; have them sneeze; and so forth. This manner of presentation can help two-dimensional story pieces come alive for the audience, and it enables them to meld more successfully with the three-dimensional prop pieces in the story.

Choosing the Combination Prop Format

Because some of the illustrations in *The Most Wonderful Egg in the World* are rather light and small, sharing the book as it is with a large group can be difficult. The story is wonderfully funny, however, with a lesson about life and what really matters that is important to share. The book is consequently an ideal candidate for adapting as a prop story.

Helme Heine's chicken illustrations for *The Most Wonderful Egg in the World* exude personality, and it is important to retain that element in a prop adaptation. Dotty, Stalky, and Plumy's special features (feathers, legs, and crest) are vital to the story's plot, so those must be dramatically shown. Another significant element is certainly the "egg laying," because it is the dramatic focal point of the story.

When deciding what format would work best for a prop adaptation, it is important to design pieces that will be clear and visible for large audiences as well as logical in terms of any required manipulations. Choose what makes the most sense: some parts can be three-dimensional and others two-dimensional; some pieces may need to be constructed, but others can be purchased objects; it may work best to combine several formats to produce the most seamless prop retelling of the story.

In *The Most Wonderful Egg in the World,* the chickens must be able to be displayed together, because they argue as a group and also go as a group to see the king. Although puppets or stuffed animal chickens are a possibility, they would need to be adapted to reflect the chickens' special features. Creating the chickens as two-dimensional characters enables you to easily place them up on a flannel or Velcro board where they can remain in clear view. You are also able to model the chickens more closely after Heine's illustrations. Using white fake fur for the chickens' bodies is reminiscent of feathers, and it gives the chickens enough firmness to be easily removed from the board and set on the nest when they lay their respective eggs.

Certainly the entire story could be done as a flannel board adaptation, with wadded-up felt eggs hiding behind the chickens. It is very dramatic and realistic, however, to have the chickens settle on a special royal nest and lay three-dimensional eggs. Although there is no nest in the original story, including one does not detract from the chickens' competition in any way. Designating it as the king's royal golden nest—complete with purple straw—makes it special. It is of course necessary for hiding the eggs, but it doesn't detract from the story in any way.

The company Book Props (*see* chapter 10) has created prop pieces for this story in which the chickens are very colorful. The three-dimensional eggs that Book Props' chickens lay are actually stored inside each chicken and then released by pulling a Velcro tab as the egg is laid. This method of egg laying is certainly realistic, although the size of the eggs is necessarily restricted by the size of the chickens. Audiences enjoy the Book Props pieces immensely. The pieces included here utilize an alternate egg-laying method, as the chickens produce the eggs while sitting on an official royal nest. This adaptation enables you to retain the surprise element of Stalky laying a really huge egg, reinforcing the wonder that such an enormous egg could come out of a comparatively small chicken.

The time invested in creating the following props for *The Most Wonderful Egg in the World* is well worth it; the story itself is immensely satisfying, and the props impart both drama and immediacy.

The Most Wonderful Egg in the World

Helme Heine

(Atheneum, 1983)

Summary

The king must choose the most beautiful egg laid by three hens, one of which he will then make a princess.

Possible themes

Babies, Birds, Chickens, Eggs, Families, Royalty

Approximate running time for combination prop story

7 minutes

Recommended audience interest level

Preschool (age 3 and older) through grade 2; intergenerational family programming

Please note that the story prop pieces are designed as professional resources, not as playthings. They do not conform to child safety play standards, and they could easily become damaged if used in a manner other than that for which they were intended.

Prop Pieces

3 adult chickens with Velcro (Dotty, Stalky, and Plumy)
1 adjustable king's crown
1 royal golden nest with purple straw
3 eggs in nest: 1 small egg, 1 giant egg, 1 cube egg
3 golden chicken crowns
3 baby chickens with Velcro

Use with

Velcro or flannel board on easel or table
light blue flannel board felt covering
table or TV tray on which to set the nest

cloth covering for table or tray (optional)

table or cart on which to lay out story prop pieces

a copy of the book to show the audience both before and after presenting the story

Setup

Start out with the three eggs buried in the purple straw in the nest so they can't be seen. Make sure you know which one is where, though, so you can pull it out at the appropriate point in the story!

T-pin the light blue felt covering over the flannel board.

Hide all of the prop pieces behind the Velcro/flannel board so the audience can't see them until that point in the story but where you can easily pull them out one at a time as the story progresses.

Presentation

Story narration is delineated in regular type; movement notes and miscellaneous directions are shown within the script in *[bracketed italics]*.

Learn the story and tell it to your audience from memory, using the prop pieces.

The script calls for you to be five characters: the Narrator, Dotty, Stalky, Plumy, and the King. The character who is talking is designated by his or her name at the beginning of the text, except for the Narrator.

Although it is not essential to use different character voices when presenting the story, it can truly help maintain the children's interest as well as help them distinguish which character is talking. Try out different voices to figure out which sounds the best for the different characters. All voices must feel natural for you after practice so that you will be able to use and maintain them successfully during an actual performance.

It is a very good idea to practice clucking and talking loudly like a chicken. Practice on your own until you are comfortable with it. Your audience will love it!

Including the audience in general as chickens in the kingdom is intended as an opportunity for audience participation (they cluck and nod at certain points). You can certainly prepare the audience for this role before starting, although it is not really necessary to do so; they will figure it out naturally as you go with just a little encouragement and gesturing on your part.

Please note: The following script is a slightly adapted story version for telling as a prop and participation story, and it includes notes for the storyteller on how and when to manipulate the prop pieces. Learn the story and tell it to your audience from memory, using the prop pieces. Please look at the book so that you know what adaptations have been made in this script; you may well prefer to tell the story verbatim from its exact original text. Show a copy of the book to your audience both before and after sharing the story with the props, and give the complete title, author/illustrator, and publication information.

SCRIPT

The Most Wonderful Egg in the World

by Helme Heine

Once upon a time, a long time ago, three chickens were quarreling about which one of them was the most beautiful.

DOTTY, STALKY, PLUMY

"Bawk, bawk, bawk! I'm the most beautiful! No, I am! No, I am!"

[Look behind Velcro board at hidden chickens as if startled to hear the loud quarreling emanating from there.]

The first chicken *[bring Dotty out and hold her up for audience to see]* was named DOTTY, for her beautiful feathers *[fluff her netting feathers]*.

DOTTY "I am the most bee-yoo-tee-ful chicken!" clucked Dotty. "Bawk, bawk! I have the most beautiful feathers; therefore, I am the most beautiful chicken! Bawk, bawk, bawk!"

And that was Dotty.

[Stick Dotty up on board, closest to you.]

The next chicken *[bring Stalky out and hold her up]* was named STALKY, for her amazing legs *[stretch/move her legs to show them off]*.

STALKY "I am THE most beautiful chicken!" clucked Stalky. "I have the most beautiful legs; therefore, I am the most beautiful chicken! Bawk, bawk!"

And that was Stalky.

[Stick Stalky up in center position on board.]

The third chicken *[bring Plumy out and hold her up]* was named PLUMY, for the remarkable crest on top of her head *[point it out]*.

PLUMY "Bawk, bawk!" said Plumy. "I have the most beautiful crest; therefore, I am clearly the most beautiful chicken! Bawk, bawk, bawk!"

And that was Plumy.

[Put Plumy on board, furthest from you.]

DOTTY, STALKY, PLUMY

"I'm the most beautiful, bawk!" "No, I am!" "No, I am!" "Bawk, bawk, bawk, bawk, bawk!"

[Make a cacophony of "bawking."]

Script adapted by Beth Murray and Kimberly K. Faurot, *Books in Bloom: Creative Patterns and Props That Bring Stories to Life* (ALA, 2003).

Well, they argued and argued and *argued,* and could not agree, so at last they decided to ask the king for his advice. They all went off together to the king's palace.

[Put on your king crown.]

When they got there, they explained their problem.

The king listened carefully *[rub your chin as if thinking deeply]*, and then this is what he said *[in deep kingly voice]:*

KING "It doesn't matter what you look like. What matters is what you do with what you've got. Therefore, I hereby declare that we shall have a contest, and whichever one of you lays the most wonderful egg will be the winner, and I will declare her the most beautiful and make her a princess, and she will live here in the palace with me."

So they got out the royal nest for the contest *[hold up nest from where it has been hidden],* the golden one with the purple straw *[tip nest forward with one hand holding the straw in so nothing falls out, but so the audience sees it and thinks there's nothing in the nest],* and there in the palace park with the king *[gesture to self]* and all of the chickens in his kingdom *[gesture to audience as if they are the chickens in the kingdom]* watching, the contest began.

[You may want to set the nest down on a table or TV tray to free your hands; just make sure the audience can't look down into it.]

Dotty was to be first. *[Remove her from the board and hold her up.]* She settled herself on the royal nest *[wiggle her back and forth at front edge of nest, with legs sticking forward over the edge of the nest as if she's sitting there],* and she concentrated very hard.

DOTTY "Bawk, bawk!" said Dotty. "Bawk, bawk, bawk! Bawk, bawk!"

And when they looked, there in the purple straw was an egg, right where Dotty had laid it. *[Stick Dotty back on board and then pick out the small Styrofoam egg and hold it up.]* A beautiful egg. A spotless egg. A perfect egg, the eggshell shimmering like polished marble. Nobody could believe it. Such a remarkable egg!

At last the king cried out,

KING "Why, it's perfect! The most perfect egg I have ever seen!"

All of the chickens nodded. *[Gesture at audience, nodding.]* It was indeed perfect. Surely this would be the most wonderful egg. Everyone felt a little bit sorry for Stalky and Plumy. *[Look at them pityingly.]* How could they possibly beat a perfect egg like Dotty's?

[Set egg down on table or shelf so it can still be seen but so your hands are free.]

Nevertheless, it was Stalky's turn *[take her down from the board and settle her on nest],* and she settled herself carefully on the nest. She concentrated very hard.

STALKY "Bawk, bawk!" said Stalky. "Bawk, bawk! Bawk, bawk, BAWK, BAWK, BAWK!"

And Stalky stood up. *[Stick her back in place in the middle of the board.]* There in the nest was the egg she had laid. *[Hold up the giant cardboard egg.]* There was a gasp from the king and the crowd, for there was an egg of such size and weight that even an ostrich would have been jealous. It was enormous! Nobody had ever seen such a large chicken egg before.

KING "This is the biggest egg I have ever seen!" cried the king, and all of the chickens nodded. *[Gesture at audience, nodding.]* Truly this was also a wonderful egg—this wonderful enormous egg *[set it down by Dotty's egg],* and right next to it Dotty's wonderful perfect egg.

Now everybody felt *extremely* sorry for Plumy. *[Gesture her direction with your thumb and look worried.]* She was last. *[Take her down from board.]* There was surely no way she could lay a more perfect egg than Dotty's and no way she could possibly lay a bigger egg than Stalky's. It was unthinkable. Poor Plumy.

But Plumy settled herself calmly on the royal nest *[sit her down on nest]* and concentrated.

She gave a very small cackle,

PLUMY "Bawk-bawk!" and stood up.

[Place Plumy back on board.]

And there, laid in the straw *[look down in surprise into the nest; the kids can't see yet],* was an EGG *[hold up cube on the word* EGG*]* that would be talked about for the next hundred years. It was a square. It was a cube! Each side was straight, as if drawn with a ruler, and each surface shone in a different color.

KING "This," cried the king," is indeed the most FANTASTIC, UNUSUAL EGG I have ever seen!"

All of the other chickens nodded in amazement *[gesture at audience, nodding].*

Well, it was of course impossible to say which egg was the most wonderful. Dotty's egg was a PERFECTLY WONDERFUL egg *[hold it up];* Stalky's egg was an ENORMOUSLY WONDERFUL egg *[hold it up, too];* and Plumy's egg was a FANTASTICALLY, UNUSUALLY WONDERFUL egg *[hold it up, too, balancing all three].*

The king said,

KING "These are all truly wonderful eggs. Each is wonderful in its own way. Therefore, I hereby declare that you are all three winners in this contest, and you shall all be princesses and live here in the palace with me."

[Set down eggs, hidden behind board or somewhere they can't be seen anymore.]

So the king gave each of the chickens a golden crown—one for Dotty *[leaving chickens on board, wrap crown around the front of her comb where crest joins her head, tucking it in on both sides],* one for Stalky *[wrap her crown],* and one for Plumy *[wrap her crown],* and he made them all princesses, and they lived together there in the palace as the best of friends—Dotty and all of her babies *[hold up little Styrofoam chick from where he is hidden behind the board, and then stick him onto the board by Dotty—maybe up by her head if there are tiny children who will come up and grab!],* Stalky and all of her babies *[bring out and hold up giant chick, and then stick him to board by Stalky],* and Plumy and all of her babies *[bring out and hold up cube chick, and then stick him by Plumy]*—and they all lived

HAPPILY
EVER
AFTER.

[The audience can/will likely say this with you.]

[Show audience back cover of book with the baby chicks and then the title page of book with the king and chickens standing happily together.]

THE END

Other Activities

Immediately following or preceding *The Most Wonderful Egg in the World,* try doing an adapted version of the "Chicken Dance" with your audience (Kimbo Educational has a good version). Do the beak, flap, shake tail, and clapping parts as usual; then simply flap and cluck noisily while revolving in place during the "swing your partner" part. For a special handout, punch out die-cut crowns from card stock or purchase gold foil cardboard crowns for the children to wear home, "just like the chickens." (*See* chapter 10.)

PATTERN INSTRUCTIONS

Combination Prop Story (Sample Pattern)

The Most Wonderful Egg in the World by Helme Heine

Patterns

Prop story pieces designed by Beth Murray

Estimated difficulty

Medium

Estimated construction time

10 hours

Estimated cost for supplies

$50–$75

You Will Need These Tools

ballpoint pen
fabric shears
small sharp-pointed scissors
Aleene's Original "Tacky" Glue
hand-sewing needle
straight pins
steam iron and thin cloth for fusing interfacing
sewing machine (*or* may be hand sewn)
needle nose pliers
wire cutters
electric drill or sharp awl

You Will Need These Supplies

SUPPLIES TO MAKE THE THREE ADULT CHICKENS

thread: white, red
1 yard white fake fur (45" wide fabric)
1/4 yard red close-weave fabric such as flannel (45" wide fabric)
1/4 yard interfacing (45" wide interfacing)
3/4 yard sparkly red lace trim for Plumy's crest, approximately 1 1/2" wide
1/4 yard sparkly white netting (with metallic or colored flecks) for Dotty's cape (45" wide fabric) *or* 6" wide sparkly tulle netting on a roll
2/3 yard sparkly ribbon for cape tie, 3/8" wide
3" × 9" piece of yellow flannel-backed vinyl or shiny nonfray yellow fabric for beaks

6 shiny rounded black shank buttons for eyes, size 9/16"

11 orange pipe cleaners/chenille stems

4 1/2" length of self-adhesive red or white hook Velcro, 3/4" wide (cut into three 1 1/2" lengths)

2/3 yard sparkly gold trim for chicken crowns, 3/4" wide (cut into three 8" lengths)

SUPPLIES TO MAKE THE EGGS AND BABY CHICKENS

thread: bright yellow

2 Styrofoam eggs, approximate size 3 1/16" × 2 5/16" (*not* pressed Dylite)

2 cardboard eggs, approximate size 6"

2 lightweight cubes, approximate size 2 1/2" square (Styrofoam, cardboard, small square boxes—whatever you can find)

white matte-finish spray paint

acrylic craft paint: red, yellow, blue, green, purple, white

2 "solid black eyes" with shank, 8 mm size

2 "solid black eyes" with shank, 9 mm size

2 "solid black eyes" with shank, 12 mm size

1 yellow felt square

3 orange pipe cleaners/chenille stems

brightly colored craft feathers (guinea feathers are especially nice as they have polka dots)

3 1/2" length of self-adhesive white hook Velcro, 3/4" wide (cut into one 1 1/2" length; one 2" length)

7" length of self-adhesive white hook Velcro, 1" wide (cut into two 3 1/2" lengths)

SUPPLIES TO MAKE THE ROYAL NEST

1 round, deep basket with close-woven sides (big enough and deep enough to hide the three eggs in it)

shiny gold spray paint

purple artificial grass or shredding

SUPPLIES FOR THE KING

1 adjustable novelty king's crown (plastic or cardboard)

Directions

How to Make the THREE ADULT CHICKENS

Step 1

Photocopy patterns *at sizes specified*. (*See* chapter 2, "Enlarging the Patterns in This Book.") Cut out all of the photocopied patterns along the outside of the pattern outlines.

Step 2

Lay the cut-out paper patterns onto the designated fabrics and interfacing and pin. Cut out all fabric and interfacing pieces, as specified on the patterns. *Make sure to cut out fabric with right sides together when cutting out two or more pieces so that the pieces will be mirror images of each other.* When cutting out the white fake fur ADULT CHICKEN BODIES, lay the patterns on the fur so that the fur will point *downward* on the finished chickens.

Figure 7-1

Step 3

Fuse interfacing to red CREST pieces (see fusing instructions on interfacing packaging).

Figure 7-2

Step 4

With right sides together, pin and stitch the three CRESTS with red thread. Seam allowance is 1/4". Make sure you leave the bottom sides open. Trim seams and clip between crest protrusions. Turn crests right side out and press. (*See* figure 7-1.)

Step 5

Pin the red lace trim along the edge of Plumy's large crest. Topstitch along the edge of the crest with red thread to secure the trim to the crest. (*See* figure 7-2.)

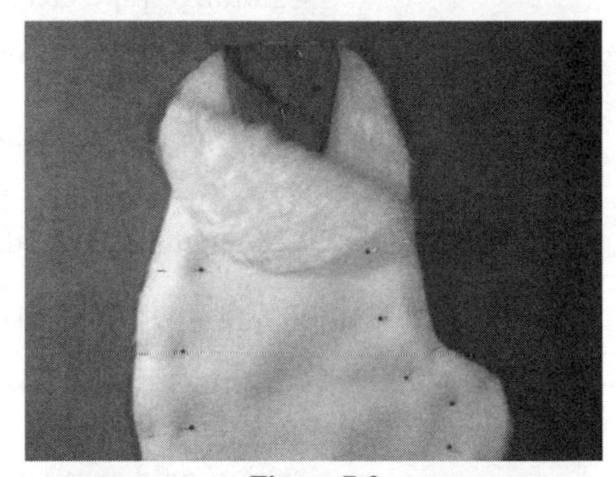

Figure 7-3

Step 6

Pin the chicken crests inside their respective chicken bodies, with crests pointing downward so that when you turn the bodies inside out, the crests will stick up. Fold in the edges of the crest and pin to reduce the chance of them getting caught in your chicken body side seams. (*See* figure 7-3.)

Stitch around CHICKEN BODIES with white thread, leaving an open place at the bottom for the legs, as shown on the pattern. Seam allowance is 1/4". Trim seams. (*See* figure 7-4.)

Turn bodies right side out. (*See* figure 7-5.)

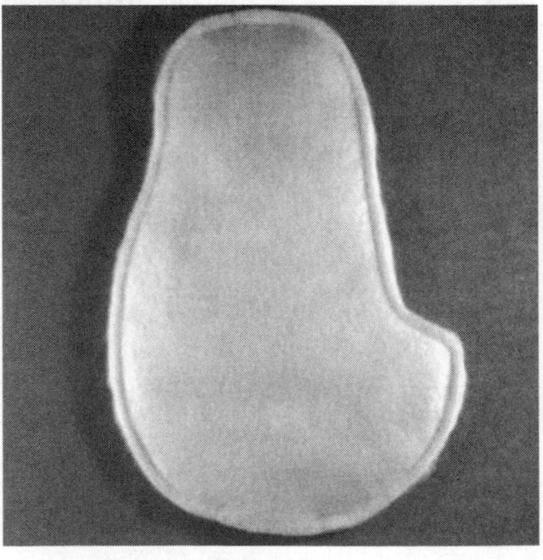

Figure 7-4

Step 7

Make six adult chicken legs, two of which will be much longer than the others (for Stalky).

To make legs, cut orange pipe cleaners into the following lengths using your wire cutters:

8 leg pieces 5" long

4 leg pieces 10" long

12 toe pieces 3" long

Twist the pieces together in pairs, by length. (*See* figure 7-6.)

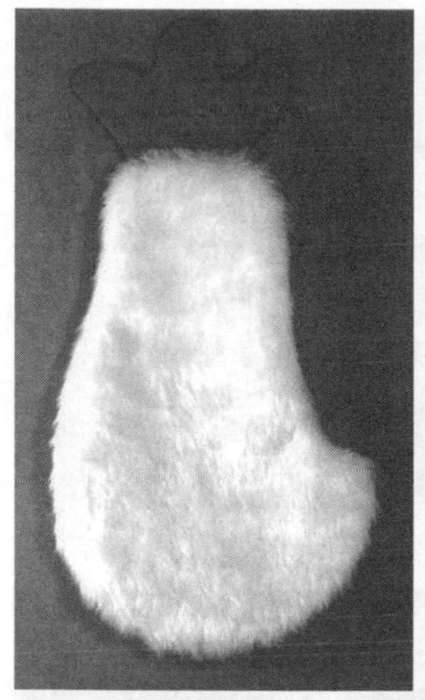

Figure 7-5

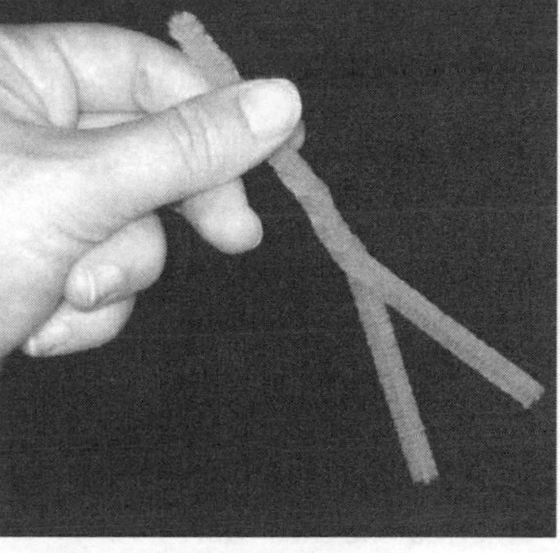

Figure 7-6

You will now have four twisted 5" leg pieces, two twisted 10" leg pieces, and six twisted 3" toe pieces. At one end of each of the 5" and 10" pipe cleaner twisted sets, make a 90-degree angle bend about 1 1/2" up. Wrap one of the twisted 3" pieces around each "ankle" at the bend, with pipe cleaner sticking out on each side. Bend the ends of the pipe cleaners at a 90-degree angle downward to make "toes": middle toes are 1/2" long; outer toes are 1/4" long. Crimp the very end of each pipe cleaner under with your needle nose pliers so that there aren't any protruding sharp wire points. (*See* figure 7-7.)

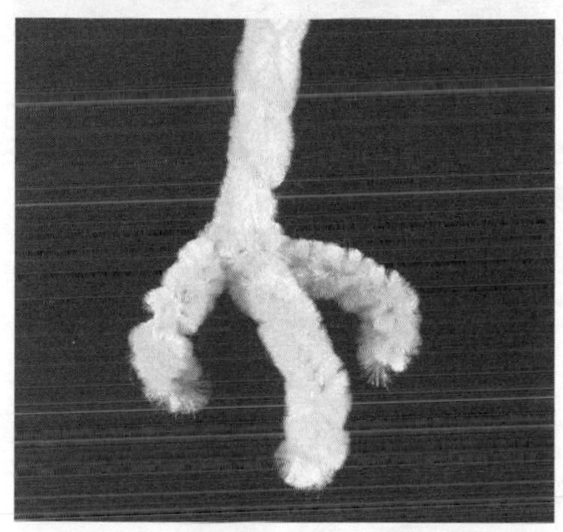

Figure 7-7

Step 8

Fold over fur along chickens' bottom edges. Using white thread, hand stitch pipe cleaner legs into bottom of chickens. This should both attach the legs to the chicken and also close the bottom opening. The stitches essentially disappear into the fur, so they aren't noticeable.

Step 9

Trace the adult chicken BEAK patterns onto the yellow flannel-backed vinyl with a ballpoint pen. Cut out the beaks *inside* the pen lines so they will not appear on the finished beaks. If you pin the beak patterns to the vinyl, it will leave permanent holes in the vinyl. Glue the adult chicken beaks onto all three chickens, following the pattern placement guidelines.

Hand sew eyes onto all three chickens, following the pattern placement guidelines.

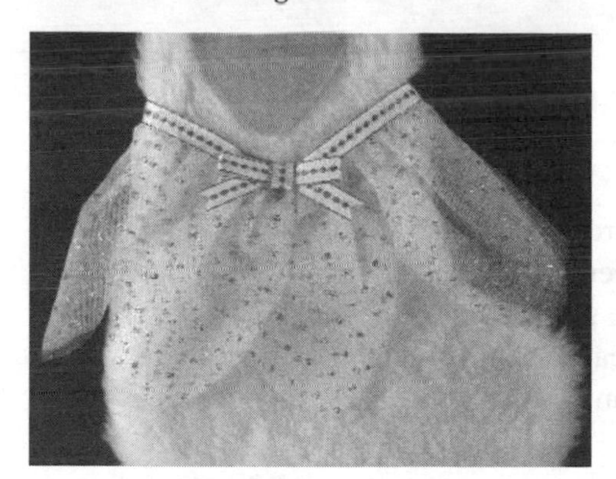

Figure 7-8

Step 10

Cut the sparkly netting into a 5" × 26" strip. Fold netting in half lengthwise, in half again, and so on until it is folded into a piece 5" × 3 1/4". Pin Dotty's feather CAPE pattern onto the netting, with the sides of the pattern placed along the places where the netting is folded. Cut out pattern, taking care to cut only bottoms of "feathers" and not separating the folds holding the sides together. You should end up with eight cape feather "petals."

Fold the cape in half, so you now have four double-thick petals. Pin the cape in the center of the shiny ribbon and stitch.

Drape netting cape around Dotty's shoulders, and hand tack with white thread at sides and in center back. Tie ribbon at front; take a hand-stitch in bow to make sure it doesn't come undone. Trim ends of ribbon tie. (*See* figure 7-8.)

Step 11

Using tacky glue, affix a 1 1/2" length of red hook Velcro vertically to the back of each chicken's crest, toward the top. Even though the Velcro is self-adhesive, you should still use the glue. When adhering Velcro to fabric, the combination of the Velcro adhesive plus the glue works much better than either one on its own. Allow glue to dry completely. (*See* figure 7-9, three finished adult chickens.)

Figure 7-9

Step 12

Cut trim for chickens' golden crowns into three equal pieces, 8" each. If trim is a type that will fray over time, seal the ends with tacky glue or fold them under and stitch. (*See* figure 7-10.)

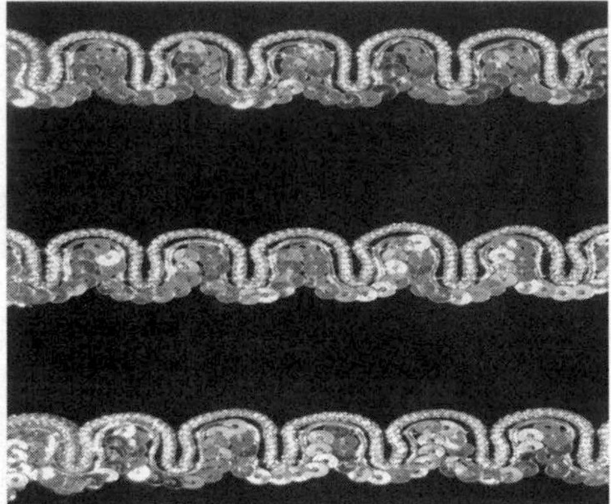

Figure 7-10

How to Make the EGGS and BABY CHICKENS

Step 1

Spray paint the two 6" cardboard eggs white. (One way to do this is to set the egg upright on an old cardboard tape ring or on a disposable plastic cup weighted with rocks, and spray the end of the egg and let it dry; then turn it over and spray it from the other end.) You may need to apply several coats. Allow paint to dry completely.

Step 2

Paint the two cubes to match each other exactly. One side each: red, yellow, blue, green, purple, and white. Allow paint to dry completely.

Step 3

Cut out the BABY CHICKEN BEAKS from yellow felt; fold over on dotted lines. Hand stitch across the folds with yellow thread so they will hold their position when attached.

Glue the beaks onto one each of the Styrofoam eggs, cardboard eggs, and cube eggs. Put the Styrofoam and cardboard chicken beaks in the centers of the small ends of the eggs, and put the cube chicken beak in the center of the green side of the cube. If the felt won't stick well to the eggs while they are drying because of the rounded egg shapes, put straight pins in to hold them at the corners—you can pull out the pins when the beaks are dry. Allow glue to dry completely.

Step 4

Attach the baby chicken eyes to the Styrofoam, cardboard, and cube eggs that are going to be the baby chickens. If you are using flat buttons or felt pieces, just glue them on. If you are using the "solid black eyes" or buttons with shanks, they may press in and stay securely because of the ridges in the shanks. If they seem loose in any way, however, attach them as follows:

Small Styrofoam egg—(8 mm solid black eyes) press shank into Styrofoam in place you want to put each eye. Pull the shank back out and put tacky glue in the indent; then press the shank back into the gluey indent. Allow eyes to dry with the baby chicken on his back so that gravity keeps the eyes from sliding while they are drying.

Big cardboard egg—(12 mm solid black eyes) repeat the process for the Styrofoam egg, except you will need to punch the eyeholes with your awl or drill. Put glue in the holes and insert the shanks.

Cube egg—(9 mm solid black eyes) duplicate the above procedures depending on what material the cube is (if it is Styrofoam, you can make the indents with the shanks; use the awl or drill if it is cardboard).

Step 5

Make six baby chicken legs, two of which will be longer than the others (for Stalky's baby).

To make legs, cut orange pipe cleaners into the following lengths using your wire cutters:

4 leg pieces 2" long

2 leg pieces 4" long

6 toe pieces 2" long

At one end of each 2" leg piece and 4" leg piece, make a 90-degree angle bend about 1" up. Wrap one of the 2" toe pieces around each "ankle" at the bend, with pipe cleaner sticking out on each side. Bend the ends of the pipe cleaners at a 90-degree angle downward to make "toes": all toes should measure approximately 1/4" long. Crimp the very end of each pipe cleaner under with the needle nose pliers to prevent any protruding sharp wire points.

Attach legs to baby chickens by poking holes for them, putting glue into the holes, and then reinserting the legs.

Step 6

Attach colorful chicken feathers to baby chickens with glue, creating a feather wing, tail, and top "hair" for each as you like. *(Leave one side of the egg-shaped baby chickens free of feathers so they can be stuck onto the Velcro/flannel board; the cube baby chicken will be stuck to the Velcro/flannel board on his back side.)* To make the feathers stick out, poke small feather-seating holes in the baby chicken bodies with the awl or with a pin. Fill the holes with glue and insert the feather quills. Allow glue to dry completely.

Step 7

Using tacky glue, affix the 1 1/2" length of white hook Velcro horizontally to the side of the Styrofoam baby chicken and the 2" length of white hook Velcro vertically to the back of the cube baby chicken. Even though the Velcro is self-adhesive, you should still use the glue. When adhering Velcro to Styrofoam, the combination of the Velcro adhesive plus the glue works much better than either one on its own. If the Velcro doesn't adhere well to the Styrofoam egg while it is drying because of the rounded egg shape, put straight pins in to hold it. Allow the glue to dry completely; then remove the pins when the glue is dry.

Step 8

Affix the two 3 1/2" lengths of white hook Velcro horizontally to the side of the giant cardboard baby chicken. Put one of the lengths along the exact center of the egg baby's side, and put the other length horizontally *up above* it. Otherwise, the baby will sag too much when stuck to the board. You may not need to use any glue, as the Velcro adhesive sticks exceptionally well to smooth cardboard. (*See* figure 7-11, three finished baby chickens.)

Figure 7-11

How to Make the ROYAL NEST

Step 1

Spray paint basket *gold,* inside and out. Allow to dry completely.

Step 2

Thinly line royal nest with purple grass. Hide three eggs in grass (Styrofoam egg, giant cardboard egg, and cube egg). (*See* figure 7-12.)

Cover with a solid layer of purple grass so the eggs are completely hidden.

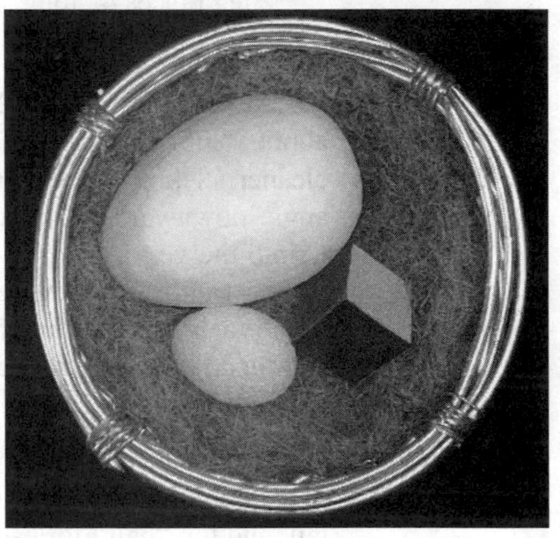

Figure 7-12

Combination Prop Story Finished Product

Figure 7-13

Stitch CREST between these dots.

EYES

Glue BEAK here.

Photocopy this page at size 135%.

Photocopy at size 135%.

This line should measure exactly 3" when pattern is photocopied correctly.

The Most Wonderful Egg in the World
Adult Chicken BODY 1 (Dotty)
Cut 2 from white fur.
Seam allowance 1/4"

Stitch to here.

Stitch to here.

Photocopy this page at size 135%.

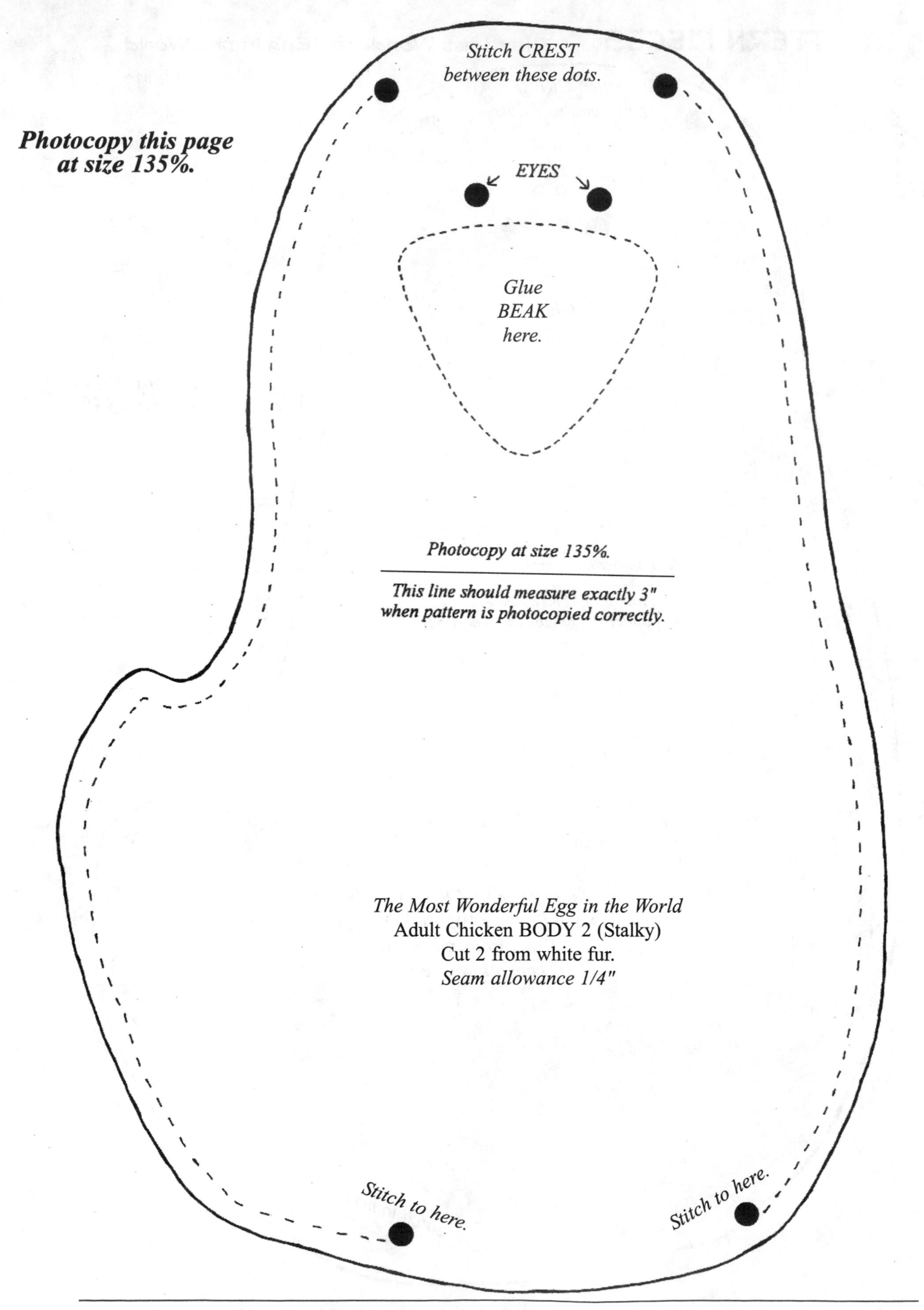

Photocopy this page at size 135%.

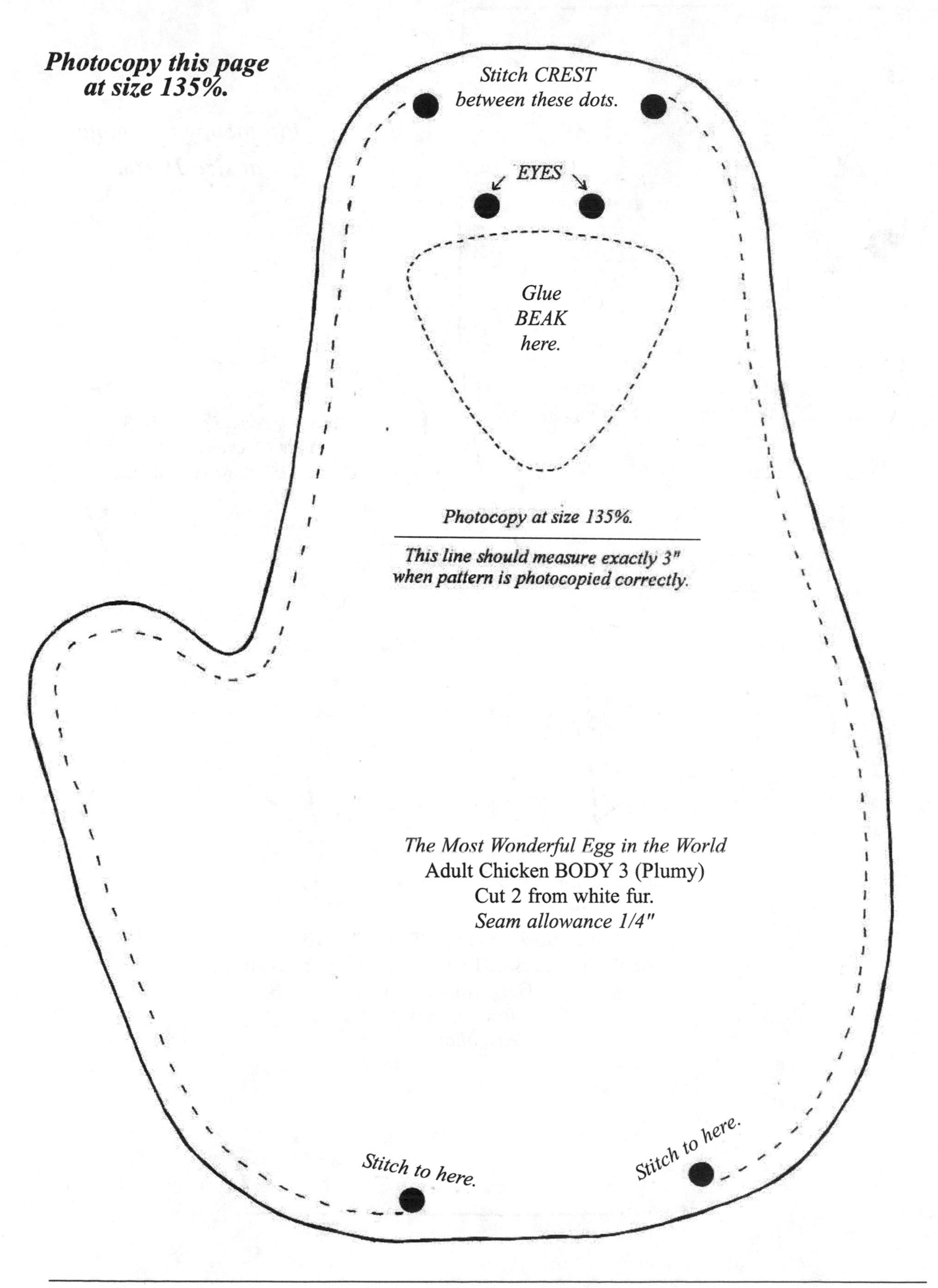

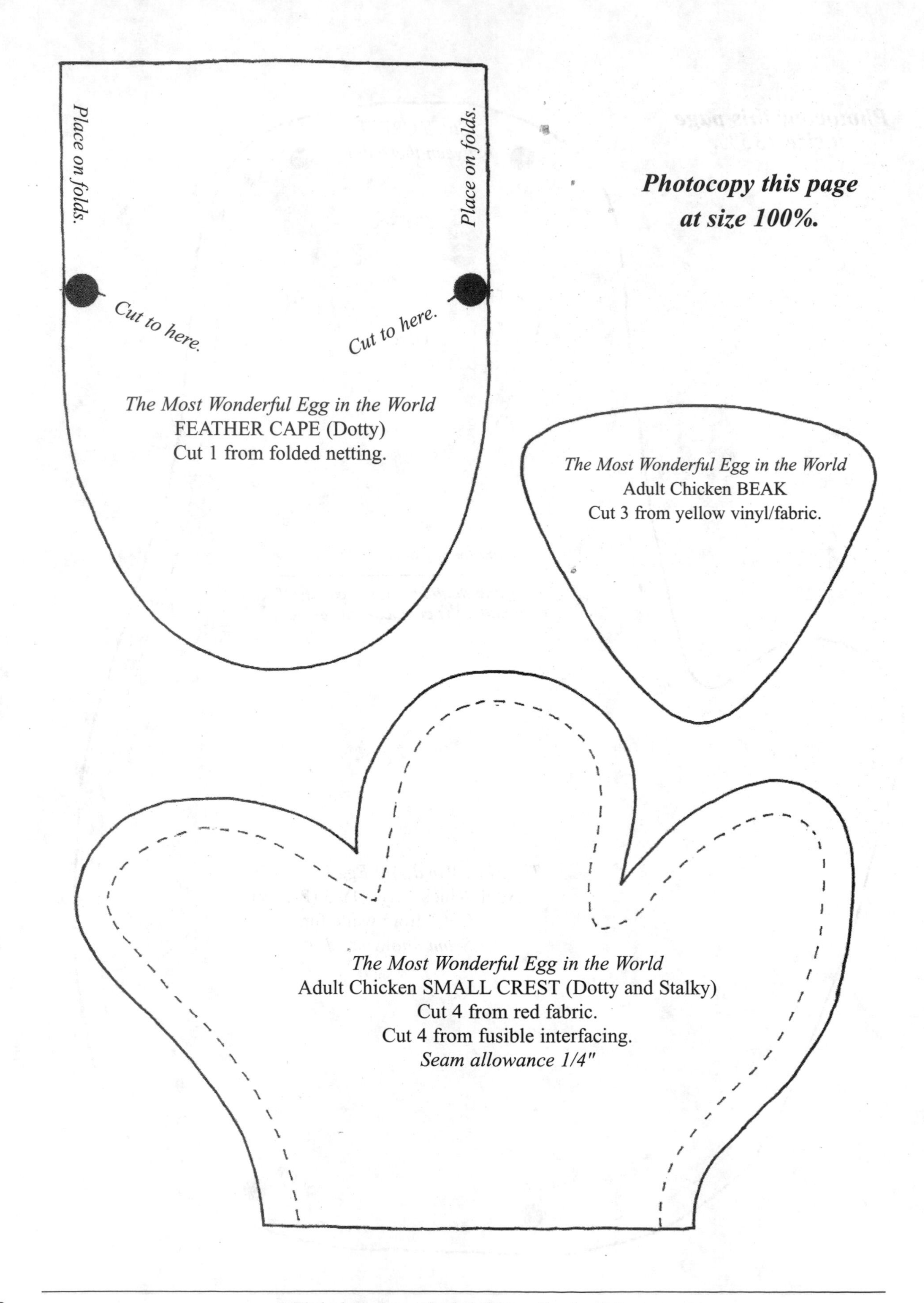

Photocopy this page at size 100%.

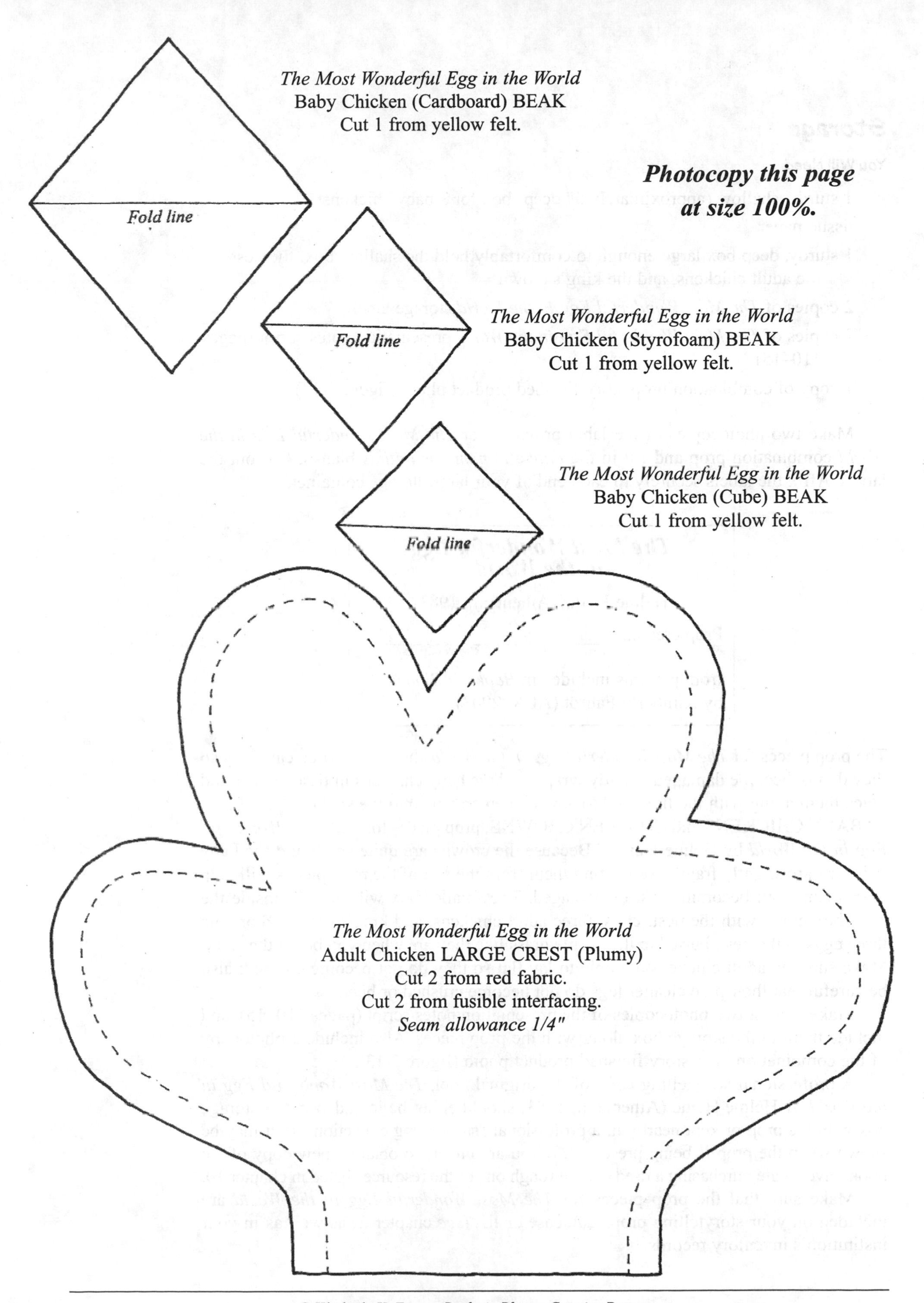

The Most Wonderful Egg in the World
Baby Chicken (Cardboard) BEAK
Cut 1 from yellow felt.
Fold line
Photocopy this page at size 100%.
The Most Wonderful Egg in the World
Baby Chicken (Styrofoam) BEAK
Cut 1 from yellow felt.
Fold line
The Most Wonderful Egg in the World
Baby Chicken (Cube) BEAK
Cut 1 from yellow felt.
Fold line
The Most Wonderful Egg in the World
Adult Chicken LARGE CREST (Plumy)
Cut 2 from red fabric.
Cut 2 from fusible interfacing.
Seam allowance 1/4"

Storage

You Will Need

1 sturdy, shallow (approximately 5" deep) box for 3 baby chickens

tissue paper

1 sturdy, deep box large enough to comfortably hold the shallow box, the nest, the adult chickens, and the king's crown

2 copies of *The Most Wonderful Egg in the World* storage label

2 copies of *The Most Wonderful Egg in the World* presentation notes/script (pages 110–15)

1 copy of combination prop story finished product photo (figure 7-13)

Make two photocopies of the label provided for *The Most Wonderful Egg in the World* combination prop and fill in the *date* and *name or initials* blanks. Cut out the labels. Affix the labels securely to each end of your large storage container.

The Most Wonderful Egg in the World

Helme Heine (Atheneum, 1983)

Prop created ________ by ________________
DATE NAME OR INITIALS

from patterns included in *Books in Bloom*
by Kimberly Faurot (ALA, 2003)

The prop pieces for *The Most Wonderful Egg in the World* should be stored carefully so they do not become damaged. Gently wrap the three baby chickens in tissue paper and place them along with the three gold-trim chicken crowns into the shallow box. Label it "BABY CHICKENS and CHICKEN CROWNS; prop pieces for *The Most Wonderful Egg in the World* by Helme Heine." Because the crowns are quite small and the baby chickens are slightly fragile, separating them from the rest of the prop pieces will help keep them from becoming lost or damaged. The smaller box will then fit inside the deep box along with the nest, eggs, three adult chickens, and king's crown. Store the three eggs in the nest, buried in the purple grass like they are when you begin the story. Make sure the adult chickens are able to lay flat so they do not become creased; also be careful that their pipe cleaner legs do not become crushed or bent.

Make at least two photocopies of the presentation notes/script (pages 110–15), and include them in the storage box along with the prop pieces. Also include a photocopy of the combination prop story finished product photo (figure 7-13).

A professional storytelling copy of the original book *The Most Wonderful Egg in the World* by Helme Heine (Atheneum, 1983) should either be included in the storage box with the prop or kept nearby in a professional "storytelling collection" so it may be shown when the prop is being presented. If you are unable to obtain a new copy of the book, investigate purchasing a used copy through one of the resources listed in chapter 10.

Make sure that the prop pieces for *The Most Wonderful Egg in the World* are included on your storytelling props database or list (*see* chapter 2) as well as in your institution's inventory records.

Notify other staff members who might be able to include *The Most Wonderful Egg in the World* in their programming or classrooms that it is ready for use, and demonstrate it for them if at all possible.

Summary

Combination props are fun to create and to use. The combination of multiple formats and presentation methods effectively attracts and retains the attention of even very young children. It can be both challenging and exhilarating to determine the best way to adapt a story as a combination prop. A careful evaluation of the demands of the story's action is essential; you can then select the media accordingly for each portion of the story. As a result of this combined approach, you are able to share stories with multiple elements in a manner that effectively retains the spirit of the originals.

8 Stick Puppets/ Rod Puppets

Includes script and pattern for

The Nightgown of the Sullen Moon
by Nancy Willard, illustrated by David McPhail (Harcourt, 1983)

Pattern difficulty level

Advanced

Construction time estimate

20 hours

One of the easiest types of puppets to make is the stick puppet. Essentially, the puppet consists of a two- or three-dimensional picture cutout or figure that is supported by a stick held by the puppeteer. These puppets can be elaborate, with jointed parts and trigger mechanisms or multiple rods to manipulate them, or extremely basic, just a picture on a stick. A stick puppet with multiple rods would be considered a "rod puppet."

Simple stick puppets can be easy enough for even very small children to both make and use. You can also readily prepare quantities of such puppets in advance to enable participation opportunities by a large group or class.

Techniques and Considerations

Creating

The methods of creating stick puppets are endless, limited only by your imagination. Picture cutouts mounted on stiff paper such as card stock, or paper die figure cutouts can be affixed to craft sticks using glue or double-stick tape. Household objects can be transformed into simple stick puppets: for example, decorating the scoop end of a wooden spoon or a feather duster's top with hair, eyes, mouth, and so forth can enable the object to be brought to life as a puppet. Simple stick puppets can be made in any size. For large puppets, flat cardboard or sturdy matte board may be cut into shapes and painted, then mounted on a thick supporting dowel rod with duct or fabric tape. I have two large matte board sun and moon stick puppets that I constructed in this way, and I use them regularly for various stories, poems, and songs.

Three-dimensional stick puppets may be created from a Styrofoam ball on a stick or from foam rubber, papier-mâché, clay, or any number of other materials. Once the basic figure is made, you can give it a body or appendages or decorations as you like, either jointing the additions and making them manipulable or allowing them to simply ornament the creation. Always consider whether and how the additions or ornamentation will enhance the puppet's appearance and illusion as you animate it. For example, a solid papier-mâché goldfish stick puppet will likely be far more believable and interesting as you make it "swim" if you add some wire-supported gauze fabric fins and a tail.

The pattern included in this chapter is for two simple Styrofoam ball stick puppets without any moving parts. Decoration includes carving the Styrofoam with a pottery carving tool and painting it to give it additional depth and texture; accoutrements such as bead eyes, buttons, and a craft fur "nimbus" are also added. This type of Styrofoam ball "head" can be used to make many other puppets as well. Many people stick puppets are made with this "head-on-a-stick" technique, with a draping fabric "body" attached to the puppet's neck to cover the stick support. Some puppets also have a manipulable hand on a second stick, fastened near the wrist region. The truly giant puppets that are commonly created for parades and large theatrical events are a variation on this theme; they have enormous papier-mâché or cardboard heads and faces, with hands often shaped of wire that is covered with plumbing pipe foam insulation tubes and painted. The heads and hands are all connected with a loose fabric robe that covers the back of the head and provides a body.

Another type of multiple-stick puppet consists of an elongated form such as a caterpillar or snake manipulated by two primary sticks, one connected to each end of the puppet. The rear stick is brought up close to the front stick, then the front stick is moved forward and away, and the movement is repeated to make the figure inch or slither along.

Stick puppets may be presented as individual characters, or they may be mounted as a group into a base and manipulated as a unit. For example, a "school of fish" can be achieved by mounting individual fish stick puppets in a row in a slightly flexible base material. Manipulating the base allows the fish to "swim" together as a group.

Presenting

The success of a stick puppet is entirely dependent upon the puppeteer who gives it life. While animating the puppet, the puppeteer must believe in it and its personality and sell it to the audience. Whether the puppeteer is hidden from or visible to the audience, he or she should *watch the puppet when animating it.* If a visible puppeteer is watching the puppet, then the audience will watch it, too. If a puppeteer is maintaining direct eye contact with the audience while attention is supposed to be on the puppet, it is confusing for the audience. The puppeteer is essentially competing with the puppet for the audience's attention. Another advantage to the puppeteer of watching the puppet while animating it is the opportunity to monitor the puppet's movements and believability.

It is important for your puppet to "look" at the audience when it is interacting with them. Make sure that the eyes are actually pointed toward the audience's eyes—not just staring over their heads or down at the floor. This will contribute enormously to your puppet's believability and to its ability to hold the audience's attention. As the stick puppet speaks to the audience, move it deliberately so that it mirrors the motions a person's head would make as he or she was talking. If the puppet is an animal, make it reflect the motions of the real animal in the way you make it bob or turn. Don't ever just bounce the puppet up and down or wave it wildly back and forth—such a non-practiced presentation will quickly destroy any illusion of believability and will lose the audience's attention. If your students or audience will be participating in a story with stick puppets, model manipulation techniques for them to demonstrate the difference between wild bobbing and deliberate movements. Teach them to watch their puppets while animating them.

If your puppet has connecting or manipulable parts or appendages, employ them to enhance the puppet's believability (such as by having the puppet scratch its head, pat its cheek or chest, etc.). If your puppet is just a simple stick puppet with no moving parts, you can still animate it so it is believable and interesting for your audience. Make the puppet turn sideways, have it pause, turn it gradually in an arc so it can look across at your entire audience (making sure it is maintaining "eye contact"). If or when the puppet talks, make sure it is facing the audience and bob its head deliberately so it is clear that the puppet is "talking." Have the puppet interact with the audience so you can gauge their level of involvement and connection.

It is always a good idea to practice with puppets in front of a mirror. By doing so, you will quickly learn how best to position your puppet and what types of movements are the most effective. When positioning the mirror for practice, consider where your audience will be sitting. If they will be on the floor while you are seated on a chair with the puppet, make sure to angle the puppet so that it will achieve eye contact at the audience's eye level.

Much of the art of puppetry involves *suggesting* aliveness to your audience and then allowing their imaginations to fill in the rest. If you believe in and value the illusion you are creating and concentrate on building that illusion for your audience, they will enthusiastically join you in the effort.

Choosing the Stick Puppet Format

David McPhail's vivid illustrations for *The Nightgown of the Sullen Moon* are detailed and painterly, making them ideally suited to cozy, small group reading. Sharing the story with a large group consequently works well as a prop adaptation.

In determining what format might best reflect the story for such an adaptation, it is important to consider, as always, both the spirit and the action of the story. *The Nightgown of the Sullen Moon* is lyrical and magical, and any props must retain that element as well as the intensity of McPhail's original illustrations. The moon, as the main character of the story, must be truly special and arresting in some way. She must be able to “travel,” so flexible staging is necessary. It is also important for the moon and the sun to be able to talk with each other in a believable manner. All of these requirements suggest puppetry of some sort as a possible format. The magic and wonder of the moon interacting directly with people (such as the salesgirl), and the exploration of those proportions and fantasies, are further advantages of the puppetry medium. The scene at the “Slumber Shop,” when the moon tries on various nightgowns and finally finds the one that she has been wanting all along, is one of the book’s most satisfying, climactic moments. Sharing the scene with the props allows you to highlight this entire exchange, which in the book is necessarily restricted to just a double-page spread and one more page. After putting on her new nightgown and telling the salesgirl that she “shall wear it home,” the moon soars out of the store and up into the sky, where she looks down on the audience and on the entire world.

After determining that puppetry is a good overall choice for the story, the stick puppet technique suggests itself for several reasons. Certainly the shape of the moon and sun are well suited to the suspended round heads of simple ball-shaped stick puppets. The story’s manipulations also require that the puppets remain in view of the audience several times when you as the puppeteer are unable to hold them. This can be managed easily with stick puppets by clipping them onto the back of the lap/tabletop theater as needed, whereas such manipulations would be difficult to achieve with many other simple puppetry techniques.

The Nightgown of the Sullen Moon

Nancy Willard

(Harcourt, 1983)

Summary

On the billionth birthnight of the full moon, the moon finally gets what she has really wanted—a nightgown such as people on earth wear.

Possible themes

Bedtime, Birthdays, Clothes, Moon and Sun, Night, Shopping, Washing/Laundry

Approximate running time for stick puppet/prop story

8 minutes

Recommended audience interest level

Preschool (age 4 and older) through grade 4; intergenerational family programming

Please note that the story pieces are designed as professional resources, not as playthings. They do not conform to child safety play standards, and they could easily become damaged if used in a manner other than that for which they were intended.

Story Pieces

- cardboard lap/tabletop theater
- lap theater grass covering
- clothesline on supports
- 2 small spring clothespins (approximately 1 3/4" long)
- star nightgown
- moon stick puppet
- sun stick puppet
- 4 nightgowns on doll hangers (small animal print, large flowered, pale, dark)
- "sky drawer"

Use with

- fine-tooth comb
- small table or TV tray on which to place lap/tabletop theater
- chair (optional)
- box to hide the moon and sun rod puppets
- a copy of the book to show the audience both before and after presenting the story

Setup

Set the cardboard lap theater on the small table or TV tray. Clothespin the two clothesline supports to the front corner side edges of the lap theater, with the dowel rods *inside* the lap theater and the clothesline stretched between the two supports.

Clip green felt "grass covering" over lap theater, with middle flap hanging down the front of the lap theater and the other two hanging down the two sides. If you have trouble with the grass covering slipping around during the story, pin the covering's back straight edge to the back edge of the lap theater.

Clip the two miniature clothespins to the laundry line, about as far apart as the two shoulders of the star nightgown.

Hide the star nightgown just inside the lap theater so you can grab it very quickly when the story begins.

Hide the four slumber-shop nightgowns on doll hangers inside the lap theater so they can be easily grabbed and hung as a group by their hangers onto the clothesline.

Hide the sky "drawer" far inside the lap theater for end of story.

Comb the sun's nimbus so it stands out around his head (it tends to become matted down during storage).

Hide the moon and sun rod puppets nearby in a box where you can easily pull them out and hide them again as needed as the story progresses.

Presentation

Story narration is delineated in regular type; movement notes and miscellaneous directions are shown within the script in *[bracketed italics]*.

Learn the story and tell it to your audience from memory, using the prop pieces.

The script calls for you to be a variety of characters: the Narrator, the Moon, the Sun, the Salesgirl, and the "people of the world." The character who is talking is designated by his or her name at the beginning of the text, except for the Narrator.

When the stick puppets are talking, move them gently to give them the appearance of being alive.

When trying the four nightgowns on hangers on the moon puppet, the metal loop of the hanger should slip through the moon's chin eyehook easily. Do not allow the hanger to scrape or press into the moon's Styrofoam head! If you have difficulty, you may need to tip the puppet forward to alter the angle a bit.

When using puppets, it is a good idea to practice the story before a mirror so that you can work on the puppet's movements and believability.

Although it is not essential to use different character voices when presenting the story, it can truly help maintain the children's interest as well as help them distinguish which character is talking. Try out different voices to figure out which sounds the best for the different characters. All voices must feel natural for you after practice so that you will be able to use and maintain them successfully during an actual performance.

The story has a number of "costume changes," so be sure that you are well rehearsed and can smoothly manipulate the pieces at an appropriate pace.

Please note: The following script is a very slightly adapted story version for telling as a prop and participation story, and it includes notes for the storyteller on how and when to manipulate the puppet and prop pieces. Learn the story and tell it to your audience from memory, using the prop pieces. Please look at the book so that you know what adaptations have been made in this script; you may well prefer to tell the story verbatim from its exact original text. Show a copy of the book to your audience both before and after sharing the story with the puppets, and give the complete title, author, illustrator, and publication information.

SCRIPT

The Nightgown of the Sullen Moon

by Nancy Willard

The nightgown started it all.

[Hold up star nightgown and clothespin it by both shoulders to the laundry line.]

It belonged to Ellen Fitzpatrick, who took the clean laundry off the line for her mother and left her own nightgown, blue flannel and stitched with stars, shining, dancing *[gently tap nightgown from behind so it appears to be blowing in a breeze]*, on the billionth birthnight of the full moon.

[Lift up moon stick puppet in your left hand as if she is rising into the sky for the evening, and then angle her so she is looking down at the nightgown; continue to hold her there.]

The moon watched the nightgown kick and shine.

MOON *(thoughtful and petulant)* "Women have danced for me. Men have worshipped me. Poets have praised me. No one has ever given me what I really want."

The sun *[lift sun stick puppet up in your right hand and then around and down as if he is sinking in the sky for the evening]* heard her.

SUN "What do you really want?"

MOON "I want a nightgown such as people on earth wear when they sleep under warm featherbeds at night."

SUN "But where will you get a nightgown, dear Moon?"

MOON "Oh, the same place they do."

[With your right hand, sink the sun puppet the rest of the way down and hide him where the audience can't see him but where you can easily get him later in the story. Still with your right hand, remove star nightgown from laundry line and hide it and the clothespins in the back of the lap theater.]

And she sank slowly *[sink moon puppet lower in your left hand, and then keep weaving her slowly back and forth as if she is going along a winding road]* to the tops of the hills and followed the black road into the valley.

She passed a laundry, a school, a library . . . *[let the audience suggest more places]* and came early in the morning, when the brightness was off her, to a shop where she had often tracked puddles of light.

[Clip moon onto back left corner of lap theater so she faces the audience but so your hands are free. Remove nightgowns from inside lap theater and hang them as a group by their hangers on the laundry line as if it was a clothes rack.]

The salesgirl stepped forward.

SALESGIRL "May I help you?"

[Unclip and hold moon in your left hand again.]

MOON "I want a nightgown."

The salesgirl brought a nightgown printed with small animals.

[Hold up small animal print nightgown for audience to see.]

She helped the moon try it on.

[Hook doll hanger through eyehook under the moon puppet's chin, and hold moon so audience can see.]

MOON "It is too small" *[shake moon's head back and forth]*.

[Remove doll hanger with nightgown, and quickly hide it in back of lap theater.]

The salesgirl brought a *[PINK—audience will say color]* pink nightgown printed with big flowers. The moon tried it on.

[Hook doll hanger through eyehook and hold moon so audience can see.]

MOON "It is too big! Help!" *[shake moon's head back and forth]*.

[Remove doll hanger with nightgown, and quickly hide it in back of lap theater.]

The salesgirl brought a *[YELLOW—audience will say color]* yellow, plain nightgown. The moon tried it on.

[Hook doll hanger through eyehook and hold moon so audience can see.]

MOON "It is too pale" *[shake moon's head back and forth]*.

[Remove doll hanger with nightgown, and quickly hide it in back of lap theater.]

The salesgirl brought a *[BLACK—audience will say color]* black nightgown. The moon tried it on.

[Hook doll hanger through eyehook and hold moon so audience can see.]

MOON "It is too dark" *[shake moon's head back and forth]*.

[Remove doll hanger with nightgown, and quickly hide it in back of lap theater.]

SALESGIRL "We have no other nightgowns in the store."

MOON *(petulant and upset, very animated)* "Not *one?* Not one more nightgown hidden in a drawer at the back of the shop?"

SALESGIRL "Madame, to please you, I shall look."

[Clip moon onto back left corner of lap theater so she faces the audience but so your hands are free.]

And there, hidden in a drawer at the back of the shop *[reach into back of lap theater and hold up star nightgown for audience to see, show to moon]* was one more nightgown, blue flannel and stitched with stars, shining and shimmering on the billionth birthnight of the full moon.

[Help moon try on nightgown as you are saying this—hook the elastic loops over the two buttons on the moon's neck so it's a close fit.]

SALESGIRL "Shall I gift wrap it?"

[Unclip moon from lap theater for her reply.]

MOON *(happy)* "No, thank you, I shall wear it home."

Joyfully, the moon sailed outside. *[Raise moon into air just a little, then weave her back and forth as if following the road again.]* She passed the library and the school and the laundry and . . . *[say the places the audience had suggested earlier]* and followed the black road out of the valley and rose into the sky.

[Raise moon higher into air in your left hand, angling her so she is looking downward and outward at the audience; continue to hold her there.]

In the evening, people looked for the moon and did not find her. The moon's new nightgown looked just like the night sky, and when she was wearing it, people could not see her! There was no moon shining down to give light and help through the night.

Men walking on the black road lost their way.

Owls crossing the woods lost theirs.

Women forgot the words to their songs, and Ellen Fitzpatrick, waking at night, saw no dear face in the sky. Outside her window every singing thing grew still.

High and away in her new nightgown, the moon heard people crying for the moon that they thought had left them. All over the world, in many languages, people called her name.

[Put your right hand up to your mouth as if calling loudly, and peer upward as if looking unsuccessfully for the invisible moon.]

English: "Moon!" French: *"Lune!"*

Spanish: *"Luna!"* German: *"Mond!"*

Hungarian: *"Hold!"*

Chinese: *"Yueh-lianq!" (Romanized transliteration)*

American Sign Language: "Moon" *(pictograph)*

American Sign Language: *MOON*

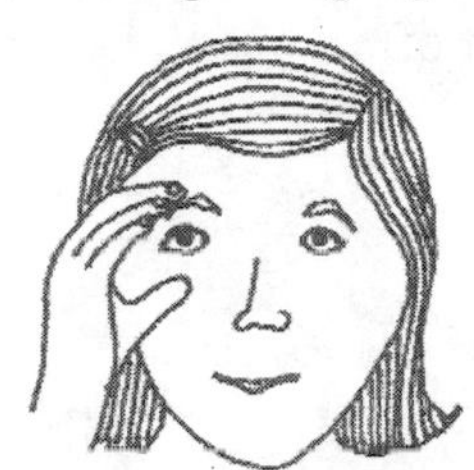

Make the shape of the letter C with your dominant hand, and position it briefly to the side of your head near your eye.

[Raise the moon up high in your left hand, angled as if looking down on everyone; then have her begin to sink lower in the sky. With right hand pick up the sun puppet and have him rise slowly low to higher as if rising for the new day.]

Slowly the moon passed the sun.

[Have them stop here, opposite one another for their conversation.]

MOON *(querulous)* "Does no one love my new nightgown?"

SUN "O Moon, people on earth want my gold face in the day and your silver face in the night. So many things change on earth that they want nothing to change in the sky. Take the nightgown back."

MOON *(vehement)* "I won't take it back!" *[shake moon's head back and forth]*.

SUN *(firm but gentle)* "You must take it back. Promise me you will take it back."

MOON *(sulky)* "Oh, very well, I promise."

But the moon's promises, what are they worth?

[Clip sun puppet to stage right back corner of lap theater so he is looking at the audience, and then clip the moon puppet to the stage left back corner so your hands are free.]

She took the nightgown off *[unhook the nightgown from the moon's neck and hold it up in one hand; with the other hand reach into the lap theater and pull out the "sky drawer"]*, and she hid it in a drawer at the back of the sky.

[Fold star nightgown into the "sky drawer," put the lid on and then balance it on the front corner of the lap theater.]

And on those nights when you look up into the sky *[look upward as if looking for the moon]* but see no moon *[shake your head and hold out your hands]*, you can be sure it's because she is trying on her nightgown and dreaming that she is back on earth sleeping under the warmest featherbed in the world.

[Show last page of book, with the moon and Ellen Fitzpatrick asleep.]

THE END

Script adapted by Kimberly K. Faurot, *Books in Bloom: Creative Patterns and Props That Bring Stories to Life* (ALA, 2003).

PATTERN INSTRUCTIONS

Stick Puppet Story (Sample Pattern)

The Nightgown of the Sullen Moon by Nancy Willard, illustrated by David McPhail

Patterns

Stick puppets and patterns designed by Kimberly Faurot

Estimated difficulty

Advanced: The successful creation of this prop requires basic knowledge of sewing construction techniques and basic craft techniques.

Estimated construction time

20 hours

Estimated cost for supplies

$50

You Will Need These Tools

pencil
Sharpie permanent black marking pen (Fine Point)
sharp utility knife
hack saw
pottery "strip-turning" carving tool, small
electric drill or sharp awl
wire cutters
needle nose pliers
fabric shears
pinking shears
small-sharp-pointed scissors
Aleene's Original "Tacky" Glue
Fray Check
straight pins
hand-sewing needle
sewing machine (may be completely hand sewn if necessary)
steam iron and pressing cloth
standard-sized spring clothespins for anchoring glued items while drying (optional)
electric fan to speed drying time as needed (optional)

You Will Need These Supplies

SUPPLIES TO MAKE THE LAP/TABLETOP THEATER AND COVERING

box bottom (the kind of box that comes with a lid), approximate size 14" wide × 10" deep × 7" high or a bit bigger

spray paint: turquoise blue satin finish

grass green felt from the bolt, approximate size 18" × 28" (sized to fit your box, covering the top, front, and two sides)

3 large T-pins

SUPPLIES TO MAKE THE STICK PUPPETS

MOON

1/4" diameter dowel rod, 16" long section

1 standard-sized wooden spring clothespin

Styrofoam ball, 4" diameter (*not* pressed Dylite)

acrylic craft paint: royal blue, cornflower blue, white, yellow, light pink, light blue

3 white star-shaped buttons, size 1/2"

3 lengths of 20-gauge or 24-gauge hobby wire, each 2 1/2" long

2 clear faceted beads, size 1/4"

1 small "screw eye" (zinc plated to resist corrosion), size 1/2" long; inside eye opening 1/8"

SUN

1/4" diameter dowel rod, 21" long section

1 standard-sized wooden spring clothespin

Styrofoam ball, 6" diameter (*not* pressed Dylite)

acrylic craft paint: royal blue, bright yellow, desert pink (a deep yellowish pink), cornflower blue, metallic gold, white

(*See* "How to Cut Craft Fur" in step 6 under "Sun" below.)

1/4" wide × 19" long strip of long craft fur, bright orange (You may need to piece two strips together if the craft fur is not long enough.)

1/4" wide × 19" long strip of long craft fur, bright yellow (You may need to piece two strips together if the craft fur is not long enough.)

1/16" wide × 4" long strip of long craft fur, bright yellow

1/16" wide × 2" long strip of long craft fur, bright yellow

2 bright blue faceted beads, size 1/4"

SUPPLIES TO MAKE THE NIGHTGOWNS

4 doll hangers with straight-edge hanger hooks (so they will slip easily in and out of the 1/8" screw eye opening in the moon's chin); hangers should measure approximately 4 1/2" across at the widest point

(Hangers should be available from craft stores; however, you can also create your own from heavy-gauge floral wire. *See* nightgown pattern instructions for the hanger pattern guide under "How to Make the Nightgowns, All Nightgowns.")

STAR NIGHTGOWN

thread: royal blue, red

12" × 24" length of nightgown fabric—either royal blue preprinted with stars (cotton or flannel) or plain royal blue cotton

fine gold paint pen (if you are using plain blue nightgown fabric only)

gold foil stars *or* small star stencils (if you are using plain blue nightgown fabric only)

red double-fold bias tape, 1/4" wide

white narrow "round cord elastic," 4" length (cut into two 2" lengths)

SMALL ANIMAL PRINT NIGHTGOWN

thread: white

12" × 24" length of nightgown fabric—cotton flannel babyish-looking small animal print

LARGE FLOWERED NIGHTGOWN

thread: white, light pink

12" × 24" length of nightgown fabric—small-flowered pink flannel

1/2" wide white eyelet lace, 14 1/2" length (cut into three 4 3/4" lengths)

3 pink ribbon rosebuds with green ribbon leaves

PALE NIGHTGOWN

thread: white, light yellow

12" × 24" length of nightgown fabric—plain, pale yellowish cotton fabric

1/4" wide light yellow grosgrain ribbon, 33" length (Cut into two 9" lengths to tie for ribbon bows and one 15" length for bottom hem.)

DARK NIGHTGOWN

thread: black, green

thin black gauzy fabric, 18" × 7" piece

2 1/2" wide black lace, 18" length

1 1/2" wide black satin ribbon, 8" length (Cut into two 4" lengths.)

3/8" wide green satin ribbon, 21" length

3/8" wide pink satin ribbon, 21" length

1 pink ribbon rosebud with green ribbon leaves

SUPPLIES TO MAKE THE MISCELLANEOUS ADDITIONAL STORY PIECES

5/16" diameter dowel rod, two 20" long sections

2 small spring clothespins (size 1 3/4" long)—from craft stores

2 standard-sized spring clothespins

medium-weight cotton rope for clothesline, 16" length (The small clothespins should be able to clip comfortably onto the rope.)

acrylic craft paint: periwinkle, royal blue

fine gold paint pen

small cardboard box with removable lid (approximate size 4" × 6") (Check unpainted cardboard boxes at craft stores to possibly find a small star- or moon-shaped plain cardboard box.)

gold foil stars (optional)

Directions

How to Make the Lap/Tabletop Theater and Covering

Step 1

Spray paint the outside of the cardboard box bottom turquoise blue. Apply multiple coats of paint as necessary to cover any graphics on the cardboard and for an even appearance. Allow paint to dry completely.

Step 2

Measure and mark the cutting lines for the entry "flap" on the back of the box/lap theater: on the back side of the box, draw pencil lines approximately 2 1/2" from each side of the box and 2" down from the top edge of the box. These will be your cutting guidelines. Use the utility knife to cut along the three lines, leaving the fourth side along the bottom of the box as a "hinge." (*See* figure 8-1.)

This flap will be the entry point for your arm and hand when using the box as a lap theater.

Figure 8-1

Step 3

Lay the green felt out flat and place the box upside down on top of it, matching one long side of the box to one of the long sides of the felt. Center the box between the two shorter edges of the felt. Lightly trace the edge of the box onto the felt with the Sharpie marker.

Step 4

Using the shape of the small "grass shape guideline" diagram as a guide, cut your green felt to fit your lap theater box.

The felt should hang down most of the way in the front as well as on the two sides. The covering's back straight edge can be T-pinned to the back edge of the lap theater box if it slips around during the story. (*See* figure 8-2.)

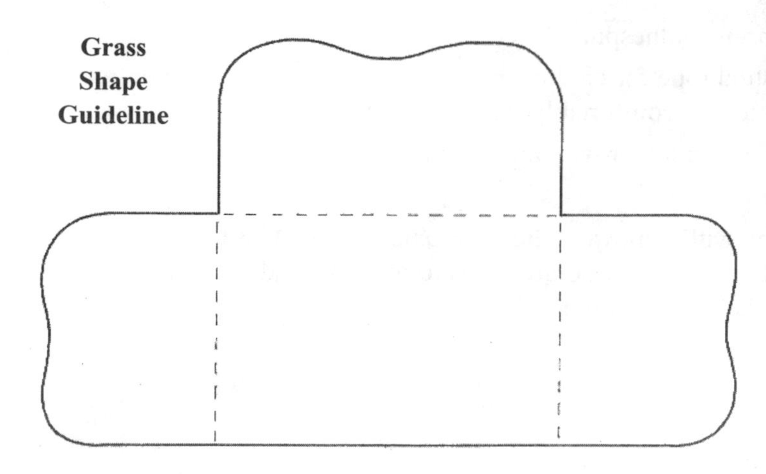

Figure 8-2

How to Make the Stick Puppets

MOON

Step 1

Paint the 16" dowel rod and the regular-sized wooden spring clothespin royal blue. Allow paint to dry completely. Glue clothespin to the bottom of the dowel rod, lining up the bottom edge of the clothespin and the bottom of the dowel. If necessary, use another spring clothespin to hold the two together as they dry. Allow glue to dry completely. (*See* figure 8-3.)

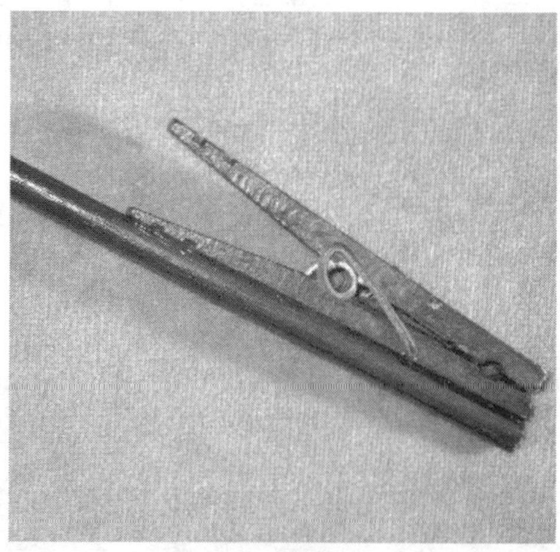

Figure 8-3

Step 2

Following the "MOON Carving template" pattern, lightly sketch the moon's facial features onto the 4" Styrofoam ball with thc Sharpic marker. Using the strip-turning pottery carving tool, carefully carve out the features. The carving tool is held sideways to essentially scoop out the strips where you are choosing to indent the moon's features. The mouth and eye sockets should be the deepest of the indentations. (*See* figure 8-4.)

Step 3

Slightly *behind* (about 1/4") the bottom center of the moon's head, mark the point where you will mount the Styrofoam ball onto the dowel rod. Make a small starter hole with a high-speed drill or with a pointed awl or a nail. Once the hole is started, insert the dowel rod into the hole, working it in gently until it is at least 2" inside the Styrofoam. After establishing the hole for the dowel rod in this way, gently slide the dowel back out of the Styrofoam ball. Fill the hole half full with tacky glue, and reinsert the dowel rod. Make sure that the clip clothespin is positioned at the bottom *back* of the dowel rod. Allow glue to dry completely.

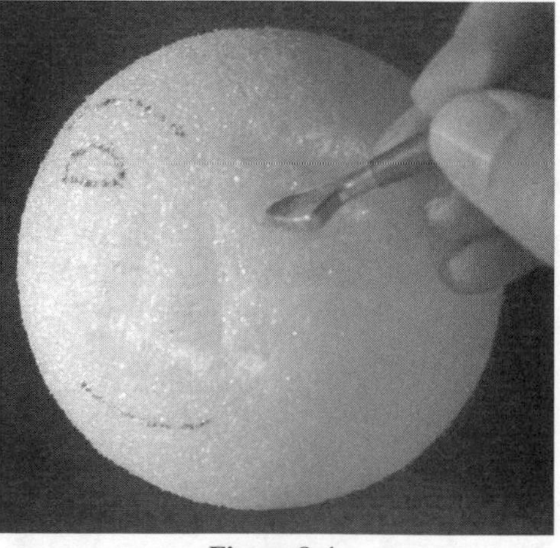

Figure 8-4

Figure 8-5

Step 4

Very slightly *in front of* (about 1/4") the moon's supporting dowel rod, push in the eyelet screw. Pull it gently back out and fill the hole with tacky glue. Reinsert the eyelet screw. Make sure that it is turned sideways, so the round opening faces toward the side. Allow glue to dry completely.

Step 5

Following the "MOON Painting template" pattern, paint the moon's facial features onto the 4" Styrofoam ball. Use the plain cornflower blue paint to highlight the carved portions, painting it along the inside of the carved channels. Use a thin rim of white paint around the outside of the moon's mouth and nose, above her eyebrows, and to underline her eyes. Lightly sponge a thin wash of yellow paint along her cheeks and down near her "jaw," and paint a thin rim of yellow along the top of her eyes above the rim of white paint. Finally, sponge a very thin wash of light pink paint and then light blue paint onto the moon's cheeks to highlight them further. Allow paint to dry completely.

Figure 8-6

Step 6

Place a drop of tacky glue in the center of each of the moon's eye sockets. Gently place one of the clear faceted beads on each drop of glue for the moon's eyes. Make sure the beads are both positioned in the same direction (normally with the facets turned horizontally). Allow glue to dry completely. (*See* figure 8-5.)

Step 7

Bend each of the three 2 1/2" lengths of hobby wire in the middle. Slide a white star button onto each piece of wire, to the middle bend. Loosely twist the wire ends together.

With the Sharpie marker, lightly mark the placement of the three star buttons on the Styrofoam ball. Press each of the wire twists deep into the Styrofoam at the points marked. The forehead button's shank should also be pressed into the Styrofoam. The two chin buttons should not be pressed in as deeply—those buttons' shanks should still show. This is necessary so that the STAR NIGHTGOWN's elastic loops can be hooked over the chin buttons without too much difficulty. (*See* figures 8-6 and 8-7, finished moon stick puppet.)

Figure 8-7

SUN

Step 1

Paint the 21" dowel rod and the regular-sized wooden spring clothespin royal blue. Allow paint to dry completely. Glue clothespin to the bottom of the dowel rod, lining up the bottom edge of the clothespin and the bottom of the dowel. If necessary, use another spring clothespin to hold the two together as they dry. Allow glue to dry completely.

Step 2

Following the "SUN Carving template" pattern, lightly sketch the sun's facial features onto the 6" Styrofoam ball with the Sharpie marker. Using the strip-turning pottery carving tool, carefully carve out the features. The carving tool is held sideways to essentially scoop out the strips where you are choosing to indent the sun's features. The mouth and eye sockets should be the deepest of the indentations.

Step 3

Slightly *behind* (about 1/4") the bottom center of the sun's head, mark the point where you will mount the Styrofoam ball onto the dowel rod. Make a small starter hole with a high-speed drill, or with a pointed awl or a nail. Once the hole is started, insert the dowel rod into the hole, working it in gently until it is at least 2" inside the Styrofoam. After establishing the hole for the dowel rod in this way, gently slide the dowel back out of the Styrofoam ball. Fill the hole half full with tacky glue, and reinsert the dowel rod. Make sure that the clip clothespin is positioned at the bottom *back* of the dowel rod. Allow glue to dry completely.

Step 4

Paint Styrofoam ball yellow. Allow paint to dry completely. (The painted Styrofoam may take a while to dry because of the solid coat of paint; set it in the path of an electric fan to speed drying time if necessary.)

Step 5

Following the "SUN Painting template" pattern, paint the sun's facial features onto the 6" Styrofoam ball. Paint the eye sockets and mouth indentation with the metallic gold paint. Add desert pink paint to the mouth indentation over the metallic gold. Lightly paint the front of the nose, the mouth side channels, the eyebrow groove, and the bottom of the cheek channels with the desert pink paint; also lightly sponge a thin wash of desert pink paint onto the surface of the cheeks. With the cornflower blue paint, lightly rim around the edge of the inside of the sun's mouth and along the bottom inside edge of the eyebrow groove. Outline the two sides of the nose with cornflower blue, and make two cornflower blue lines under each eye. Lightly sponge a thin wash of cornflower blue near the outside of the cheek circles as well. Finally, use white to lightly rim the mouth, cheeks, and the upper outside edge of the eyebrow channel. Allow paint to dry completely.

Step 6

How to Cut Craft Fur

To cut craft fur, use your small sharp-pointed scissors to cut along the fur material at the very base of the fur. Find the fabric weave and snip along the woven line, taking care not to cut the fur itself. After snipping through the base fabric, you should be able to gently separate the long fur strands of the cut strip from the rest of the fur.

Glue the thin 2" strip of long yellow craft fur just under the sun's mouth as a sort of goatee, with the fur pointing wispily *downward.* To hold the fur in place while it is drying, insert straight sewing pins through the fur and into the Styrofoam ball in three or four places along the fur strip.

Glue the thin 4" strip of long yellow craft fur just above the white stripe over the sun's eyebrows, with the fur pointing wispily *upward.* Insert straight pins to hold the fur strip in place while drying.

Glue the 19" strip of long yellow craft fur around the perimeter of the sun, in front of the supporting dowel rod. Join the ends on the side of the sun, near where an ear would be. Insert straight pins to hold the fur strip in place while drying.

Finally, glue the 19" strip of long orange craft fur around the perimeter of the sun, immediately in front of the yellow craft fur. Again, join the ends on the side of the sun, near where an ear would be. Insert straight pins to hold the fur strip in place while drying.

Allow glue to dry completely. Remove straight pins.

Step 7

Place a drop of tacky glue in the center of each of the sun's eye sockets. Gently place one of the bright blue faceted beads on each drop of glue for the sun's eyes. Make sure the beads are both positioned in the same direction (normally, with the facets turned horizontally). Allow glue to dry completely.

Figure 8-8

Step 8

Gently comb the sun's furry goatee, eyebrows, and nimbus to stand out from the ball before using. (*See* figure 8-8, finished sun stick puppet.)

How to Make the Nightgowns

ALL NIGHTGOWNS

General Step 1

If the doll hangers you have located are partly unfinished wood, paint those portions with acrylic craft paint in colors to match the nightgowns. If ready-made doll hangers are unavailable in the correct size, you can create your own from heavy-gauge floral wire following the pattern guide that follows.

General Step 2

Photocopy nightgown patterns *at sizes specified.* (*See* chapter 2, "Enlarging the Patterns in This Book.") Cut out all of the photocopied patterns along the outside of the pattern outlines.

HANGER PATTERN GUIDE

Hanger Option 1:
Twist hanger from heavy-gauge floral wire.

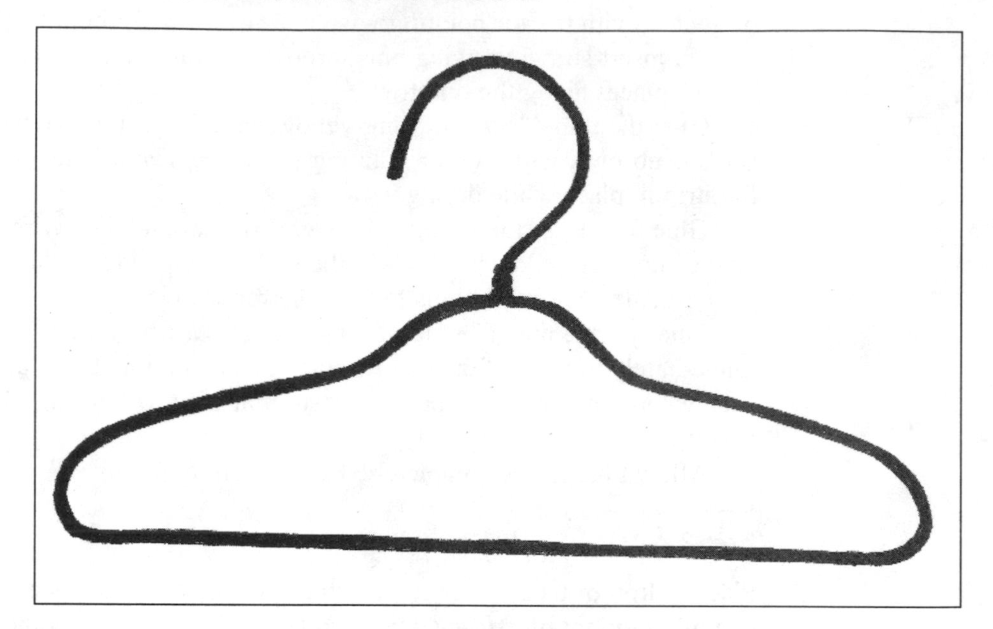

Hanger Option 2:
Create hanger base from craft wood or cardboard and affix a heavy-gauge floral wire hanger hook.

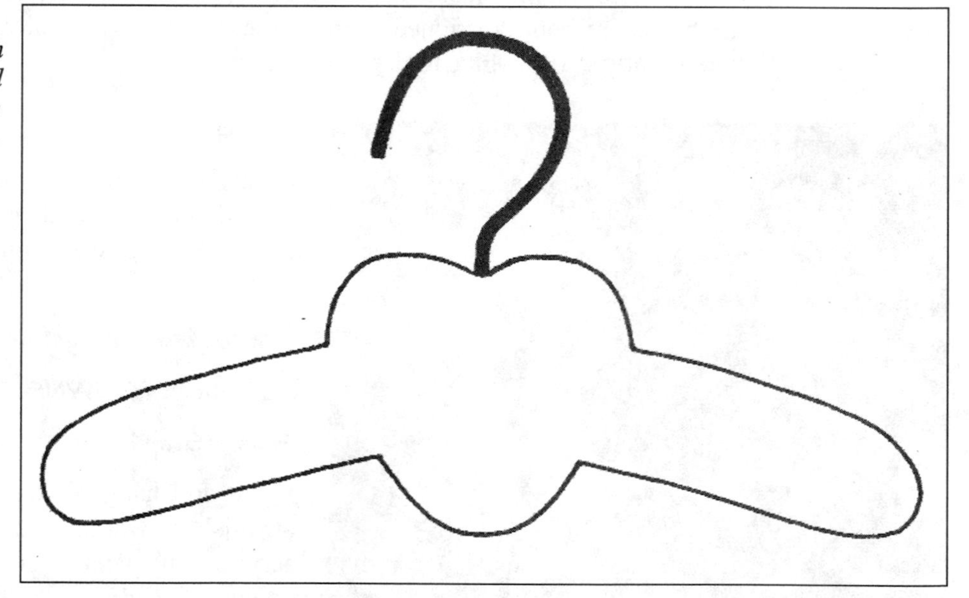

STAR NIGHTGOWN

Step 1

If you are using royal blue fabric with preprinted stars, proceed directly to step 2.

If you are using plain blue fabric for the nightgown, draw stars on the fabric with the gold paint pen and fill them in. If you do not feel confident drawing the stars free-hand, stick foil stars onto the fabric and trace; then remove the stickers and fill in the star outlines with the gold paint pen. You may also use small star stencils to trace stars onto the fabric. Allow the gold paint to dry completely.

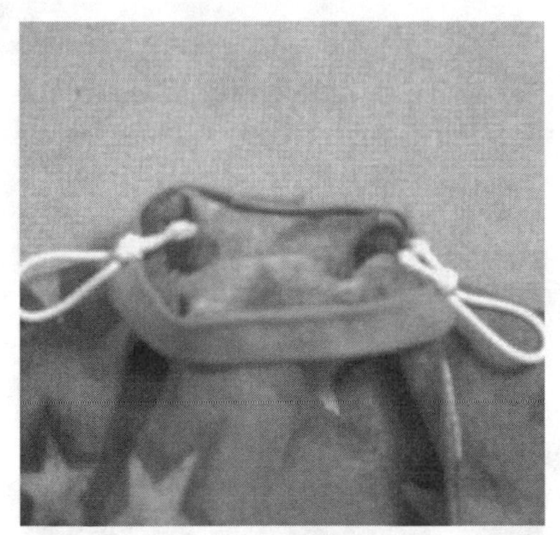

Figure 8-9

Step 2

Cut out the nightgown pattern from the blue star fabric, as specified on the pattern.

Pin the nightgown with right sides together, and machine stitch top of arm and underarm/side seams using blue thread. Seam allowance is 1/4". Do not sew across neck or wrist openings. Turn nightgown right side out; press with steam iron. (If you drew stars onto the fabric, you should definitely use a pressing cloth.)

Step 3

Pin red bias tape around the bottom of the nightgown, wrist openings, and neck opening. Hand stitch in place using red thread.

Figure 8-10

Step 4

Loop and *overhand loop knot* (*see* chapter 2, "Terms and Techniques") the white cord elastic to create two small loops that extend 1/2". Apply Fray Check to the cut ends of the elastic; allow to dry.

Using red thread, hand stitch the loops securely to the two sides of the nightgown's neck opening. (*See* figure 8-9; *see also* figure 8-10, finished star nightgown.)

SMALL NIGHTGOWN

Step 1

Cut out the nightgown pattern from the animal print flannel, as specified on the pattern. Place the bottom edge of the nightgown on the fabric selvage if possible so you won't need to hem it.

Pin the nightgown with right sides together, and machine stitch top of arm and underarm/side seams using white thread. Seam allowance is 1/4". Do not sew across wrist or neck openings. Turn nightgown right side out; press with steam iron.

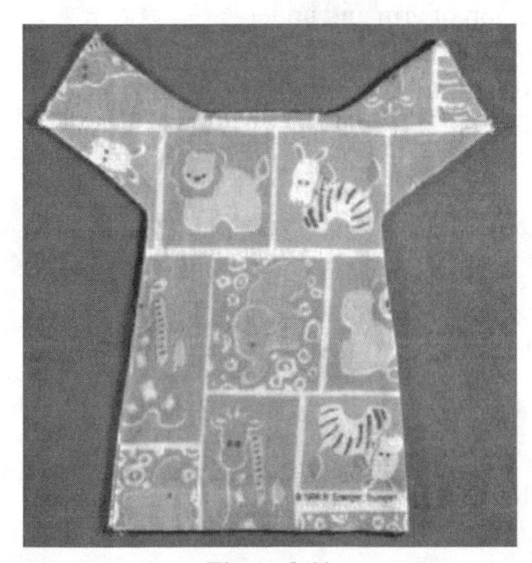

Figure 8-11

Step 2

Turn under fabric at neck; hand stitch around opening.

Step 3

Apply Fray Check to the unfinished wrist edges; allow to dry completely. (*See* figure 8-11, finished small nightgown.)

LARGE NIGHTGOWN

Step 1

Cut out the nightgown pattern from the flowered flannel, as specified on the pattern.

Pin the nightgown with right sides together, and machine stitch underarm/side seams only using white thread. Fold under wrist edges 1/4" and pin eyelet lace along the straight edge. Machine stitch lace to wrist edge using white thread.

Pin the nightgown with right sides together again, and machine stitch along top of arms. Seam allowance is 1/4". Do not sew across neck or wrist openings. Turn nightgown right side out, press with steam iron.

Figure 8-12

Step 2

Turn neck edge under 1/4". Pin eyelet lace around neck so that it will stick up, overlapping it slightly to join at the back. Hand stitch in place using white thread.

Step 3

Fold under bottom of nightgown 1/4" and pin; machine stitch hem using white thread.

Step 4

Using light pink thread, hand stitch three ribbon rosebuds in place as marked on pattern. (*See* figure 8-12, finished large nightgown.)

PALE NIGHTGOWN

Step 1

Cut out the nightgown pattern from the pale fabric, as specified on the pattern. Place the bottom edge of the nightgown on the fabric selvage if possible so you won't need to hem it. Pin the nightgown with right sides together, and machine stitch top of arm and underarm/side seams using light yellow thread. Seam allowance is 1/4". Do not sew across neck or wrist openings. Turn nightgown right side out; press with steam iron.

Step 2

Turn neck and wrist edges under 1/4"; hand stitch using light yellow thread.

Step 3

Pin light yellow grosgrain ribbon around bottom of nightgown, approximately 1/4" up from the bottom edge. Machine stitch ribbon using light yellow thread.

Step 4

Cut remaining grosgrain ribbon in half, and tie into two small bows, approximately 1 3/4" across. Using light yellow thread, hand stitch the bows in place as marked on pattern. (*See* figure 8-13, finished pale nightgown.)

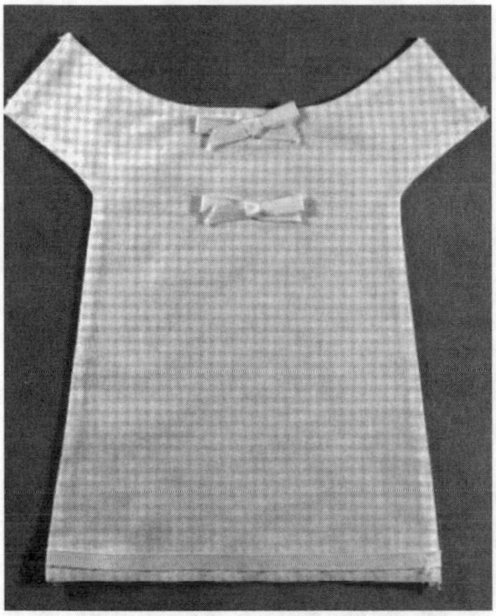

Figure 8-13

DARK NIGHTGOWN

Step 1

Using black thread, machine stitch the black lace along the bottom 18" edge of the black gauze fabric. With right sides together, machine stitch the fabric and lace square along the short side into a tube. Fold the top 18" edge of the gauze fabric under 1/4"; machine stitch with black thread.

Step 2

Baste a gather stitch around the top edge of the gauze fabric in the 1/4" hem. Gather the fabric evenly so that it measures 4" across the front and 4" across the back. Tie off the basting stitch to temporarily secure the gather.

Step 3

Cut the wide black satin ribbon into two 4" lengths; apply Fray Check to the cut edges and allow to dry completely. Position the ribbon pieces to form the nightgown's shoulders: pin the two pieces so they meet in a slight V at the back and then loop forward over the "shoulders" to join the front of the gown, leaving a center space of approximately 3/4". Hand stitch ribbon in place, both front and back, using black thread.

Figure 8-14

Step 4

Overlap the green and pink satin ribbon, with the green ribbon on the outside. Pin double ribbon layer in place as a "belt" around the middle of the nightgown, covering the gather stitching. At the center front of the nightgown, fold the ribbon at 90-degree angles so that the double layers now point downward and so the pink ribbon becomes forefront. Hand stitch the belt in place with a straight stitch, using green thread through the double green and pink ribbon layers, the black gauze fabric, and the satin shoulder pieces. Hand stitch the pink ribbon rose to the center front of the belt. Trim the bottom of the pink and green ribbon lengths in an inverted V. (*See* figure 8-14, finished dark nightgown.)

How to Make the Miscellaneous Additional Story Pieces

Step 1

Paint the two 20" dowel rod sections and the two regular-sized wooden spring clothespins with the periwinkle craft paint. Allow paint to dry completely. Glue one clothespin partway down each dowel rod, with the bottom edge of the clothespin about 5" up from the bottom of the dowel. If necessary, use another spring clothespin to hold the two together as they dry. Allow glue to dry completely.

Step 2

Tie one end of the cotton rope clothesline to the top of one of the periwinkle dowel rods with a *double knot,* and tie the other end of the rope to the other dowel rod. You will need to adjust the length of your clothesline to match the width of your lap theater box. Position the clothesline at the front of the lap theater, clipping the dowel rods to the box's front corner side edges. The dowel rods should be *inside* the lap theater, with the clothesline stretched between the two supports. (*See* figure 8-15.)

Clip the two small spring clothespins to the laundry line, about as far apart as the two shoulders of the star nightgown.

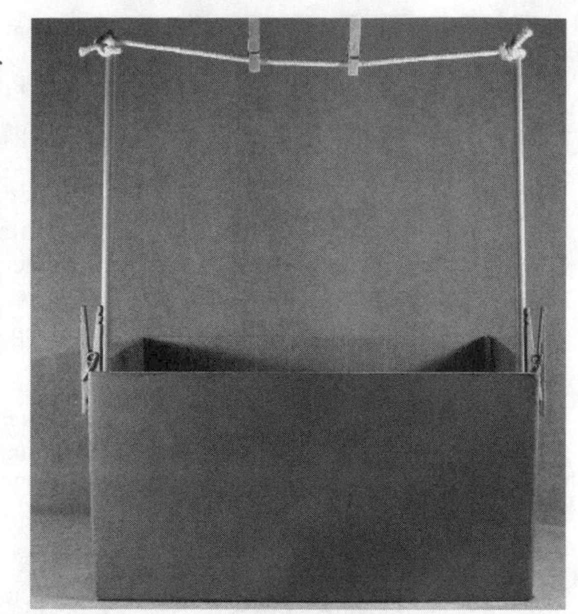

Figure 8-15

Step 3

Paint the small cardboard box and lid royal blue, both inside and out. Using the gold paint pen, draw stars on the box and fill them in. If you do not feel confident drawing the stars freehand, stick foil stars lightly to the box and trace them with a sharp pencil; then remove the stickers and fill in the outlines with the gold paint pen. You may also use small star stencils to trace stars onto the box. Allow the gold paint to dry completely. (*See* figure 8-16, finished "sky drawer.")

Figure 8-16

Stick Puppet Story Finished Product

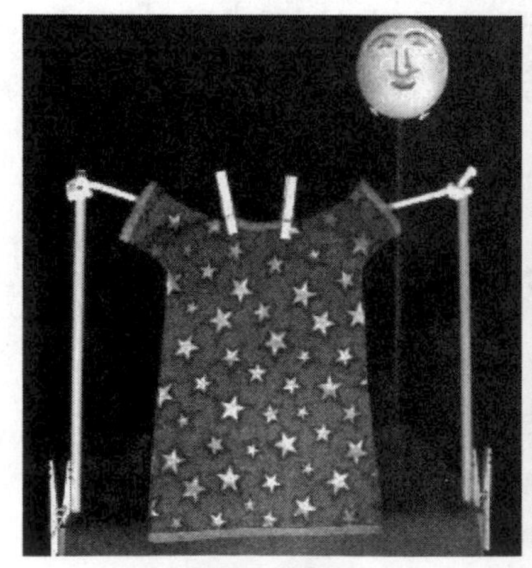

Figure 8-17

Figure 8-18

Figure 8-19

Figure 8-20

Figure 8-21

Figure 8-22

Figure 8-23

Figure 8-24

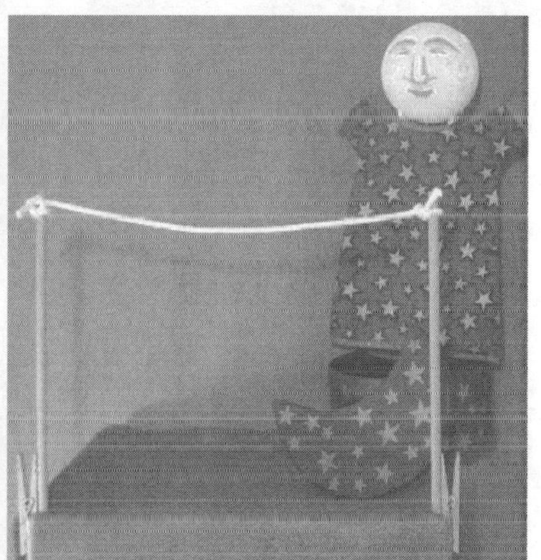
Figure 8-25

Figure 8-26

PATTERN PIECES

The Nightgown of the Sullen Moon

by Nancy Willard, illustrated by David McPhail

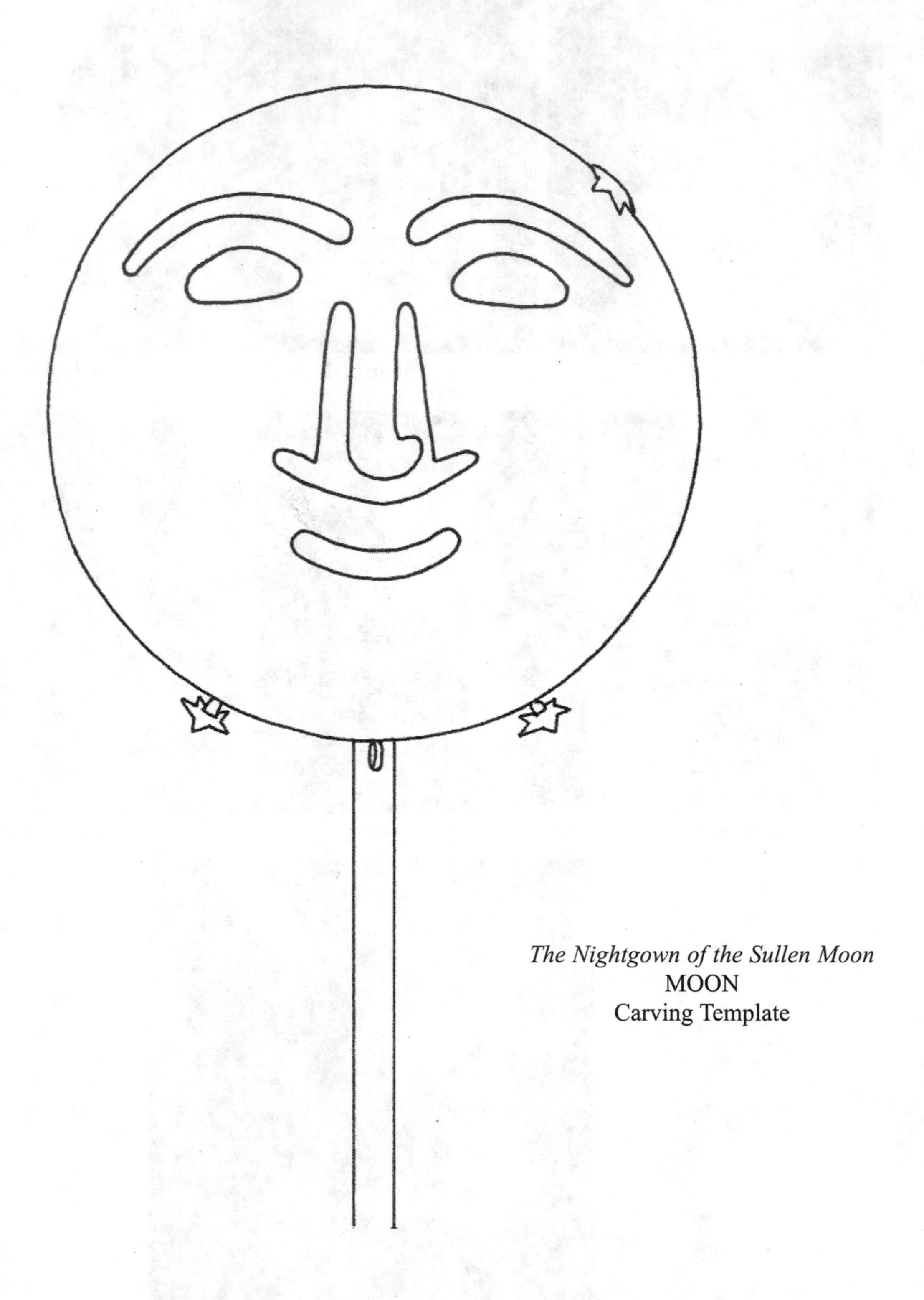

The Nightgown of the Sullen Moon
MOON
Carving Template

The Nightgown of the Sullen Moon
MOON
Painting Template

The Nightgown of the Sullen Moon
SUN
Carving Template

The Nightgown of the Sullen Moon
SUN
Painting Template

Photocopy this page at size 135%.

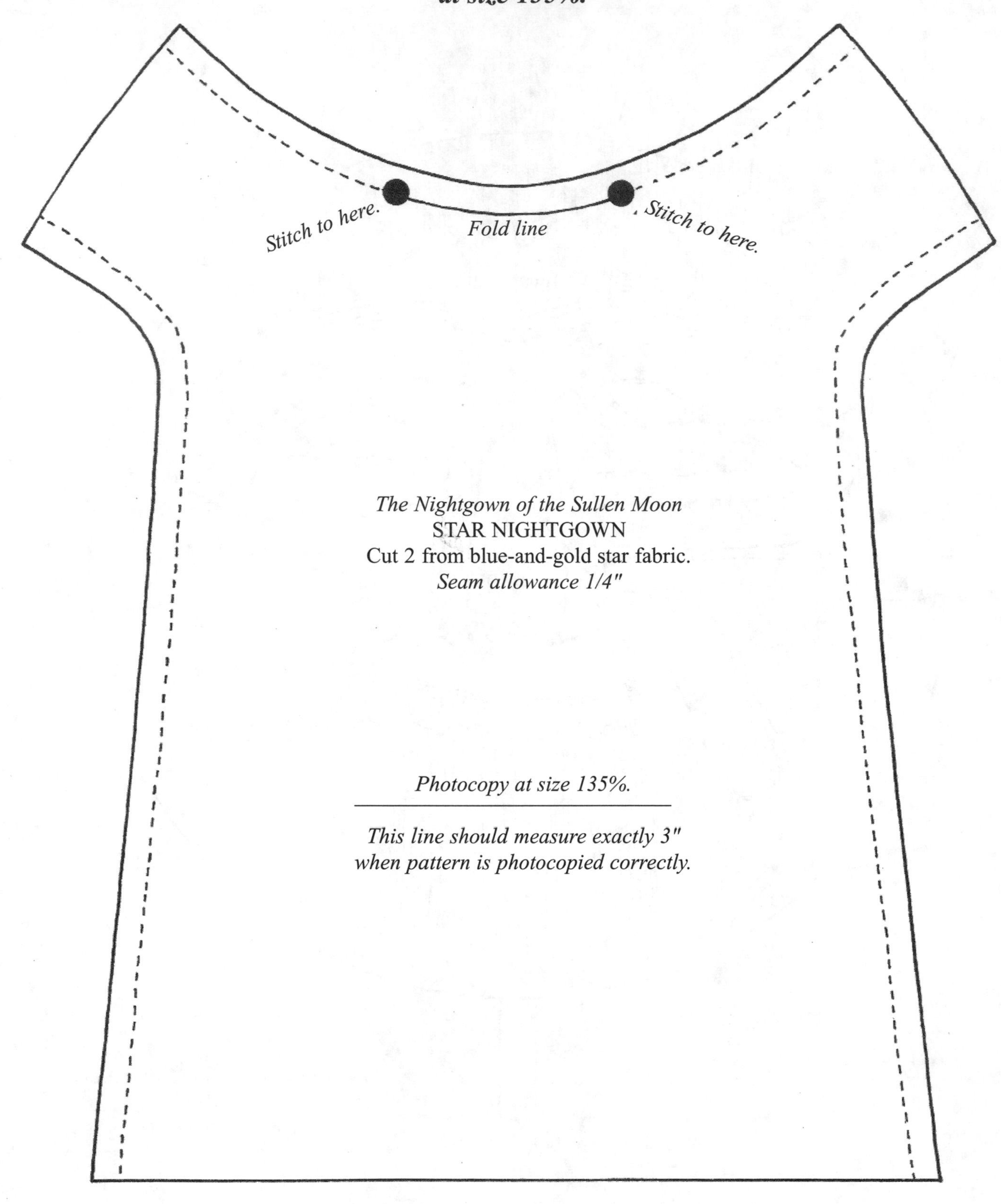

Photocopy this page at size 135%.

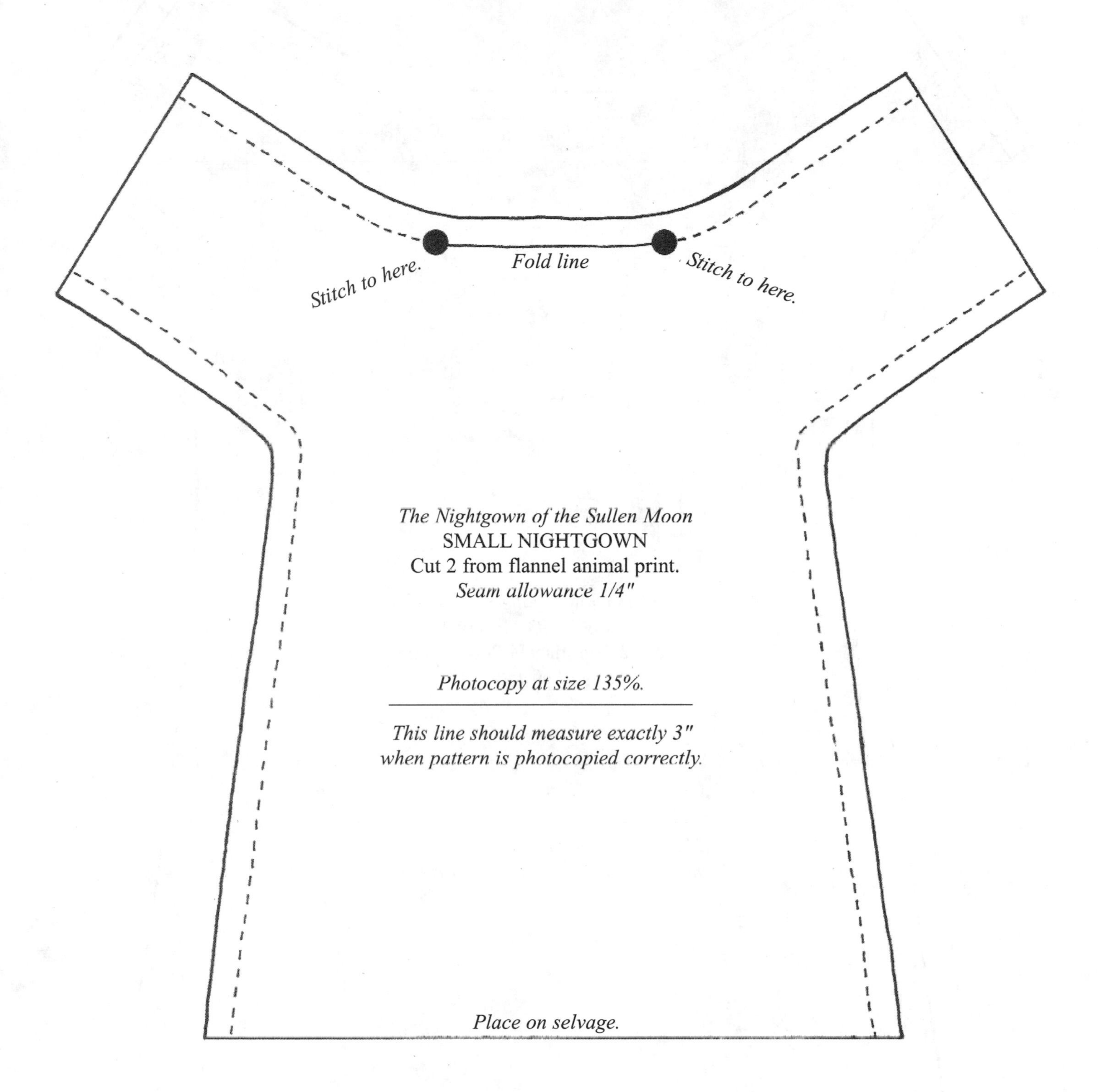

Photocopy this page at size 135%.

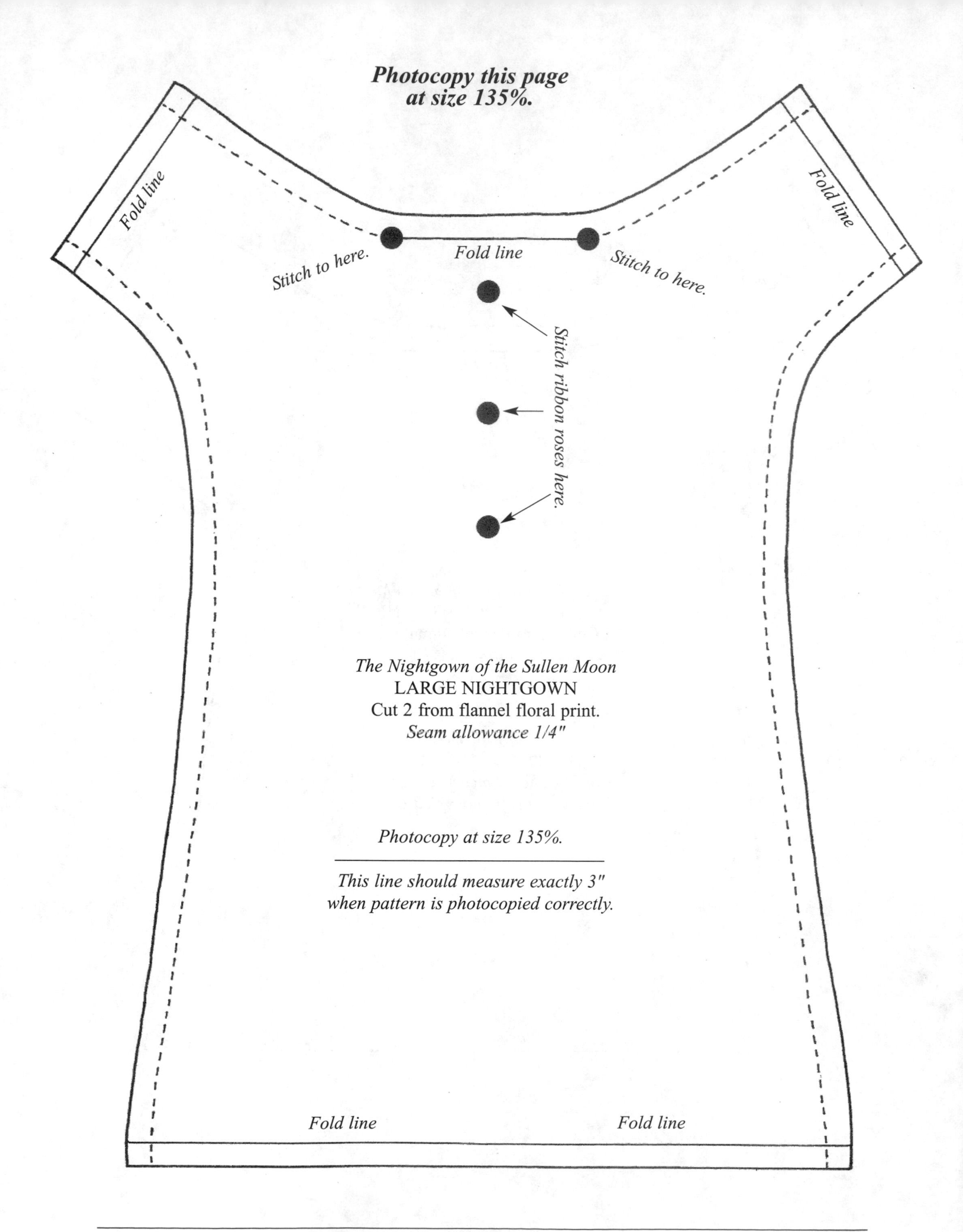

Photocopy this page at size 135%.

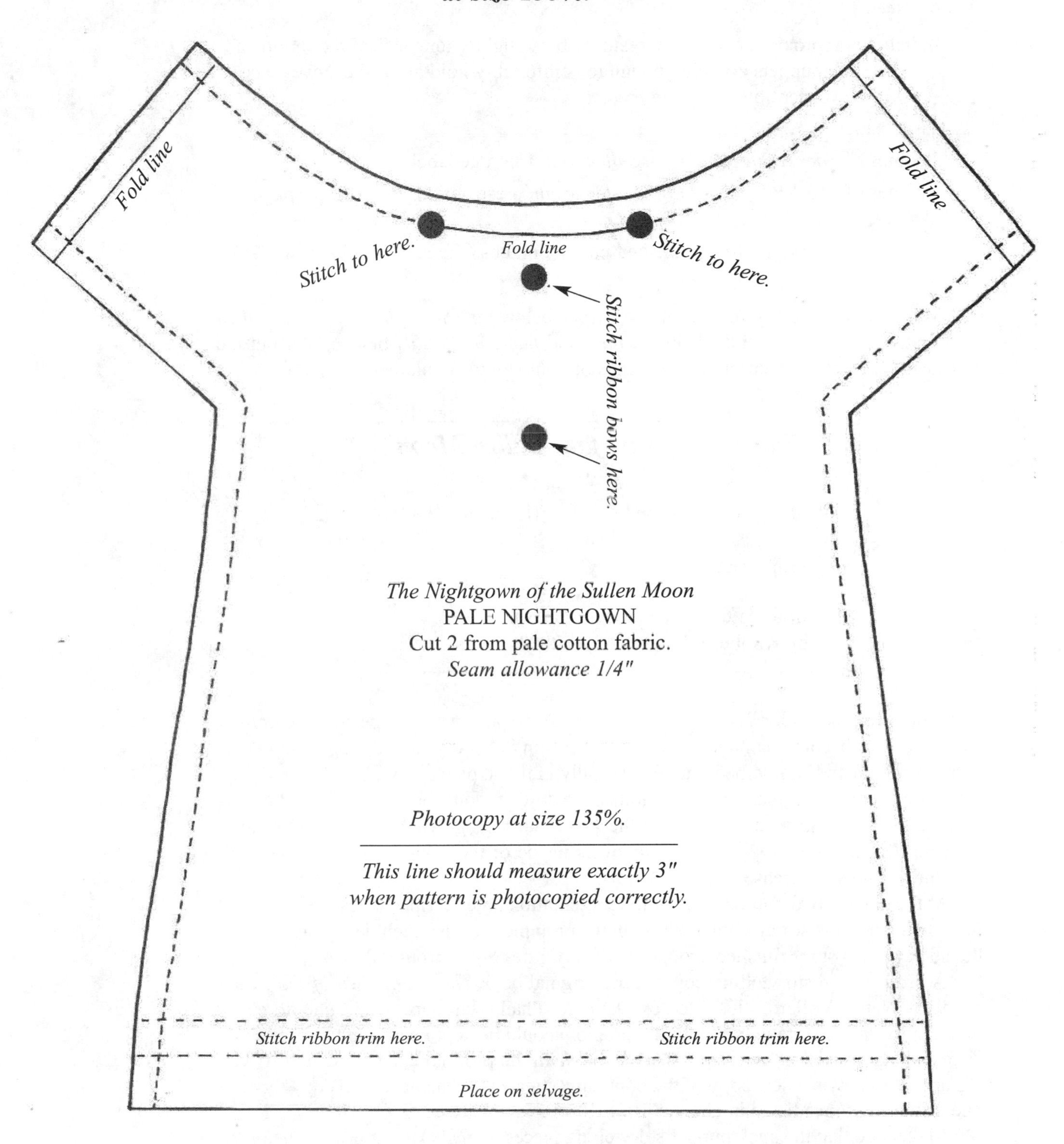

Storage

You Will Need

1 shallow (approximately 8" deep) sturdy box, slightly longer than the moon and sun stick puppets and big enough to comfortably hold all of the story pieces with the exception of the lap theater

tissue paper

2 copies of *The Nightgown of the Sullen Moon* storage label

2 copies of *The Nightgown of the Sullen Moon* presentation notes/script (pages 134–39)

1 copy of stick puppet story finished product photos (figures 8-17 through 8-26)

Make two photocopies of the label provided below for *The Nightgown of the Sullen Moon* stick puppet/prop and fill in the *date* and *name or initials* blanks. Cut out the labels and affix them securely to both ends of your storage container.

The Nightgown of the Sullen Moon

Nancy Willard

Illustrated by David McPhail (Harcourt, 1983)

Prop created ________ by ____________________
DATE NAME OR INITIALS

from patterns included in *Books in Bloom*
by Kimberly Faurot (ALA, 2003)

The story prop pieces for *The Nightgown of the Sullen Moon* should be stored carefully so they do not become damaged. The moon and sun Styrofoam stick puppets in particular are fragile and should be wrapped carefully in tissue paper when being stored. The clothespins can be clipped onto the clothesline so they don't become lost, and everything else should just be laid flat in the box. The nightgowns can be left on their hangers. Do not store any of the nightgowns inside of the "sky drawer" or they will become wrinkled or creased.

Make at least two photocopies of the presentation notes/script (pages 134–39), and include them in the storage bin along with the prop pieces. Also include a photocopy of the stick puppet story finished product photos (figures 8-17 through 8-26).

A professional storytelling copy of the original book *The Nightgown of the Sullen Moon* by Nancy Willard, illustrated by David McPhail (Harcourt, 1983), should either be included in the storage box with the prop or should be kept nearby in a professional "storytelling collection" so it may be shown when the prop is being presented. If you are unable to obtain a new copy of the book, investigate purchasing a used copy through one of the resources listed in chapter 10.

Make sure that the stick puppet storytelling pieces for *The Nightgown of the Sullen Moon* are included on your storytelling props database or list (*see* chapter 2) as well as in your institution's inventory records. Make sure that the location of the lap theater is also designated.

Notify other staff members who might be able to include *The Nightgown of the Sullen Moon* in their programming or classrooms that it is ready for use, and demonstrate it for them (along with proper storage caveats) if at all possible.

Summary

Although simple stick puppets are one of the easiest types of puppets to make, they offer limitless performance possibilities. Such puppets can help bring songs, poetry, and stories to life for audiences in a new and exciting way. Because the simplest stick puppets can be basic enough for even very small children to make and to use, they provide excellent opportunities for both creation and participation in the classroom and library.

9 Hand Puppets

Includes script and pattern for

Lunch by Denise Fleming (Holt, 1992)

Pattern difficulty level

Expert

Construction time estimate

40 hours

Hand puppets are one of the most well known types of puppets in the United States, for a variety of reasons. Several popular children's television shows have featured regular hand and body puppet characters for years, and many toy stores sell a wide range of beautiful hand puppets at relatively affordable prices. These hand puppets generally have soft bodies and heads, and their basic movements can be controlled fairly easily. This ability to display delicate, nuanced movements makes such puppets good candidates for low-key interactive settings as well as for public performances. There is something innately intriguing about an animated inanimate object, and even beginning puppeteers will likely experience the "power" of puppets. A puppet will frequently be able to manage a crowd in an almost magical way, and it can enable you to gain and retain the attention of even very young or unfocused audiences.

Techniques and Considerations

Creating

Hand puppets can be extremely simple or unbelievably complex. As with the other formats included in *Books in Bloom,* the methods of creating hand puppets are ultimately limited only by your imagination and skill. Numerous pattern books and resources exist that can help give you ideas and guide you through various techniques (*see* chapter 10). Possibilities include basic paper bag hand puppets; flat "mitt" or simple hand puppets made from felt or fabric; three-dimensional sewn fabric puppets; "sock puppets"; hand puppets with Styrofoam or papier-mâché heads; foam rubber/polyurethane hand puppets; and many, many more.

There are also numerous ready-made puppets available for purchase (*see* chapter 10) that you can adapt for your purposes. I often dress purchased puppets with clothing and doll accessories or add features such as a wig or different eyes so that they more closely approximate the characters in a particular book. It is extremely difficult to design puppets from scratch that both function effectively and also look like specific characters in a book (such as this chapter's *Lunch* Mouse hand puppet). I advise working from and adapting existing patterns until you begin to internalize the rudiments of basic hand puppet construction.

Whether making a puppet from scratch or adapting an existing puppet or stuffed animal, make certain that both the materials you use and your end product take into account the manipulations you need the puppet to perform in the story. Remember that simple, well-constructed designs are always effective, and make sure that your basic puppets exhibit these qualities. As you gain confidence in your creative abilities and facility with the medium and materials of hand puppetry, you will be able to achieve more sophisticated and elaborate creations.

Presenting

As mentioned in the previous chapter (chapter 8, "Stick Puppets/Rod Puppets"), effective eye contact between a puppet and the audience is essential to a performance's success. Think of how disturbing it is when a real person talks to you without looking at you! The situation is the same with a puppet. If a puppet is unintentionally staring over the audience's head, at the ceiling, or down at the floor, the audience is less likely to give the puppet their full attention. When performing, make certain that your puppet is making intentional eye contact with the audience, looking from person to person. Because most simple hand puppets have fixed eyes, the puppets' head movements tandem with their eye movements. Tilting a puppet's head one way or another can help express various emotions; just make sure that the audience is able to see the puppet's face or they will quickly lose interest.

As with the stick puppets, the puppeteer should *watch the puppet when animating it,* whether he or she is hidden from or visible to the audience. Again, if a visible puppeteer is watching the puppet, then the audience will watch it, too. The performer may surreptitiously glance at the audience while manipulating the puppet to gauge responses; however, direct eye contact between the puppeteer and the audience should be avoided when attention is supposed to be on the puppet. Otherwise, the puppeteer is directly competing with the puppet for the audience's attention. Certainly some performers have a comical contest with their puppets in a supposed competition for the audience's attention, but such "contests" are actually carefully orchestrated to spotlight the puppet's antics, not detract from them. Watching the puppet while animating it also enables the puppeteer to monitor the puppet's movements and believability.

Manipulating your puppet's arm or hand (or tail) can also help convey emotion and add interest to the puppet's performance. The construction of some hand puppets enables you to do this using your fingers inside the puppet's arms, hands, and so forth, whereas other puppets (such as *Lunch* Mouse) require such manipulations externally. When external manipulation is needed, you can either just use your hand (gloved or not) to move the puppet or you can employ wire rods attached to the puppet's wrist or tail. Move the puppet so that it mirrors the type of movements that people commonly make while talking, such as having it scratch its head or neck, sneeze or cough with hand to mouth, and so forth. Small details like these sharply enhance your puppet's believability, and they make the performance far more memorable and enjoyable for the audience.

Hand puppets without movable mouths must depend entirely upon the eye contact, head, and appendage movement mentioned. If your hand puppet's mouth is articulated (movable), on the other hand, you will need to pay attention to the points already mentioned as well as to the puppet's mouth movements. An articulated mouth puppet provides wonderful opportunities for the puppet to eat, chew, and taste as well as to exhibit surprise, yawn, laugh, and of course the chance to "speak" believably.

All of these movements require practice, but particular care is needed in developing the puppet's speech mouth movements. Improper mouth manipulation can be truly disconcerting and even painful for an audience to watch, and it can dash all previous efforts at believability in a single sentence. Many new and even some veteran puppeteers manipulate their puppets' mouths so that the puppet appears to be "biting" or "eating" the words rather than speaking them. This is extremely distracting. Another common mistake occurs when a puppeteer simply flaps his or her hand wildly inside a puppet to make its mouth open and close without any rhyme or reason.

Think about what happens when you speak: you essentially open your mouth to let a word or syllable out, then close your mouth after the word gets out, and then open it again for the next one. The puppet should likewise open its mouth to release a word or syllable, then close it, then open it again for the next, and so on. To achieve this manipulation in a smooth and believable manner, it is necessary to keep your wrist and hand inside the puppet flexible and loose. Your hand moves very slightly forward with each word or syllable as the puppet ejects/releases it; then your hand returns to its original position. The motion is almost like you are lightly flicking water off the ends of your fingertips.

It is also extremely important to try and move the puppet's lower jaw more than the top. Although this technique will at first feel somewhat unnatural for your hand, it enables the puppet to maintain better eye contact with the audience and also to appear more natural. If you move the top of the mouth too much, the top of the puppet's head essentially keeps rearing back again and again each time it opens its mouth. Try to move the upper part of the puppet's head about 30 percent or so, and move the bottom jaw 70 percent.

For a practice exercise, try counting to five with your puppet. As the puppet says each number, your wrist moves gently forward and your hand/the puppet's mouth opens on the number; then your wrist returns to its original place and your hand/the puppet's mouth closes. Repeat with each successive number. Once you understand and have practiced this basic mouth movement with monosyllabic words, begin to practice with longer words. You won't be able to open and close the puppet's mouth on every single syllable, or the mouth will begin to appear "flappy." A great way to practice puppet mouth manipulation is to subtly "lip sync" with your bare hand to songs or to other people's conversations. You will develop an understanding of when to combine syllables in a puppet's mouth movement and when to preserve each syllable individually. Your efforts will be well worth it in making your puppet's performance believable and enjoyable for your audiences.

Make the most of your puppet's ability to speak to the audience: use a toy microphone to "interview" the puppet performer; have the puppet thank the audience for coming; use the puppet to make an announcement (the audience will likely pay closer attention to the puppet than they would to you!).

Practice presenting your story as well as your introduction, any segues, and so forth. If at all possible, practice in front of a mirror at first so you can evaluate the success of your puppet's movements and synchronicity. Puppets often seem to take on a life of their own; a good puppeteer simply tries to help the puppet come to life for the audience.

Your puppet's availability to speak provides you with a great opportunity to give him or her a unique character voice. If you do give the puppet a particular voice, however, it is imperative that you maintain it. It is bewildering for an audience to watch and listen to a puppet that has two completely different voices. A unique character voice can help define a puppet's personality, and it helps maintain audience interest. Decide what general tone you think your puppet should have, and experiment with different voices to figure out which sounds the best for him or her. Perhaps the puppet has an accent or energy level in addition to a unique-sounding tone. Practice speaking in the voice you have chosen for your puppet when you are alone in your car or house until it comes naturally to you, and you are able to switch into and out of the voice with ease. Remember that the audience will love it if you wholeheartedly embrace and present your characters with abandon. The only way you will look stupid in front of an audience is if you act like you feel stupid or self-conscious. Enjoy the story and your audience, and recognize that you are simply serving as the vehicle for the wonderful and important gift of story.

Choosing the Hand Puppet Format

Denise Fleming's picture books, employing vibrant handmade paper techniques, are ideal just as they are for sharing with groups of children. The illustrations are bright and clear and can be seen from a distance, and the text is rhythmic and provocative. The book *Lunch* engages children both visually and verbally in naming colors as well as guessing from visual clues what the next food Mouse finds will be. Because *Lunch* is wonderful shared just as it is in book form, it is important to carefully evaluate whether adapting it to another medium will truly add anything to significantly enhance an audience's experience. The book's key elements do suggest several good opportunities for interactivity that could be provided by creating a story prop. For example, children love the fact that Mouse becomes so messy, and they would delight in actively putting food parts on Mouse; they would also thoroughly enjoy being able to feed him.

The story could certainly be adapted in many different ways. Presenting *Lunch* as a flannel/felt board story would allow audiences to place "messy" felt food pieces onto Mouse, though feeding him might then be problematic. Mouse is such a lively, animated character in the book, however, that it seems desirable to reflect as much of that motion as possible. A puppet enables you to achieve this in a way that a static adaptation could not.

As a puppet, *Lunch* Mouse necessarily has several important design requirements. He must be able to have food pieces stuck onto him that are also removable, and he should be able to "eat" in some way. Velcro is a good attachment possibility for the food pieces, which consequently means that Mouse must be constructed from a Velcro-compatible fabric. If he is going to "eat," his mouth should open, and it would be nice if he could somehow "swallow" his food. His mouth must be fairly sturdy and of a non-Velcro-compatible fabric so he is able to swallow the food pieces without them sticking to his mouth. The food pieces should also be mostly non-Velcro-compatible so that they don't stick together in Mouse's tummy.

When determining whether sharing *Lunch* with props allows it some desirable new dimension(s), it is also necessary to consider whether doing so eliminates some other important aspect that the author and illustrator intended. If *Lunch* is shared only as a puppet/prop set, you will gain the desirable opportunity for interactivity but lose the anticipation and joy that Fleming offers in the original illustrations. In this type of situation, consider using both the book and the prop with your audience: read the story aloud first while showing the pictures; then share the story again using the props.

Although creating the following prop pieces for *Lunch* is a fairly major undertaking, the end result is well worth the effort and offers endless possibilities. The pieces may be used in many ways to extend the book *Lunch* as well as be used for other nutrition and color discussions. Many of the pieces can have alternate lives: the turnip may be used in *The Great Big Enormous Turnip* by Alexei Tolstoy; the carrots can appear in *The Carrot Seed* by Ruth Krauss; and the Mouse puppet can guest in *The Mouse and the Apple* by Stephen Butler, to name just a few possibilities. Mouse is also the star of *Alphabet under Construction* by Denise Fleming, so the Mouse puppet can happily reappear to introduce and dramatize that title as well.

Lunch

Denise Fleming

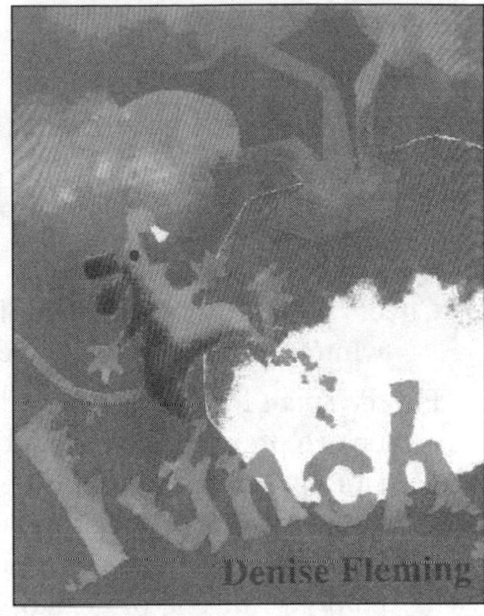

(Holt, 1992)

Summary

A very hungry mouse eats a large lunch comprised of colorful foods.

Possible themes

Colors, Five Senses, Food, Gardens, Mice, Noses, Nutrition

Presentation time for story with puppet/props (including introduction and audience participation)

8–10 minutes

Recommended audience interest level

Preschool (age 1 and older) through grade 1

Please note that the story pieces are designed as professional resources, not as playthings. They do not conform to child safety play standards, and they could easily become damaged if used in a manner other than that for which they were intended.

Story Pieces

- black and white checkered fabric/tablecloth
- *Lunch* Mouse puppet
- plastic bag or jar for the food pieces
- giant white turnip
- white turnip pieces
- giant orange carrot
- orange carrot pieces
- giant yellow corn
- yellow corn kernel pieces
- giant green pea pod with peas
- green pea pieces
- giant blueberries in bowl
- blueberry pieces
- giant bunch of purple grapes
- purple grape pieces
- giant red apple
- red apple pieces
- giant pink watermelon
- pink watermelon pieces
- giant black watermelon seeds
- black watermelon seed pieces

Use with

table
large box in which to hide Mouse and the giant food (optional)
chair (optional)

Setup

Cover the table on which you plan to set the *Lunch* story food with the black and white checkered fabric/tablecloth.

Put the small food pieces mixed up together in the plastic bag/jar, but set out one or two of each color in a hidden place where you can reach them easily as the story progresses. (This way, even if the children decide to feed all of their food pieces to Mouse instead of putting some of them on him, you can still stick a piece or two of each color onto Mouse yourself so you can review the colors at the end of the story like in the final page of the book.)

If you are using the opening behind Mouse's head to manipulate him while he's eating, you will probably need to surreptitiously remove some of the food pieces he has eaten out through his neck with your other hand (the opening down into his body is pressed closed by your arm, so the food doesn't go down into his tummy when you are using that entry point). Have a small bowl or bag in your lap or nearby into which you can drop these extra pieces. If you are using the bottom opening, the food pieces will go on down inside his body but will be stopped from dropping on through by your arm being in the way.

Hide the story pieces (giant food and Mouse puppet) out of sight inside the box or behind the table where they may be easily pulled out one at a time.

Presentation

Within the script, story narration is delineated in regular type; movement notes and miscellaneous directions are shown in *[bracketed italics]*.

Learn thc story and tell it to your audience from memory, using the prop pieces.

While telling the story, hold Mouse on your knee, on your other forearm held up for him to sit on, or on the edge of the table.

The story text only requires one character voice: the Narrator. However, Mouse may also interact verbally with the children. For example, he could say "thank you," when the children feed him, "yum, yum," and so forth. If you do have Mouse speak, give him sounds and a voice that would be appropriate to his character. Make sure that you practice beforehand, so that moving into and out of his voice will come naturally to you.

When Mouse is waiting for the food, is just sitting there, or is talking or sniffing, animate his arms and head in a realistic manner so he looks alive and excited.

When using puppets, it is a good idea to practice the story before a mirror to work on the puppet's movements and believability.

Make sure that Mouse's body language is not threatening in any way, so that the children are not afraid of him. He should take food pieces from the children carefully, so they don't feel like he's trying to "bite" them. If a child is afraid to feed Mouse, have them give you their food piece and watch while you give it to him. Mouse should then thank the child for the food and perhaps wave at him/her so the child feels important.

For guidance in manipulating Mouse's mouth and his rod hand, see the "Presenting" section of chapter 9, "Hand Puppets," pages 165–67, in *Books in Bloom* (ALA, 2003).

Slip the puppet on and off your hand as needed if you need both hands to manipulate the other props. If you do take the puppet off your hand during the story, simply hold him on your lap or carry him in your arm.

Please note: Below are a brief possible introduction and conclusion for establishing effective audience participation using the story pieces. The script that follows the introduction is the exact text of the original story, provided for ease in practicing with Mouse. This particular story works especially well if you first read the book with the audience and show them the pictures and then present the story with the puppet and the food. Learn the story and tell it to your audience from memory the second time, using the prop pieces. Show a copy of the book to your audience both before and after sharing the story with the puppet, and give the complete title, author/illustrator, and publication information.

Possible Introduction

AFTER READING THE BOOK, TELL THE CHILDREN:

"Well, we have a special visitor from our book today!"

[Bring out Mouse puppet and sit him on your knee or on the edge of the table; Mouse waves to the audience and sniffs with interest in their direction.]

TO MOUSE: "Thank you so much for coming to visit us, Mouse! We're so glad that you're here. Now, Mouse, we just read this story about you *[hold up book],* and we were so surprised at how much food you ate, and at how messy you got."

[Mouse nods.]

"Are you hungry now?"

[Mouse nods excitedly, rubs his tummy with rod hand.]

"Would you like to do the story again with the children and me?"

[Mouse nods.]

"Okay, why don't you go take a nap for a few minutes while we get your food ready. We'll call you to come back out when we're ready."

[Slip Mouse off your hand and hide him temporarily back in the box or behind the table.]

[You may want to snore surreptitiously, and ask the children if they heard Mouse snoring and if they think he is asleep.]

TELL THE CHILDREN:

"Okay, we need to get the food ready for Mouse to eat." *[Bring out the TURNIP and hold it up.]* "Do you remember what food this is?" (TURNIP)

"What color is it?" *[Point to the body of the turnip.]* (WHITE)

[Lay the turnip on the table.]

Continue along the same lines with each different food.

Tell the children that Mouse will need help with his food, and they will all get to help him. Show them the bag/jar of food pieces.

You have various options for utilizing the food pieces: it really depends on how many children are in the group, how much time you have for the activity, and what your goals are!

Each child takes just one piece out of the bag/jar.

Each child takes two pieces from the bag/jar (one to feed Mouse and one to put on him).

Each child may take all of the colors (if you do this, though, prepackage the pieces in little sets or the distribution will take forever!).

Or try any other variation that works well for your group.

Again, make sure that one or two food pieces of each color are set aside for the presenter so that Mouse is sure to end up with all of the colors stuck to him by the end.

Please note: If you have a large audience and it would be too wild to distribute the pieces, you can feed Mouse the food pieces yourself, engaging the children by having them call out what color and food the piece represents as you do so. Have Mouse show them that he "swallowed" the piece, and then put a second piece somewhere on him to make him "messy," and so on with all of the colors.

TELL THE CHILDREN:

"We had better wake Mouse up so he can come back and eat his lunch! Maybe if we say 'Wake up, Mouse' all together, that will wake him up. Let's count to three, and then call him. *[Hold up your fingers as you are counting.]* One, two, three . . . 'Wake up, Mouse!' *[Nothing happens—you may want to snore again to show that Mouse is still sleeping.]* Did you hear him snoring? I guess we need to call him a little bit louder! Okay, one, two, three . . . 'Wake up, Mouse!'"

[Slip Mouse puppet onto your hand and bring him out yawning and covering his mouth with his rod hand, rubbing his eyes, and so forth, to sit on your lap.]

TO MOUSE: "Did you have a good nap, Mouse? *[Mouse nods and yawns again.]* Are you going to be hungry enough to eat some lunch in a minute or two? *[Mouse perks up and looks excited and sniffs.]* Good. Just a minute and we'll get started."

TELL THE CHILDREN:

"We are going to tell the story again with our Mouse puppet and with the bites of food that we have for him. In the story, Mouse eats lots of food, and he also gets very messy from his food, doesn't he? When we get to the part of the story that has your food, you will get to bring it up here and give it to Mouse to help him. You can either let him eat it, like this *(hold "food" piece up in your fingers—Mouse puppet sniffs it, then eats it gently and delicately so the children aren't afraid he'll bite them when it's their turn)*, or you can stick it on him to make him messy, like this. *(Stick piece on Mouse.)* I will help you know when it's your turn if you need help. Mouse, are you ready for the story? *(Mouse nods vigorously.)* Are you all ready? *(Look questioningly at audience and nod.)* Okay!"

SCRIPT

Lunch by Denise Fleming

Mouse was very hungry.

[Mouse nods vigorously and pats his tummy with rod hand.]

He was so hungry, he ate a crisp WHITE— *[hold up turnip in your free hand]* TURNIP,

[Invite the children with white turnip pieces to come up to the front of the room by Mouse, either one at a time or as a group; ask them individually if they want to feed him their piece or if it makes Mouse messy and they want to stick it to his fur; children sit back down after their turn; if nobody sticks their food piece on Mouse, put one or two of the white pieces you had set aside onto him yourself.]

tasty ORANGE—CARROTS,

[Continue as above for each fruit and vegetable.]

sweet YELLOW—CORN,

tender GREEN—PEAS,

tart BLUE—BERRIES,

sour PURPLE—GRAPES,

shiny RED—APPLES,

and juicy PINK—WATERMELON,

crunchy BLACK SEEDS and all.

Then *[Mouse puppet yawns, covers his mouth/yawn with his rod hand],* he took a nap *[snuggle Mouse in your arms, with his face turned a little away from the audience so his eyes don't show as being open; make him snore loudly]* until . . .

. . . dinnertime!

[Mouse sits up and looks around, patting his tummy; Mouse then sniffs toward audience and toward the table of food.]

Possible Conclusion

"Oh, Mouse! You just ate! I can't believe you are hungry already! Let's see if we can remember what you had for lunch."

[Point to the various food pieces of color on Mouse; have the audience help you name the food and color of each. Mouse looks at himself as you talk about the colors, as if surprised that he is so messy. Show the children the last page of the book again, where all of the colors that Mouse got on himself are shown.]

"Mouse, it's not quite dinnertime yet—I'm afraid you'll have to wait a little while! Why don't you take another nap? You look sleepy! *[Mouse yawns, covers his mouth.]* Okay, tell everyone good-bye!"

[Mouse waves good-bye to the audience and blows them kisses; put him away in the box or behind the table.]

Script adapted by Kimberly K. Faurot, *Books in Bloom: Creative Patterns and Props That Bring Stories to Life* (ALA, 2003).

PATTERN INSTRUCTIONS

Hand Puppets (Sample Pattern)

Lunch by Denise Fleming

Patterns

Patterns designed by Kimberly Faurot

Estimated difficulty

Expert: The successful creation of this prop requires a strong fundamental knowledge of machine sewing, sewing terminology and techniques, and basic craft techniques.

Estimated construction time

40 hours

Estimated cost for supplies

$150 or less (depends largely upon your fabric choices)

You Will Need These Tools

- ballpoint pen
- Fray Check
- small sharp-pointed scissors
- fabric shears
- pinking shears
- straight pins
- hand-sewing needle
- embroidery needle
- tapestry needle
- crochet hook size I (or size required to crochet to gauge)
- steam iron and thin cloth for fusing interfacing
- sewing machine
- candle and matches/lighter (for *heat fusing* fabric edges)
- wire cutters (for clipping pipe cleaners and cable ties)
- heavy-duty wire cutters (for clipping wire wrist rod)
- needle nose pliers
- regular pliers
- hammer
- 8 1/2" × 11" square of noncorrugated cardboard (for hammering rivets)

You Will Need These Supplies

MISCELLANEOUS SUPPLIES

- black and white checkered fabric/tablecloth
- Ziploc bag or transparent plastic container for the food pieces
- approximately 20 bags of polyester fiberfill stuffing (8-oz. bags)

SUPPLIES TO MAKE THE MOUSE PUPPET

Note: The mouse puppet's body should be made from a Velcro-compatible fabric that holds its shape fairly well. Ideal fabric is "Show-a-Tale Fabric," also termed "Hook-and-Loop Fabric," currently available from Book Props (*see* chapter 10). *Please note that the company sells the fabric in 1-yard increments only.* The mouse's tooth and mouth interior should be made from fabric that is somewhat stiff and that is *not* Velcro-compatible. "Versatile Vinyl" fabric (recommended for the tooth as well as for several of the giant soft sculpture food pieces), from Vitex, is available through Hancock Fabrics stores. Flannel-backed vinyl is recommended for the mouth interior. Please also note that if you use fabrics for the mouse puppet other than those recommended here, it may be necessary to interface the pieces.

1/3 yard slate grey "Show-a-Tale Fabric," 60" wide
1/3 yard silver grey (not platinum grey) "Show-a-Tale Fabric," 60" wide
1/4 yard desert rose pink "Show-a-Tale Fabric," 60" wide
1/8 yard flame red "Show-a-Tale Fabric," 60" wide
3 inches shiny white "Versatile Vinyl" fabric
1/3 yard grey cotton lining fabric, 45" wide
5 inches raspberry pink flannel-backed vinyl, 45" or 60" wide
thread: slate grey, silver grey, desert pink, raspberry pink, white
2 "solid black eyes" (size 18 mm)
polyester fiberfill stuffing
small cable tie or zip tie (grey if available)
black wire hand rod (black wire coat hanger or Axtell Expressions' wire wrist rod)

SUPPLIES TO MAKE THE GIANT SOFT SCULPTURE FOOD AND ACCOMPANYING FOOD PIECES

TURNIP (giant white turnip, white turnip pieces)

Note: If you use fabrics for the turnip other than those recommended here, it may be necessary to interface the pieces.

1/2 yard white "pack cloth" (backpack fabric), 60" wide
1/4 yard purple "pack cloth" (backpack fabric), 60" wide
1/4 yard dark green "flag fabric," 60" wide
thread: dark green, purple, white
polyester fiberfill stuffing
1 square white felt
2 1/4" length of 3/4" wide grey sew-on hook Velcro (cut into three 3/4" lengths)

CARROT (giant orange carrot, orange carrot pieces)

Note: If you use fabrics for the carrots other than those recommended here, it may be necessary to interface the pieces.

1/2 yard orange "pack cloth" (backpack fabric), 60" wide
1/4 yard light green "flag fabric," 60" wide

thread: light green, orange
polyester fiberfill stuffing
1 square orange felt
2 1/4" length of 3/4" wide grey sew-on hook Velcro (cut into three 3/4" lengths)

CORN (giant yellow corncob with husk, yellow corn kernel pieces)

2/3 yard husk green pinwale corduroy, 45" wide
1 1/3 yard fusible interfacing (heavyweight), 22" wide
bright yellow yarn (worsted weight; 4 oz.)
crochet hook size I
thread: husk green
polyester fiberfill stuffing
1 square yellow felt
3" yellow flannel-backed vinyl backing, 45" or 60" wide
2 1/4" length of 3/4" wide grey sew-on hook Velcro (cut into three 3/4" lengths)

PEAS and PEAPOD (giant green pea pod with peas, green pea pieces)

Note: If you use fabric for the peas other than that recommended here, it may be necessary to interface the pieces. "Versatile Vinyl" fabric is from Vitex and is available through Hancock Fabrics stores.

1/4 yard bright green "flag fabric" (pea pod), 60" wide
7/8 yard fusible interfacing (heavyweight), 22" wide
6 green glass seed beads
12" length of 1/4" wide flat elastic
1/4 yard shiny light green "Versatile Vinyl" or other pea fabric, 45" or 60" wide
thread: bright green, light green
polyester fiberfill stuffing
1 square light green felt
2 1/4" length of 3/4" wide grey sew-on hook Velcro (cut into three 3/4" lengths)

BLUEBERRIES (giant blueberries in bowl, blueberry pieces)

large transparent or translucent blue plastic bowl or other large bowl, 10" diameter
1/2 yard bright blue crushed panne fabric, 60" wide
1 yard fusible interfacing (featherweight/lightweight), 22" wide
6 navy blue buttons, size 1/2" for blueberry tops
6 navy blue buttons, size 7/16" for blueberry bottoms
thread: royal blue
polyester fiberfill stuffing
2 squares heather blue felt
2 1/4" length of 3/4" wide grey sew-on hook Velcro (cut into three 3/4" lengths)

GRAPES (giant bunch of purple grapes, purple grape pieces)

2/3 yard royal purple crushed panne fabric, 60" wide
1 2/3 yard fusible interfacing (featherweight/lightweight), 22" wide
9 metal eyelets (size large, two-part eyelets)
sandpaper appropriate for sanding metal surfaces
royal purple spray paint
18 brown pipe cleaners/chenille stems, 12" long
thread: royal purple
polyester fiberfill stuffing
1 square royal purple felt
2 1/4" length of 3/4" wide grey sew-on hook Velcro (cut into three 3/4" lengths)

APPLE (giant red apple, red apple pieces)

Note: If you use fabric for the apple other than that recommended here, it may be necessary to interface the pieces. "Versatile Vinyl" fabric is from Vitex and is available through Hancock Fabrics stores.

2/3 yard shiny bright red "Versatile Vinyl" fabric, 60" wide
1 metal eyelet (size large, two-part eyelet)
sandpaper appropriate for sanding metal surfaces
bright red spray paint
1 brown flower-shaped button, size 5/8" for apple bottom
3 yards red string or crochet cotton, medium weight
3 brown pipe cleaners/chenille stems, 12" long
thread: red
polyester fiberfill stuffing
1 square red felt
2 1/4" length of 3/4" wide grey sew-on hook Velcro (cut into three 3/4" lengths)

WATERMELON and SEEDS (giant pink watermelon, pink watermelon pieces, giant black watermelon seeds, black watermelon seed pieces)

Note: If you use fabric for the watermelon seeds other than that recommended here, it may be necessary to interface the pieces. "Versatile Vinyl" fabric is from Vitex and is available through Hancock Fabrics stores.

2/3 yard bright pink heavyweight fabric (denim weight), 60" wide
1/2 yard bright green heavyweight fabric (denim weight), 60" wide
1/3 yard white heavyweight fabric (denim weight), 45" wide
2 1/2 yards fusible interfacing (heavyweight), 22" wide
1/4 yard shiny black "Versatile Vinyl" fabric, 60" wide
thread: bright pink, white, bright green, black
polyester fiberfill stuffing
1 square bright pink felt
1 square black felt
4 1/2" length of 3/4" wide grey sew-on hook Velcro (cut into six 3/4" lengths)

Directions

How to Make the Mouse Puppet

Notes: If you use fabric for the mouse puppet other than that recommended here, it may be necessary to interface the pieces.

If you have difficulty moving vinyl fabric through your sewing machine, put tissue paper under the fabric so it will slide along more easily. After stitching the seam, simply tear away the tissue paper.

Step 1

Photocopy patterns *at sizes specified.* (*See* chapter 2, "Enlarging the Patterns in This Book.") Cut out all of the photocopied patterns along the outside of the pattern outlines.

Step 2

Cut out all fabric pieces as specified on the patterns. *Make sure to cut out fabric with right sides together when cutting out two or more pieces so that the pieces will be mirror images of each other.*

Step 3

On the fabric pieces listed below, measure a 1/4" seam allowance line along the edges specified. Using a ballpoint pen, lightly draw the line on the *wrong* side of the fabric. These seams will be sewn by hand, and having the seam allowance guide will help you when you reach that point.

MOUSE BODY FRONT—neck edge

MOUSE LOWER JAW—long straight neck edge, short straight sides

MOUSE FACE SIDES—loop of nose on both sides of the face, long straight edge that will connect with the lower jaw

MOUSE FACE NOSE-TO-MOUTH JOINING STRIP—straight sides between tooth placement and nose end

Step 4

Mark the center points of:

MOUSE FACE LINING
MOUSE FACE TOP
MOUSE BODY LINING FRONT
MOUSE LOWER JAW

Step 5

Position the MOUSE HANDS Fingers template on the *wrong* side of one side each of the sets of hands. The top fingers (specified on the pattern) should end up on top, and the two finished hands should be mirror images of each other. Trace the template lightly with a ballpoint pen.

Step 6

Position the MOUSE FOOT SOLE Toes template on the *wrong* side of each MOUSE FOOT SOLE. The outer foot edge should end up on the outside, and the inner foot edge should end up on the inside (these are specified on the pattern); the two soles should be mirror images of each other. Trace the template lightly with a ballpoint pen.

Step 7

Right sides together, pin MOUSE HANDS to MOUSE ARMS at the wrists. Position the hands so that they will match up when you sew the arms together. The two silver grey arms with hands should be mirror opposites of each other; each will be stitched to one of the slate grey arms with hands. Stitch all four wrist seams with desert rose pink thread.

Step 8

Right sides together, pin arm/hand units together. Each arm should be silver grey on one side and slate grey on the other side. Stitch around hand and fingers along the template lines using desert rose pink thread.

Step 9

Stitch sides of arm seams with slate grey thread. Seam allowance is 1/4". Trim and clip arm and hand seams. Turn arm/hand units inside out and stuff firmly with polyester fiberfill. Set arm/hand units aside.

Step 10

Right sides together, pin each MOUSE FRONT HAUNCH to one side of the MOUSE BODY FRONT. Stitch with silver grey thread. Seam allowance is 1/4". Trim seams.

Step 11

Right sides together, pin the FEET separately to the FRONT HAUNCHES and the BODY BACK haunches at the ankles. Stitch all four ankle seams with desert rose pink thread.

Step 12

Right sides together, pin MOUSE TAIL together. Stitch around tail with desert rose pink thread. Seam allowance is 1/4". Trim seam. Turn tail right side out and stuff firmly with polyester fiberfill.

Step 13

Right sides together, pin the two MOUSE BODY BACK halves together. Position the MOUSE TAIL in the seam as shown on the pattern. Stitch center back seam with slate grey thread. Seam allowance is 1/4". Trim and clip seam. Fold the neck edge under 1/4"; topstitch 1/8" in from the edge using slate grey thread.

Step 14

Right sides together, pin each half of the MOUSE BODY FRONT to the MOUSE BODY BACK at the side seams, including the entire side seam as well as the seams beneath the haunches. Position the arms in the seam as shown on the pattern, pointing inward. The silver grey side of the arms should be facing the silver grey body front so that they turn out correctly. Stitch the two side seams using slate grey thread, stopping at the ankle where the pink fabric begins. Stitch the two seams beneath the haunches with slate grey thread, stopping at the ankle where the pink fabric begins. Seam allowance is 1/4". The two halves of the MOUSE BODY FRONT will extend 1/4" higher at the neck than the MOUSE BODY BACK because of the 1/4" hem already taken along the back.

Step 15

Stitch the top of the foot and along the back of the ankle using desert rose pink thread. Make sure to stop at the back of the ankle at the point shown on the pattern. Seam allowance is 1/4". Trim and clip seams.

Step 16

Right sides together, pin each MOUSE FOOT SOLE to its respective MOUSE FOOT. Stitch around foot and toes along the template lines using desert rose pink thread. If you start at the heel of the foot, you can position the ankle out of the way and then shift it over when you get around to the back again. Seam allowance is 1/4". Trim and clip seams.

Step 17

Right sides together, pin the two MOUSE BODY FRONT halves together. Stitch center front seam with silver grey thread. Seam allowance is 1/4". Trim and clip seam.

Step 18

Turn body and feet right side out.

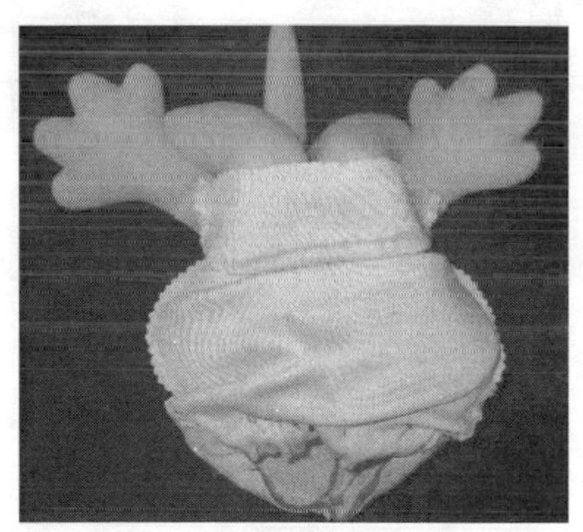

Figure 9-1

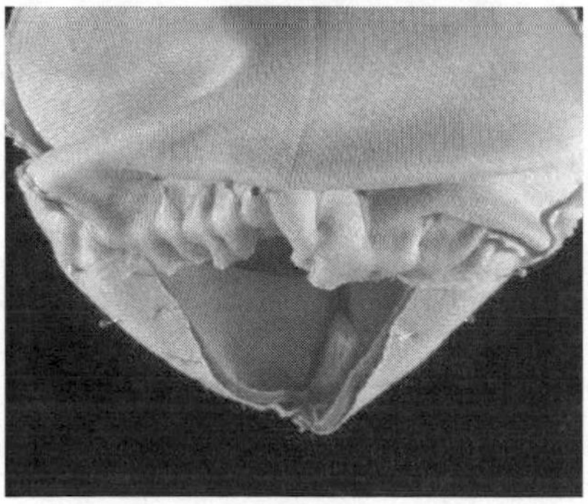

Step 19

Right sides together, pin together the two MOUSE BODY LINING BACK halves. Stitch center back seam with silver grey thread. Right sides together, pin the MOUSE BODY LINING FRONT to the MOUSE BODY LINING BACK. Stitch the side seams with silver grey thread. Seam allowance is 1/4". Trim seams.

Step 20

The body lining sleeve should still be turned inside out. Slip the body lining sleeve over the mouse's body and feet so that the body lining bottom is lined up with the mouse's body bottom. (*See* figure 9-1.)

Pin the lining to the body around the bottom, matching up the center back and side seams. (*See* figure 9-2.)

Stitch around the bottom, using silver grey thread.

Figure 9-2

Step 21

Slide body lining sleeve back down over the mouse and pull it up into the middle of the mouse's body. Seam allowances should now all be hidden, except for at the neck.

Step 22

Stuff the mouse's feet, ankles, and haunches firmly with polyester fiberfill. Take special care stuffing the ankles, as there is a tendency for narrow areas such as those to bend and become weak. (Taking several small stitches by hand through the ankle and stuffing can also help keep the fiberfill in place.)

Stuff the mouse's back and tummy lightly with polyester fiberfill to keep them pouched out. Note that the amount of fiberfill with which you stuff the puppet's torso will affect how much room you have for the puppeteer's hand.

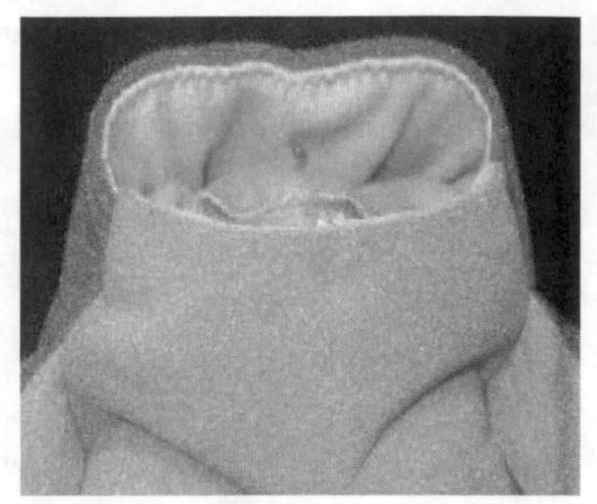

Figure 9-3

Step 23

Turn under a 1/4" seam allowance across the MOUSE BODY LINING BACK and hand stitch it with slate grey thread along the seam already taken in the MOUSE BODY BACK. (*See* figure 9-3.)

Set mouse body aside. (*See* figure 9-4.)

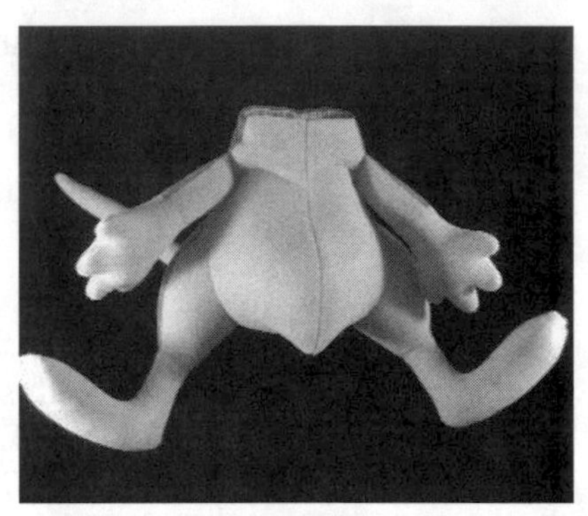

Figure 9-4

Step 24

Right sides together, pin MOUSE EARS together. Stitch around top and sides with slate grey thread. Seam allowance is 1/4". Trim seams. Turn EARS right side out and set them aside.

Step 25

Right sides together, pin the two MOUSE BACK OF HEAD halves together. Stitch center back seam with slate grey thread. Seam allowance is 1/4". Trim seam.

Step 26

Fold the marked edges of the MOUSE MOUTH TOP INTERIOR and the MOUSE MOUTH BOTTOM INTERIOR under 1/4" and top stitch 1/8" in from the edge using raspberry pink thread.

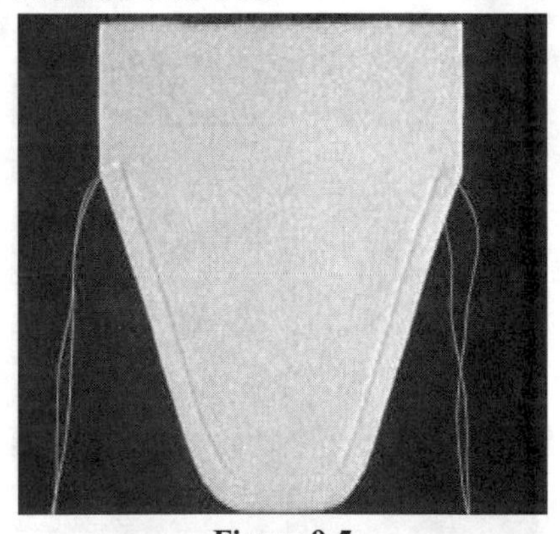

Figure 9-5

Step 27

Using silver grey thread, baste between the dots around the curved portion of the MOUSE LOWER JAW, as shown on the pattern and photograph. Seam allowance is 1/4". (*See* figure 9-5.)

Using the basting stitch, gather up the lower jaw just a little bit so that it matches up with the edges of the MOUSE MOUTH BOTTOM INTERIOR. Pin with right sides together. Stitch around the curved portion using silver grey thread; seam allowance is 1/4". Trim seam. Turn LOWER JAW/MOUTH BOTTOM INTERIOR right side out. (*See* figure 9-6.)

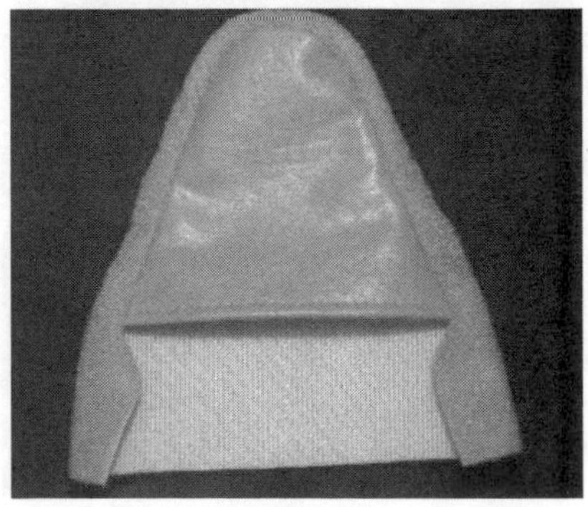

Figure 9-6

Step 28

Lay the MOUSE TOOTH pieces right sides together, and place one pin just along the top of the tooth where the pinholes won't show in the final tooth. Stitch around sides and bottom of tooth with white thread. Seam allowance is 1/4". Trim seam, making sure to clip the corners. Turn tooth right side out.

Step 29

Fold MOUSE FACE NOSE-TO-MOUTH JOINING STRIP with right sides together as shown on the pattern, and pin the MOUSE

TOOTH in the center of the fold. Stitch across fold with silver grey thread; seam allowance is 1/4".

Step 30

Right sides together, pin one of the red MOUSE NOSE pieces to the nose end of the MOUSE FACE NOSE-TO-MOUTH JOINING STRIP and stitch with red thread. Pin the other red MOUSE NOSE piece to the nose end of the MOUSE FACE TOP and stitch with red thread. Seam allowance is 1/4". Trim seams.

Right sides together, pin the MOUSE NOSE pieces to each other and stitch with red thread. Seam allowance is 1/4". Trim seam.

Step 31

Right sides together, pin the MOUSE FACE SIDES to the MOUSE FACE TOP. Stitch with silver grey thread. Seam allowance is 1/4". Trim seams.

Step 32

Right sides together, pin the MOUSE MOUTH TOP INTERIOR narrow end to the mouth end of the MOUSE FACE NOSE-TO-MOUTH JOINING STRIP. Stitch across the narrow end with silver grey thread; seam allowance is 1/4". Trim seam. (*See* figure 9-7, wrong side of face-to-mouth unit, and figure 9-8, right side of face-to-mouth unit.)

Step 33

Gather stitch the front (short) end of the MOUSE FACE LINING; seam allowance is 1/4". Pull up the gathers gently until the lining will match up to the front end of the MOUSE MOUTH TOP INTERIOR where it is connected to the MOUSE FACE NOSE-TO-MOUTH JOINING STRIP. Stitch the gathered edge of the lining *to the seam allowance* of the MOUTH TOP/JOINING STRIP seam. Seam allowance for the lining seam should be about 3/16". (*See* figure 9-9.)

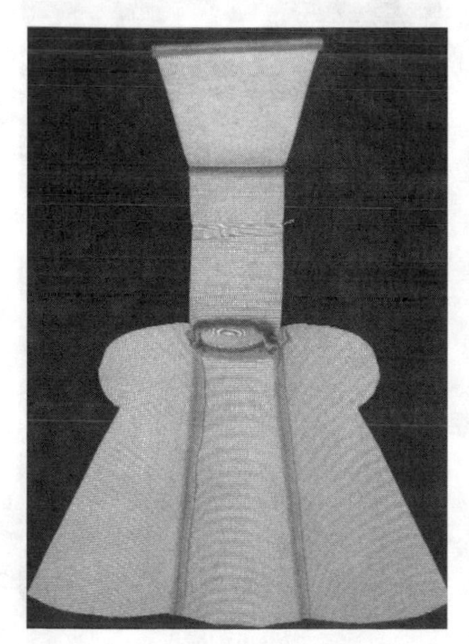

Figure 9-7

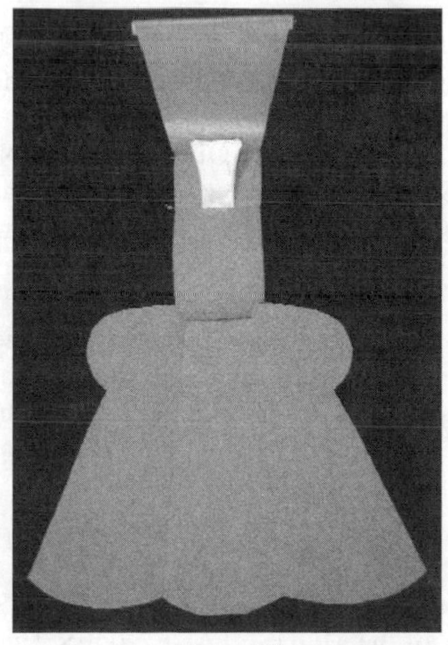

Figure 9-8

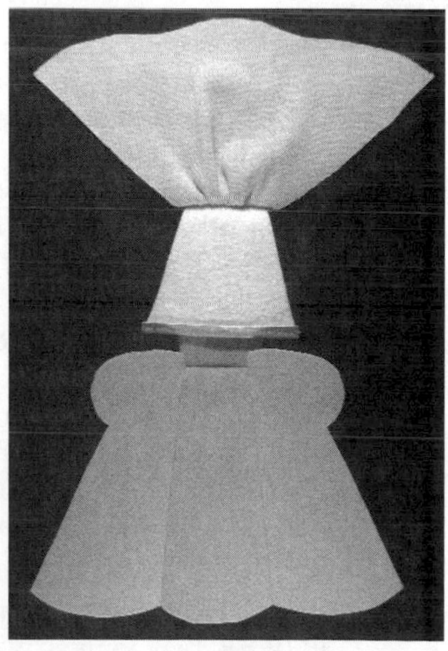

Figure 9-9

Step 34

Right sides together, pin the mouth edges of the two MOUSE FACE SIDES to the sides of the MOUSE MOUTH TOP INTERIOR and the sides of the MOUSE FACE LINING. The correct order of the fabric pieces should be MOUSE FACE on the bottom, then the MOUSE MOUTH TOP INTERIOR, then the MOUSE FACE LINING on top. Stitch through all three layers using silver grey thread. Seam allowance is 1/4". Carefully trim seams. Make sure to only stitch as far along the sides as the ends of the MOUSE MOUTH TOP INTERIOR; the extra MOUSE FACE SIDE and MOUSE FACE LINING fabric should still be loose past that point. (*See* figure 9-10.)

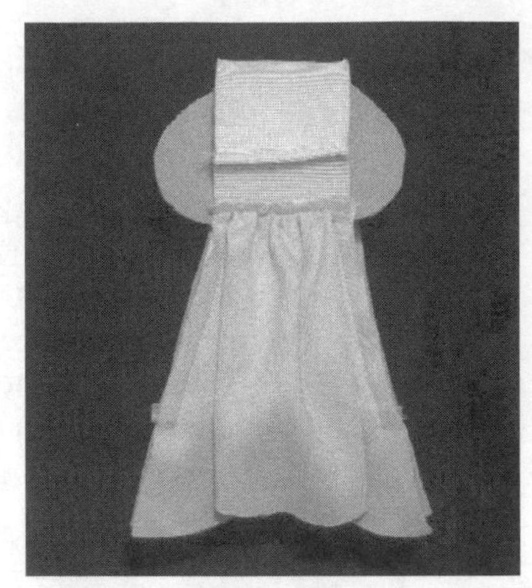

Figure 9-10

Step 35

Right sides together, pin the MOUSE FACE SIDES to the MOUSE FACE NOSE-TO-MOUTH JOINING STRIP where the nose pouches down. Hand stitch the nose seam on both sides using silver grey thread. Seam allowance is 1/4"; follow the ballpoint seam allowance markings you drew on the fabric pieces in step 3 for a guide. Trim seams. (*See* figure 9-11.)

Figure 9-11

Step 36

Turn head right side out and stuff semi-firmly with polyester fiberfill. Leave enough room for the puppeteer to comfortably slide his or her hand between the lining and the MOUSE MOUTH TOP INTERIOR. Mark EYE placement along the MOUSE FACE SIDES/MOUSE FACE TOP seams, and make a small hole in the fabric for the eye shanks just *above* the seams. Insert the 18 mm solid black EYES and firmly affix the EYE backs. (*See* figure 9-12.)

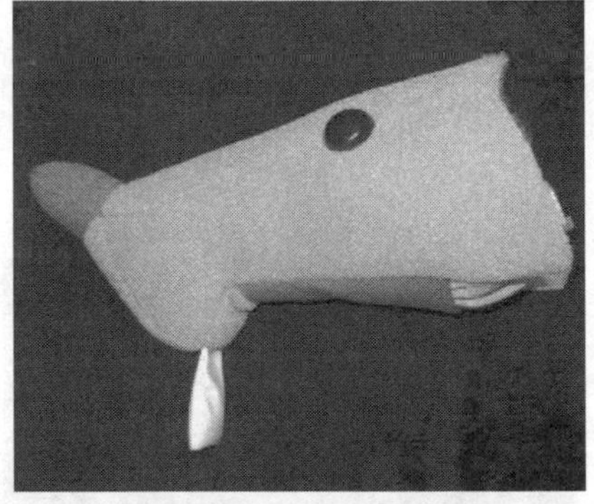

Figure 9-12

Step 37

Right sides together, pin MOUSE BACK OF HEAD LINING center back seam. Stitch using silver grey thread; seam allowance is 1/4". Trim seam.

Right sides together, pin MOUSE BACK OF HEAD LINING to MOUSE FACE LINING. Stitch using silver grey thread. Please note that the MOUSE BACK OF HEAD LINING will extend down past the MOUSE FACE LINING on both sides. Seam allowance is 1/4". Trim seam.

Pin the MOUSE EARS to the MOUSE FACE TOP as specified on the pattern. Make sure to position them so the inside edges are pointing inward and the outside edges are pointing outward. Hand stitch the ears to the MOUSE FACE TOP using slate grey thread; seam allowance is 1/4". (*See* figure 9-13.)

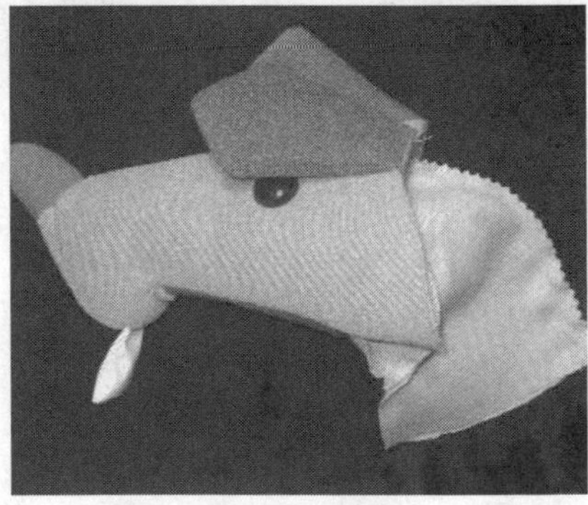

Figure 9-13

Step 38

Right sides together, pin the short side edges of the MOUSE LOWER JAW to the jaw edge of the MOUSE FACE SIDES. Hand

Figure 9-14

stitch using silver grey thread. Seam allowance is 1/4"; follow the ballpoint seam allowance markings you drew on the fabric pieces in step 3 for a guide. Make sure to connect the seams right up to the edges of the MOUSE MOUTH TOP and BOTTOM INTERIOR pieces so they will fit snugly together. Trim seams. (*See* figure 9-14.)

Step 39

Right sides together, pin the MOUSE BACK OF HEAD to the MOUSE FACE TOP and SIDES unit. The MOUSE EARS should point downward into the seam so they will turn out correctly. Please note that the MOUSE BACK OF HEAD will extend down past the MOUSE FACE on both sides. Machine stitch head seam using slate grey thread. Seam allowance is 1/4". Trim seam. Turn under the side edges of the remaining MOUSE BACK OF HEAD fabric that is hanging down on each side, and machine stitch using slate grey thread. (*See* figure 9-15.)

Figure 9-15

Step 40

Turn under the two raw jaw edges of the MOUSE FACE LINING and hand stitch them *to the seam allowance* of the jaw seams using silver grey thread.

Step 41

Turn under the side edges of the MOUSE BACK OF HEAD LINING fabric that is hanging down on each side of the mouse's head. Hand stitch to the side edges of the MOUSE BACK OF HEAD fabric through all layers using slate grey thread.

Step 42

Turn under the bottom edges of the MOUSE BACK OF HEAD fabric and the MOUSE BACK OF HEAD LINING together and pin. Machine stitch across the bottom BACK OF HEAD through all layers (fabric and lining) using slate grey thread.

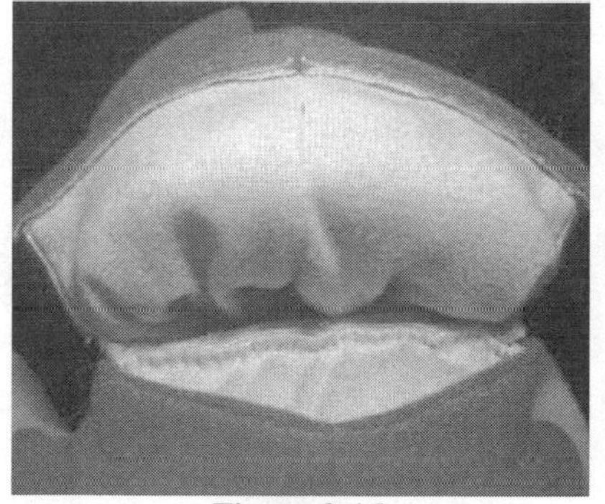
Figure 9-16

Step 43

Right sides together, pin the MOUSE LOWER JAW to the neck of the MOUSE BODY FRONT. Hand stitch with silver grey thread. Seam allowance is 1/4"; follow the ballpoint seam allowance markings you drew on the fabric pieces in step 3 for a guide. Stitching the seam may be slightly awkward, so proceed with patience.

Turn under the MOUSE BODY FRONT LINING 1/4" and hand stitch it *to the seam allowance* of the MOUSE LOWER JAW/MOUSE BODY FRONT seam using silver grey thread. (*See* figure 9-16.)

Step 44

Hand tack the MOUSE BACK OF HEAD side flaps that are hanging down on each side to the MOUSE BODY side seams using slate grey thread.

Step 45

Bend the black wire clothes hanger or black Axtell wire wrist rod into the shape shown in the diagram. It is important to twist the end of the rod into a "handle" shape for safety reasons, because the puppet will be used near small children. Attach the puppet wrist end of the rod to the puppet's wrist (at the pink/grey hand/arm seam demarcation) with a small clear-colored cable tie or zip tie.

See figure 9-17, finished mouse puppet.

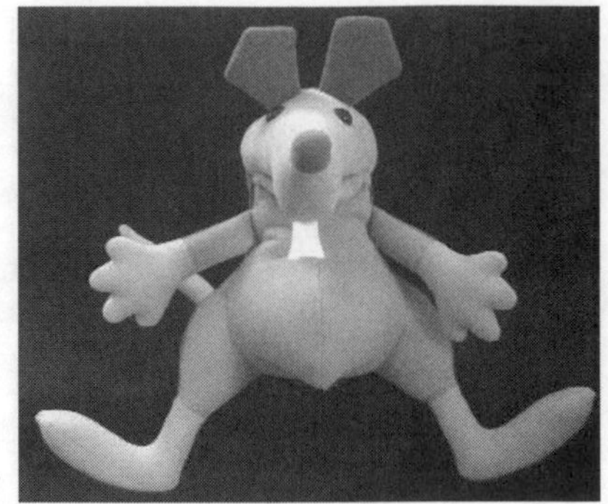

Figure 9-17

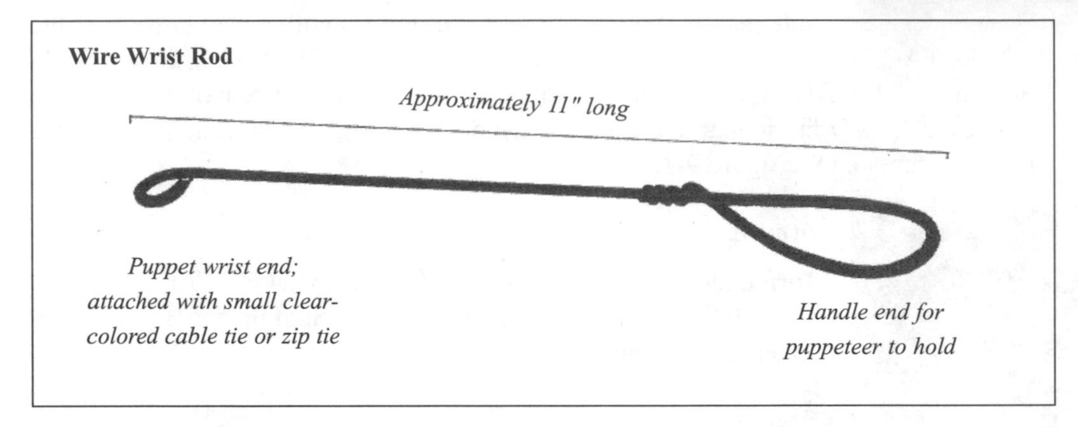

How to Make the Giant Soft Sculpture Food and Accompanying Food Pieces

General Step 1

Photocopy patterns *at sizes specified*. (*See* chapter 2, "Enlarging the Patterns in This Book.") Cut out all of the photocopied patterns along the outside of the pattern outlines.

General Step 2

Lay the cut-out paper patterns onto the designated fabrics and interfacing and pin. Cut out all fabric and interfacing pieces, as specified on the patterns. *Make sure to cut out fabric with right sides together when cutting out two or more pieces so that the pieces will be mirror images of each other.*

General Step 3

Interface all of the pieces that need interfacing.

Notes: For directions on how to use *heat fusion, see* chapter 2, "Terms and Techniques."

For directions on how to *close stitch* the finished soft sculpture pieces, *see* chapter 2, "Terms and Techniques."

If you use fabrics other than those recommended in the soft sculpture food and food pieces supplies list, it may be necessary to interface the pieces.

If you have difficulty moving vinyl fabric through your sewing machine, put tissue paper under the fabric so it will slide along more easily. After stitching the seam, simply tear away the tissue paper.

GIANT WHITE TURNIP

Step 1

With a lighted candle, carefully *heat fuse* around the edges of the three dark green turnip leaves so they will not fray.

Step 2

Fold the bottoms of two of the TURNIP LEAVES lengthwise and pin; the other leaf will remain flat. The flat leaf will be in the center. Pin one of the folded leaves on one side of the flat leaf and the second folded leaf on the other side of the flat leaf. They should be positioned opposite of each other, with their outer edges lined up with those of the center flat leaf. Stitch across the bottom edge of the leaves with dark green thread to secure them. Seam allowance is 1/4". (*See* figure 9-18.)

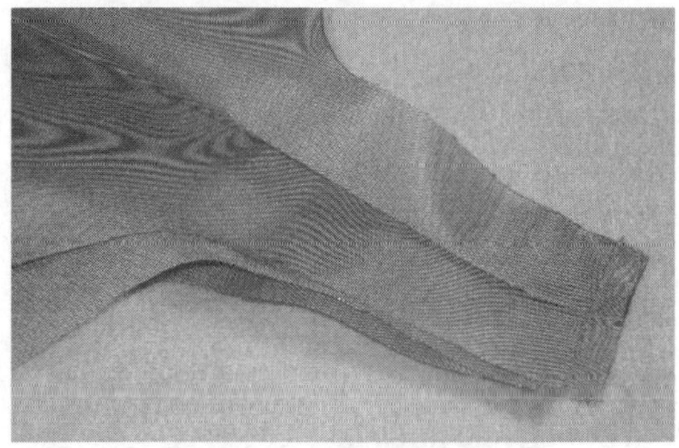

Figure 9-18

Step 3

Fold the purple TURNIP TOP in half, right (nonshiny, noncoated) sides together, as shown on the pattern guideline. Slide the stitched edge of the set of TURNIP LEAVES between the TURNIP TOP layers so the leaves are in the center with their bottom edge along the TURNIP TOP center fold. With purple thread, stitch across the folded center as shown on the TURNIP TOP pattern. Seam allowance is 1/2".

Step 4

The TURNIP BODY is made from six panels.

Right (nonshiny, noncoated) sides together, pin two panels along one side and stitch with white thread. Seam allowance is 1/4". Stitch the next two panels together and then the final two panels together in the same way.

Open up these three double-panel sets and pin, right sides together. Stitch with white thread. Leave a 3 1/2" opening along the middle of one side (so that you will be able to turn the turnip right side out and stuff it). Trim seams.

Step 5

Right sides together and green leaves pointing down into the white turnip casing, pin the purple TURNIP TOP to the white TURNIP BODY all around; stitch with purple thread. Seam allowance is 1/4". Trim seam.

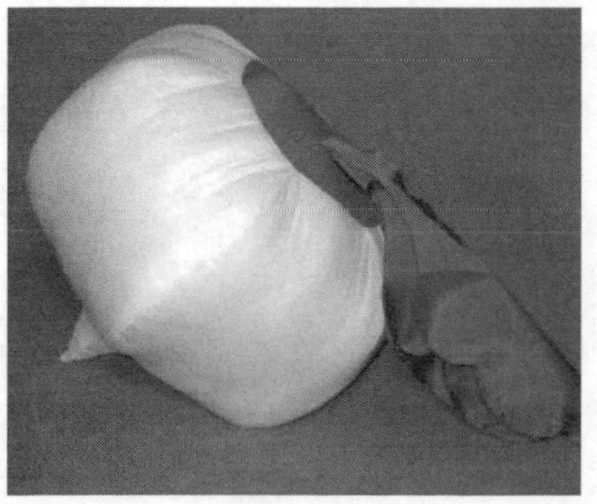

Figure 9-19

Step 6

With a lighted candle, carefully seal any cut seams that seem likely to fray with *heat fusion.*

Step 7

Turn turnip right side out; stuff with polyester fiberfill until firm. Stitch opening closed using white thread. (*See* figure 9-19, finished turnip.)

TWO GIANT ORANGE CARROTS

Step 1

With a lighted candle, carefully *heat fuse* around the edges of the six light green carrot fronds so they will not fray.

Step 2

Fold the bottoms of four of the CARROT FRONDS lengthwise and pin; the other two fronds will remain flat. For each carrot, the flat frond will be in the center. Pin one of the folded fronds on one side of each flat frond and a second folded frond on the other side of the flat frond. They should be positioned opposite of each other, with their outer edges lined up with those of the center flat fronds. Stitch across the bottom edge of the fronds with light green thread to secure them. Seam allowance is 1/4".

Step 3

Fold the two orange CARROT TOPS in half, right (nonshiny, noncoated) sides together, as shown on the pattern guideline. Slide the stitched edge of each set of CARROT FRONDS between the CARROT TOP layers so the fronds are in the center with their bottom edge along the CARROT TOP center fold. With orange thread, stitch across the folded centers as shown on the carrot top pattern. Seam allowance is 1/2".

Step 4

Baste a gathering stitch around the edge of the carrot tops, 1/4" in from the edge. This will help ease the tops onto the carrot bottoms later on.

Step 5

Right (nonshiny, noncoated) sides together, stitch small horizontal tucks along the CARROT BODIES with orange thread. (Fold carrot fabric over, right sides together, and stitch a short seam. The beginning and end of thc scams should bc at the very edges of the fold; the inner part of the seam should be 1/4" or so in from the fold.) This will help to shape the carrot bodies and give them ridges like a real carrot. (*See* figure 9-20, wrong side of fabric tucks, and figure 9-21, right side of fabric tucks.)

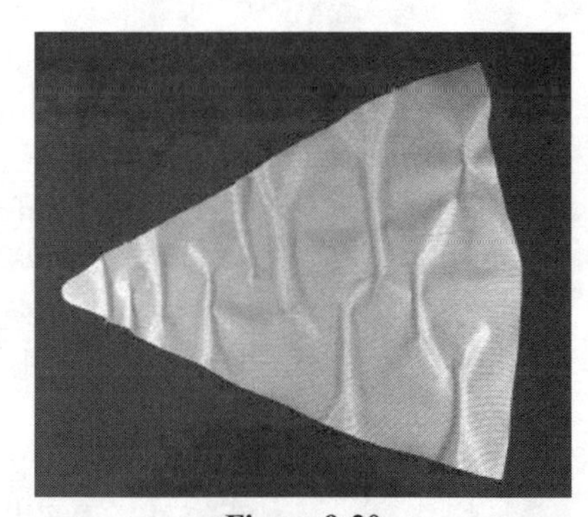

Figure 9-20

Step 6

Right sides together, stitch edge of carrots using orange thread. Leave a 3" opening along the side (about 3 1/2" down from the top of the carrot), so that you can turn the carrots right side out later on. Trim seams.

Step 7

Gather the CARROT TOPS slightly so they will ease successfully onto the CARROT BOTTOMS. Right sides together and green leaves pointing down into the carrot casings, pin the orange CARROT TOPS to the CARROT BOTTOMS all around; stitch with orange thread. Seam allowance is 1/4". Trim seams.

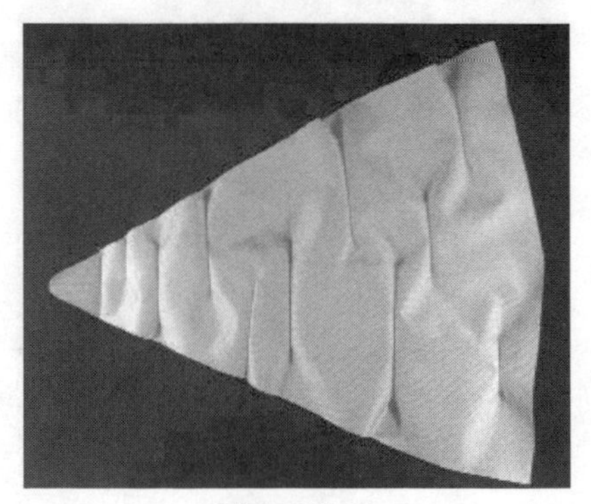

Figure 9-21

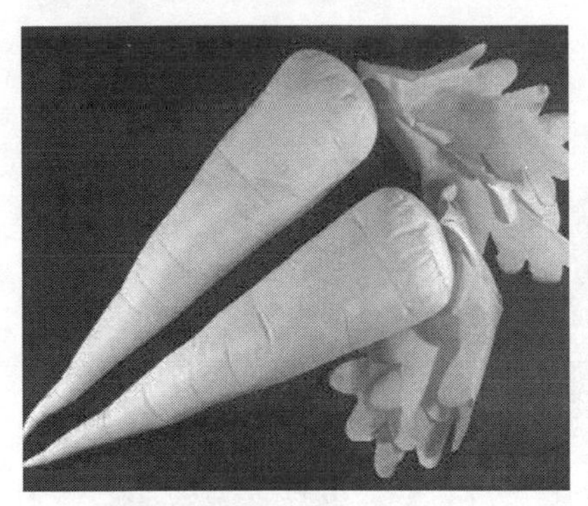

Figure 9-22

Step 8

With a lighted candle, carefully seal any cut seams that seem likely to fray with *heat fusion.*

Step 9

Turn carrots right side out; stuff with polyester fiberfill until firm. Stitch openings closed using orange thread. (*See* figure 9-22, finished carrots.)

GIANT YELLOW CORNCOB WITH HUSK

Corncob

Materials: Aluminum crochet hook size I or size required to crochet to gauge; tapestry needle; worsted weight yarn, bright yellow

Measurements: The finished crocheted and stuffed corncob should measure approximately 20" long, and it should be 20" around in circumference at its widest point, approximately halfway down the cob.

Abbreviations: sc = single crochet

Gauge: 7 sc = 2"; 7 rows = 2" in sc rounds

Directions

Begin at tip of corncob. With yellow yarn, chain 4. Join with slip stitch to form ring.

Round 1: Work 6 sc in ring. Do not join rounds, but mark beginning of rounds.

Round 2: Work 2 sc in each sc around—12 sc.

Round 3: Sc in first sc, 2 sc in next sc, (sc in next sc, 2 sc in next sc, and so on)—18 sc.

Round 4: Repeat round 3—27 sc.

Round 5: Sc in first 2 sc, 2 sc in next sc, (sc in next 2 sc, 2 sc in next sc, and so on)—36 sc.

Round 6: Sc in each sc around—36 sc.

Rounds 7 through 11: Repeat round 6—36 sc.

Round 12: Repeat round 5—48 sc.

Rounds 13 through 59 (or until corncob casing measures 20" long): Repeat round 6—48 sc.

Round 60: Sc in first 2 sc, decrease 1 sc over next 2 sc, (sc in next 2 sc, decrease 1 sc over next 2 sc, and so on)—36 sc.

Round 61: Repeat round 60—27 sc.

Turn corncob casing inside out so it appears "kernel-like." Stuff firmly with polyester fiberfill; the corncob should measure approximately 20" around in circumference at the widest point, approximately halfway down the cob.

Single crochet the corncob bottom closed in quickly decreasing stitches:

Round 62: Decrease 1 sc over each 2 sc, all the way around (include the first stitch of the next round)—14 sc.

Round 63: Repeat round 62—7 sc.

Round 64: Repeat round 62—3 sc.

Fasten yarn off and finish closing bottom using the tapestry needle.

The bottom will not show on the finished corncob.

If the finished corncob seems too rounded at its tip (compare to the corncob in *Lunch*), thread a tapestry needle with a length of the yellow yarn and weave a running gather stitch around the top approximately 1 1/2" down (just below Row 5) from the tip. Pull stitches slightly taut and tie off; weave the yarn ends through the crochet work. This gather stitch will pull the tip in a bit to resemble the *Lunch* illustrations more closely. (*See* figure 9-23, finished corncob before husk is added.)

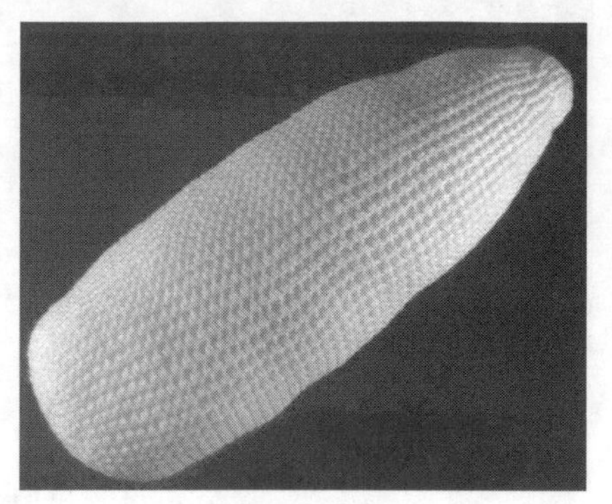

Figure 9-23

Husk

Notes: All four CORN HUSK pieces should be interfaced with heavyweight fusible interfacing.

Cut two of the CORN HUSK TOP PART pieces along the outer cutting line and two along the inner jagged cutting line.

Step 1

Right sides together, stitch the two darts near the bottom of each of the four individual CORN HUSK pieces.

Step 2

Lay the matching CORN HUSK pieces right sides together and pin. Stitch around the husk halves as shown on the patterns, using husk green thread. Seam allowance is 1/4". Leave the very bottom tips open on both halves as shown on the pattern so that you will be able to turn the husks right side out. Trim and clip seams. Turn both halves right side out; press with steam iron.

Figure 9-24

Step 3

Lay the two CORN HUSK halves together and pin at the bottom tip. Stitch the tip along the sides and bottom. Seam allowance is 1/4". Trim seams. Turn tip right side out and stuff firmly with polyester fiberfill. The corncob will rest on top of the stuffing.

Step 4

Place the corncob into the CORN HUSK casing, resting it on the stuffing in the tip. Pin the husk leaves to the corn. Hand stitch the husk to the corncob with husk green thread, arranging the leaves as shown for visual interest.

The finished length of the corncob and husk together should be approximately 25". (*See* figure 9-24, finished corncob with husk, side 1, and figure 9-25, finished corncob with husk, side 2.)

Figure 9-25

Figure 9-26

THREE GIANT GREEN PEAS AND PEAPOD

Peas

Step 1

Each PEA is made from four panels.

Right sides together, pin two panels along one side and stitch with light green thread. Seam allowance is 1/4". Stitch the other two panels together in the same way. Open up these two double-panel sets and pin, right sides together. Stitch with light green thread. Leave a 1 1/4" opening along the middle of one side (so that you will be able to turn the pea right side out and stuff it). Trim seams.

Repeat above instructions for two more peas.

Turn peas right side out; stuff with polyester fiberfill until firm. Stitch the openings closed using light green thread. (*See* figure 9-26, finished peas before peapod is added.)

Peapod

Note: All four PEAPOD pieces should be interfaced with heavyweight fusible interfacing.

Step 1

Right sides together, stitch first one half of the PEAPOD together and then the other half of the PEAPOD together. Seam allowance is 1/4". Leave a 3" opening along the middle of the back side of each so that you will be able to turn the halves right side out. Trim seams. Turn both halves right side out; press with steam iron.

Step 2

Pin the two pod halves together, matching the edges. Using a hand-sewing or embroidery needle and doubled regular green thread, *basic blanket stitch* (*see* chapter 2, "Terms and Techniques") the two halves together. This will also serve to close the 3" openings along the back of the peapod halves. Stitch most of the way around the pod, leaving a 7 1/4" opening across the front of the pod as shown on the pattern.

Step 3

Right sides together, machine stitch around the PEAPOD VINE with bright green thread. Seam allowance is 1/4". With a lighted candle, carefully *heat fuse* around the "petal" edges at the bottom of the vine so they will not fray. Right sides still together, run a gathering stitch along one side of the vine only. Tie off and apply Fray Check to the thread ends at the vine tip, leaving the gather stitch thread ends at the petal tip as they are so you can pull them for gathering. Trim seams. Carefully seal all cut seams that seem likely to fray with *heat fusion.* Turn the vine right side out. Now pull on the gather stitch ends to gently gather one side of the vine. This should make the vine curl around. When it is curled as much as you like, securely tie off the gather stitch thread ends at the petal tip and dot with Fray Check.

Step 4

Position the petal tip over the pointier end of the PEAPOD (also designated on pattern) and pin. Machine stitch across several times at stitching line to hold the vine securely to the pod. Tie off threads, using a green glass seed bead on each side of the vine to hide the knots. (*See* figure 9-27.)

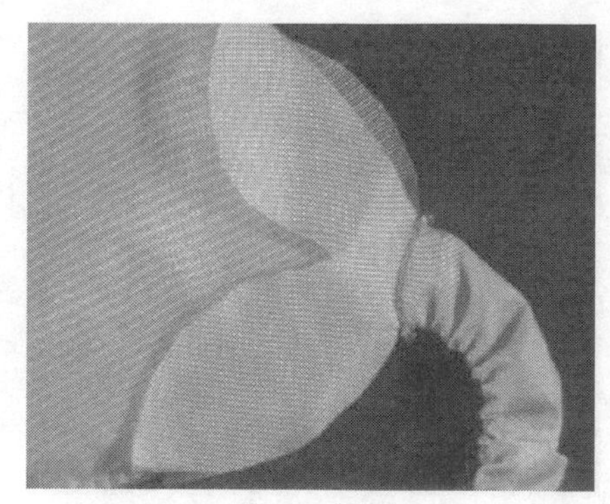

Figure 9-27

Step 5

Heat fuse around the edges of both PEA VINE LEAVES. Take a small tuck in the bottom of each leaf, and stitch each to the PEA VINE. Sew the small leaf to the vine tip and the larger leaf halfway down the vine, using a green glass seed bead on each side to anchor and hide the stitches. One bead will be positioned on the front of each leaf at the tuck; the other beads will be opposite on the back side of the vine. (*See* figure 9-28; *see* figure 9-29, finished peapod without peas.)

Place the three peas into the peapod so they are all peeking out. (*See* figure 9-30, finished peapod with peas.)

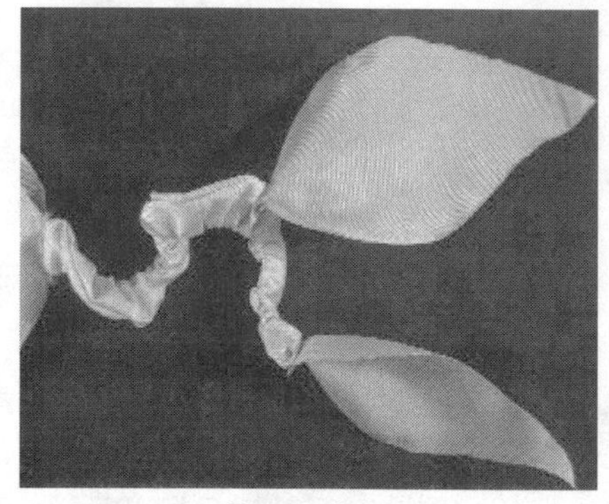

Figure 9-28

SIX GIANT BLUEBERRIES

Note: All of the blueberry crushed panne pieces should be interfaced with lightweight fusible interfacing.

Step 1

Each BLUEBERRY is made from four panels.

Right sides together, pin two panels along one side and stitch with blue thread. Seam allowance is 1/4". Stitch the other two panels together in the same way. Open up these two double-panel sets and pin, right sides together. Stitch with blue thread. Leave a 1 1/4" opening along the middle of one side (so that you will be able to turn the berry right side out and stuff it). Trim seams.

Repeat above instructions for five more blueberries.

Turn berries right side out, and stuff them with polyester fiberfill until firm. Stitch openings closed using blue thread.

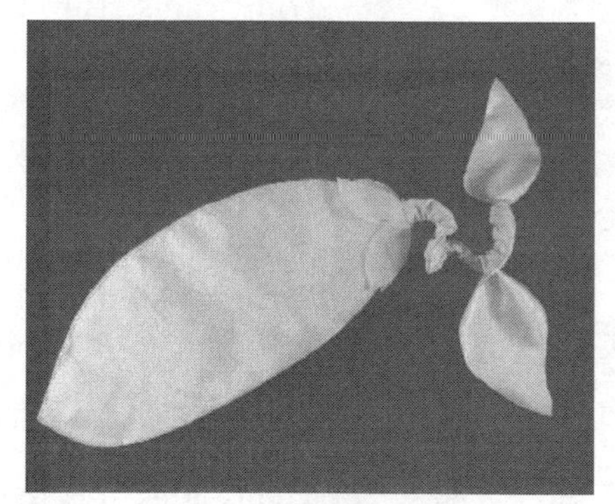

Figure 9-29

Step 2

Thread a hand-sewing needle with blue thread; knot the bottom two ends securely together. Make a loop through the holes of the smaller blue base button so that the thread is fastened to it securely. Position the small base button at the bottom center of the berry, and insert the needle into the berry until you are able to push it through the center top. Now position the larger blue button in the very center of the felt BERRY TOP, and stitch in place, plunging the needle back through the entire berry to take another stitch through the small button. Pull the thread firmly. This should help to shape and flatten the berry slightly while attaching the top and bottom "stems" at the same time. The felt BERRY TOP is connected only in its center, by the top button. Thread the needle through the entire berry one more time, ending at the top of the berry. Tie off thread and stitch through the felt to hide the thread ends and knots.

Repeat above instructions five more times.

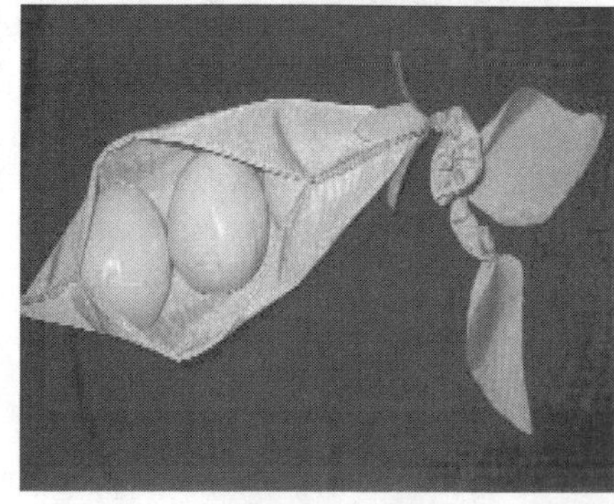

Figure 9-30

Figure 9-31

Step 3

Arrange six finished berries in large plastic blue bowl. (*See* figure 9-31, finished berries.)

NINE GIANT PURPLE GRAPES ON THE STEM

Note: All of the grape crushed panne pieces should be interfaced with lightweight fusible interfacing.

Step 1

Lightly sand the *tops* of nine large metal two-part eyelets with sandpaper so that spray paint will adhere to them. Lay the sanded eyelet tops right side up on a piece of poster board, and spray with royal purple gloss spray paint. Allow paint to dry completely.

Step 2

Each GRAPE is made from four panels.

Right sides together, pin two panels along one side and stitch with purple thread, making sure to stop a short distance in from the top end as shown on the pattern (you will need to insert the eyelet through that opening). Seam allowance is 1/4". Stitch the other two panels together in the same way.

Open up these two double-panel sets and pin, right sides together. Stitch with purple thread, again stopping a short distance in from the top end. Leave a 1 1/4" opening along the middle of one side (so that you will be able to turn the grape right side out and stuff it). Trim seams.

Repeat above instructions for eight more grapes.

Turn grapes right side out.

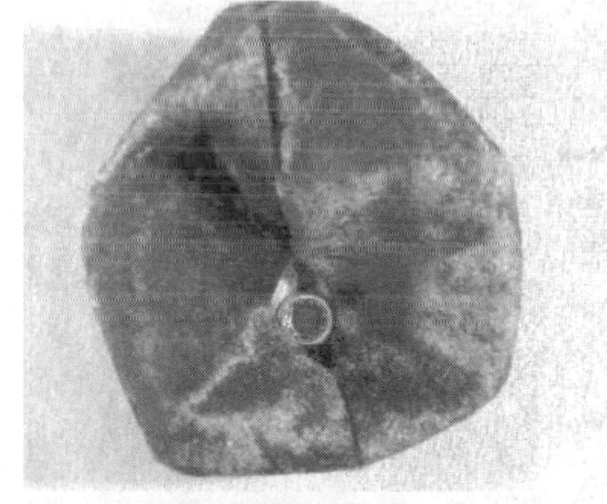

Figure 9-32

Step 3

For each grape, insert an eyelet through the narrow top opening so that the purple eyelet top will show when you are done. Turn eyelet upside down so the purple tops are face down on your eyelet-pounding cardboard. Hammer bottoms onto eyelets, following package instructions. Position the 1 1/4" side openings over the eyelets so you can successfully access the eyelets with the hammer. (*See* figure 9-32, underneath view of eyelet, and figure 9-33, top view of eyelet.)

Figure 9-33

Step 4

Tie three brown pipe cleaners/chenille stems in a knot at one end. Insert the three stems through the eyelet in one of the grapes so that the pipe cleaner lengths protrude and the knot is inside the grape. Braid the three pipe cleaners firmly together. Insert the end into another grape shell and knot the pipe cleaners.

Stuff both grapes with polyester fiberfill until firm. Stitch openings closed using purple thread. (The stuffing should hold the pipe cleaner knots firmly against the eyelets.)

Repeat above step three more times, so you have four sets of grapes connected by braided pipe cleaners.

Complete the ninth grape as if it would have an opposite, but just let its pipe cleaners protrude without connecting anywhere yet. (This ninth grape will be at the tip of the grape bunch.)

Step 5

Braid the ninth grape's pipe cleaners 3 1/2"; then connect two of the connected grape sets to the stem *by braiding them in.* Simply catch the center V of the double-grape stem in as you braid as shown in the diagram. After attaching the two sets, braid the three original pipe cleaners another 2 1/2". You will be close to running out of your end grape's pipe cleaner stems. At this point, braid three new pipe cleaners into the stem as the first three pipe cleaners run out (so you will have six stems for an inch or two). Braid 2" more; then connect the final two double-grape sets to the stem by braiding them in as you did the ones previously. Braid another 3 1/2"; then bend the pipe cleaner stems back downward and braid them over and around the existing braid to make the top of the stem thicker at that point. The tips of the pipe cleaners should end up right down near where the top sets of double-grape stems are connected to the main stem. Twist the pipe cleaner tips around and under with the needle nose pliers so they don't stick out and aren't sharp.

See figure 9-34, finished grapes.

Figure 9-34

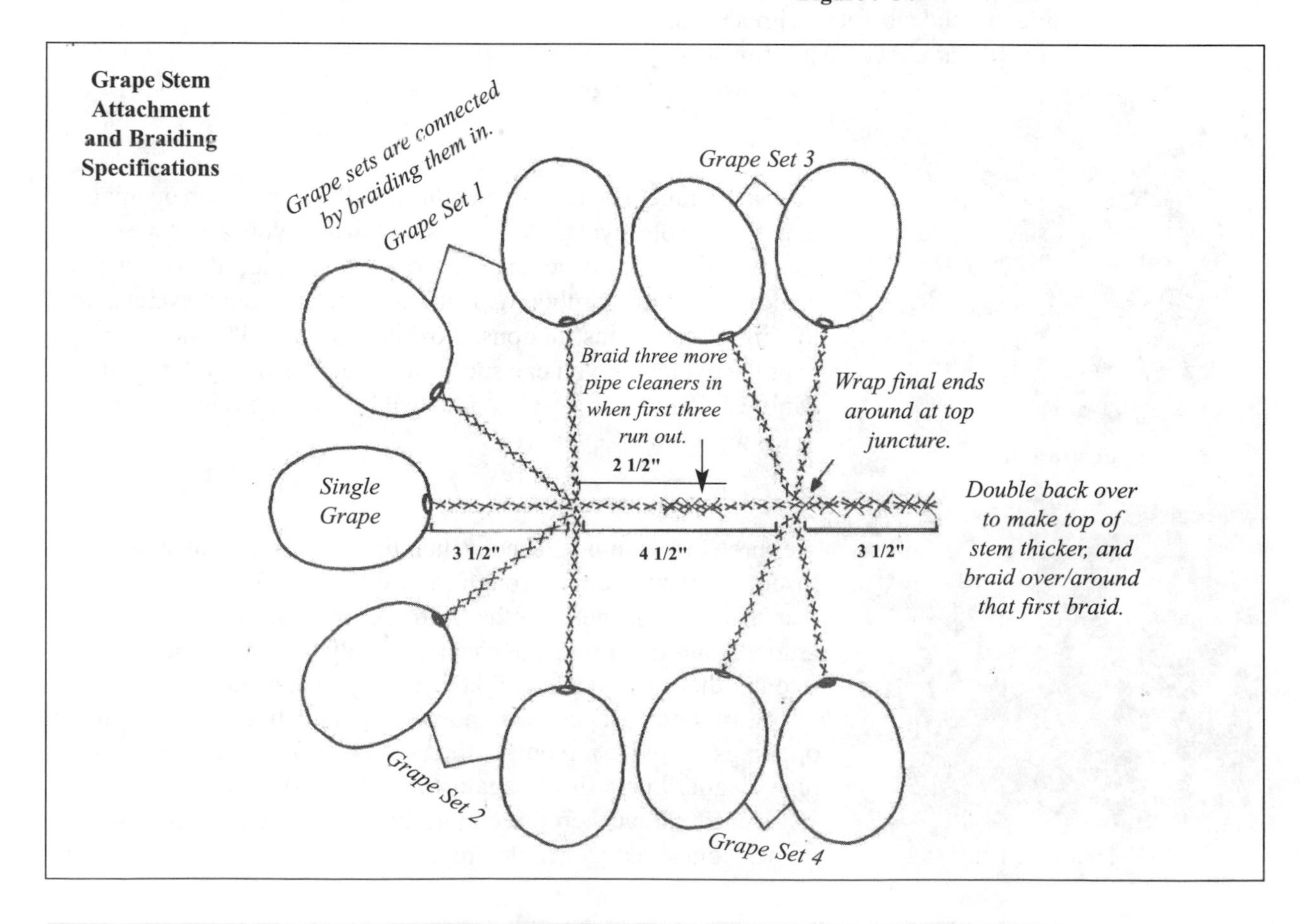

GIANT RED APPLE

Step 1

Lightly sand the *top* of one large metal two-part eyelet with sandpaper so that spray paint will adhere to it. Lay the sanded eyelet top right side up on a piece of poster board, and spray with bright red gloss spray paint. Allow paint to dry completely.

Step 2

The APPLE is made from six panels. Be careful not to get the panels turned around when stitching them—the apple top is cut differently than the apple bottom.

Right sides together, pin two panels along one side and stitch with red thread, making sure to stop a little ways in from the top end as shown on the pattern (you will need to insert the eyelet through that opening). Seam allowance is 1/4". Stitch the next two panels together and then the final two panels together in the same way.

Open up these three double-panel sets and pin, right sides together. Stitch with red thread, continuing to stop a little ways in from the top end. Leave a 4" opening along the middle of one side (so that you will be able to turn the apple right side out and stuff it). Trim seams. Turn apple right side out.

Step 3

Insert eyelet through the narrow top opening so that the red eyelet top will show when the apple is completed. Turn eyelet upside down so the red top is face down on your eyelet-pounding cardboard. Hammer bottom onto eyelet, following package instructions. Position the 4" side opening over the eyelet so you can successfully access the eyelet with the hammer as you did with the grapes.

Step 4

Tie three brown pipe cleaners/chenille stems in a knot at one end. Insert the three stems through the apple eyelet so that the pipe cleaner lengths protrude and the knot is inside the apple. Braid the three pipe cleaners halfway along their length, then bend them back downward and braid them over and around the existing braid to make the stem thicker. The tips of the pipe cleaners should end up right down near the eyelet; twist the ends around and under with your needle nose pliers so they don't stick out and aren't sharp.

Step 5

Stuff apple with polyester fiberfill until firm. (The stuffing should hold the pipe cleaner knots firmly against the eyelet so the stem doesn't slide down into the apple.)

Step 6

Thread an embroidery needle with 3 yards of medium-weight red string or crochet cotton, and knot the two bottom ends securely together. Make a loop through the holes of the brown base button so that the string is fastened to it securely.

Step 7

Position the base button at the bottom center of the apple, and insert your needle into the apple until you are able to push it through the eyelet at the center top. You will have to put your hand into the stuffing through the side opening to reach the needle partway through and push it on through the *inside center* of the eyelet in the top of the apple.

Plunge the needle back down into the apple along the *outside* edge of the top eyelet, and through the holes in the bottom button. Repeat this whole procedure one more time, coming up through the opposite side of the top eyelet and back down again. Pull the string firmly. This should help to shape the apple while attaching the base button at the same time. Tie off the string at the bottom of the apple, hiding the ends and the knots. Dot the tied-off knots with Fray Check.

Figure 9-35

Step 8

Stitch the side opening closed using red thread. (*See* figure 9-35, finished apple.)

GIANT PINK WATERMELON AND TEN BLACK SEEDS

Watermelon

Notes: All of the watermelon pieces should be interfaced with heavyweight fusible interfacing.

Cut five of the WATERMELON SEED POCKETS along the outer cutting line and five along the inner cutting line, so that half will be deep and the other half will be shallow.

Step 1

In addition to the watermelon pattern pieces you have already cut out, you will also need to cut the following from the fabric and heavyweight interfacing:

2 pink strips 4" wide by 19 3/4" long
2 white strips 4" wide by 2" long
2 green strips 4" wide by 1 1/2" long
1 green strip 4" wide by 35 1/4" long

Step 2

Using a ballpoint pen, mark 10 buttonholes (each buttonhole is 3" long) in the pink watermelon fabric as shown, marking 5 buttonholes on one of the watermelon slices, 4 buttonholes on the other slice, and 1 buttonhole a third of the way along one of the 4" by 19 3/4" pink strips. Make sure you position the markings/buttonholes high enough on the WATERMELON SLICE so that there is room for the WATERMELON SEED POCKETS to be stitched fully on the pink part of the slice and not run down into the rind. Stitch the buttonholes using bright pink thread.

Watermelon Buttonhole Placement

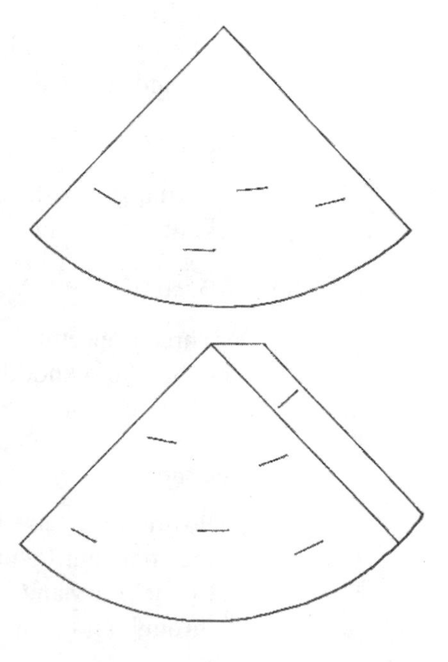

Step 3

Pin one pink pocket *behind* each buttonhole, right side of the pocket facing the buttonhole. Vary the pocket sizes so that the deep and shallow pockets are intermingled. Line up the top flat edge of the pocket so it is positioned just above (about 1/4") the top side of the

Watermelon Pocket Placement and Technique

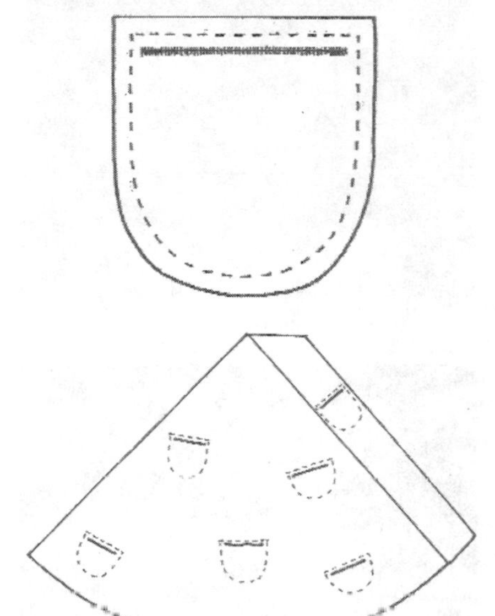

buttonhole. From the *front,* straight stitch just above the top of each buttonhole with bright pink thread so the stitching will catch in the top edge of each pocket. From the *back,* straight stitch the rest of the way around each pocket as shown using bright pink thread. Seam allowance is 1/4". Using a seam ripper, open the buttonholes, being careful not to rip the actual pockets.

Step 4

Right sides together, pin each pink watermelon slice panel to one of the watermelon curved white rind pieces. Stitch using bright pink thread. Seam allowance is 1/4".

Right sides together, pin each 4" × 19 3/4" pink strip to one of the 4" × 2" white strips. Stitch using bright pink thread. Seam allowance is 1/4". Trim seams.

Step 5

Right sides together, pin each pink watermelon slice panel with white rind to one of the watermelon curved green rind pieces. Stitch using bright green thread. Seam allowance is 1/4".

Right sides together, pin each pink and white strip to one of the 4" × 1 1/2" green strips. Stitch using bright green thread. Seam allowance is 1/4". Trim seams.

Step 6

Right sides together and lining up the white and green rind along the bottom, pin the pink/white/green watermelon side panels to the pink/white/green edge strips. Stitch with bright pink thread. Seam allowance is 1/4". Trim seams.

Step 7

Stitch across the top edge of the side strips with bright pink thread. Seam allowance is 1/4". Trim seam.

Step 8

Right sides together, pin the bottom green rind to the bottom edge of the watermelon with curved rind slices. Stitch using bright green thread, leaving a 6" opening along the middle of one side (so that you will be able to turn the watermelon slice right side out and stuff it). Seam allowance is 1/4". Trim seams.

Step 9

Turn watermelon slice right side out; stuff with polyester fiberfill until firm. Stitch opening closed using bright green thread.

TEN WATERMELON SEEDS

Step 1

Each watermelon seed is made from two seed pieces.

With right sides together, pin and stitch the seeds with black thread. Seam allowance is 1/4". Leave a 1 1/4" opening along the center bottom of the seed (so that you will be able to turn it right side out and stuff it). Trim seams.

Repeat above instructions for nine more seeds.

Figure 9-36

Step 2

Turn seeds right side out; stuff with polyester fiberfill until firm. Stitch openings closed using black thread. Dot tied-off knots with Fray Check. (*See* figure 9-36, watermelon seed in pocket, close-up view. *See also* figure 9-37, finished watermelon with seeds, side 1, and figure 9-38, finished watermelon with seeds, side 2.)

FOOD PIECES

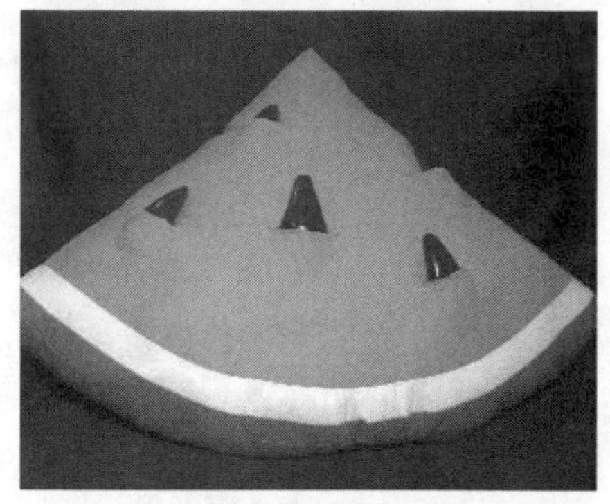
Figure 9-37

You should make at least three small food pieces for each highlighted food color: white, orange, yellow, green, blue, purple, red, pink, and black.

Use the same fabrics that you used for the pieces' corresponding giant food.

General Step 1

Photocopy FOOD PIECES patterns *at sizes specified.* Cut out all of the photocopied patterns along the outside of the pattern outlines.

Note: Make sure to cut out fabric with right sides together when cutting out two or more pieces so that the pieces will be mirror images of each other.

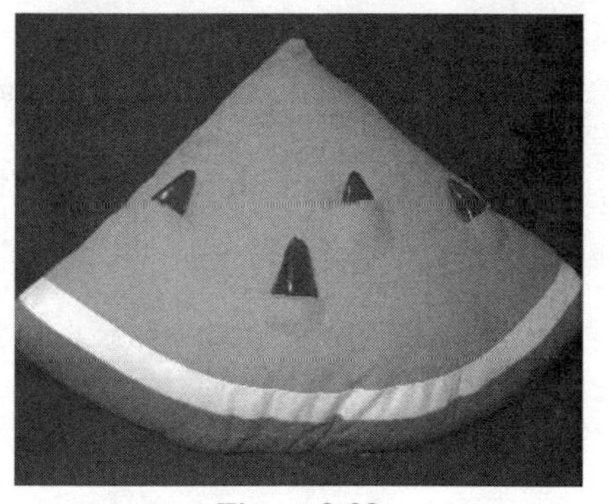
Figure 9-38

The following steps are to be used for each food piece.

Step 1

Right sides together, cut out a double layer of the original food fabric. Use heat fusion or Fray Check around the edges of each small piece as needed. Cut one layer of matching colored felt from the same pattern.

Step 2

With tacky glue, affix the bottom fabric layer, right side out, to the felt. Allow glue to dry completely. Position grey hook Velcro 3/4" square in the middle of the bottom fabric layer, and machine stitch the Velcro onto the food piece through the Velcro, fabric, and felt layers. Stitch with silver grey thread to match the color of the Velcro.

Step 3

Glue the top layer of fabric right side up over the felt/fabric/Velcro base. Allow glue to dry completely. Machine stitch around the very edge of each food piece with thread to match the fabric.

Step 4

Exception: CORN food pieces

Single crochet three small food pieces from yellow yarn that will approximately match the size of the other food pieces.

Materials: Aluminum crochet hook size I; tapestry needle; worsted weight yarn, bright yellow

Abbreviations: sc = single crochet; ch = chain

Possible Pattern Option

PIECE 1: With bright yellow yarn, chain 6. Row 1: Sc in second ch from hook and in each ch across—5 sc. Ch 1, turn. Row 2: Sc in each sc across—5 sc. Ch 1, turn. Row 3: Repeat Row 2—5 sc. Ch 1, turn. Row 4: Repeat Row 2—5 sc. Fasten off; weave yarn ends into the piece.

PIECE 2: With bright yellow yarn, chain 6. Row 1: Sc in second ch from hook and in each ch across—5 sc. Ch 1, turn. Row 2: Sc in each sc across—5 sc. Ch 1, turn. Row 3: Sc in first 2 sc, decrease 1 sc over next 2 sc, sc in last sc—4 sc. Ch 1, turn. Row 4: Sc in first sc, decrease 1 sc over next 2 sc, sc in last sc—3 sc. Fasten off; weave yarn ends into the piece.

PIECE 3: With bright yellow yarn, chain 6. Row 1: Sc in second ch from hook and in each ch across—5 sc. Ch 1, turn. Row 2: Sc in first 3 sc, decrease 1 sc over last 2 sc—4 sc. Ch 1, turn. Row 3: Decrease 1 sc over 2 sc, sc in last 2 sc—3 sc. Ch 1, turn. Row 4: Sc in first sc, decrease 1 sc over last 2 sc—2 sc. Fasten off; weave yarn ends into the piece.

Finishing the CORN Food Pieces

Using the crocheted pieces as a pattern guide, cut out a felt center layer and a yellow fabric bottom layer. Bright yellow flannel-backed vinyl fabric works well for this purpose. Follow steps 2 and 3 above, with the following exception: hand stitch the top crocheted layer to the middle and bottom layers using a straight stitch and yellow thread.

Puppet Story Finished Product

Figure 9-39
Clean Mouse with giant food.

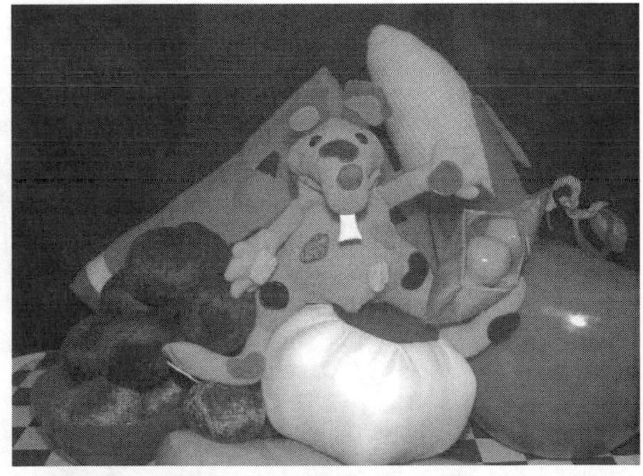

Figure 9-40
Messy Mouse (wearing food pieces) with giant food.

PATTERN PIECES

Lunch

by Denise Fleming

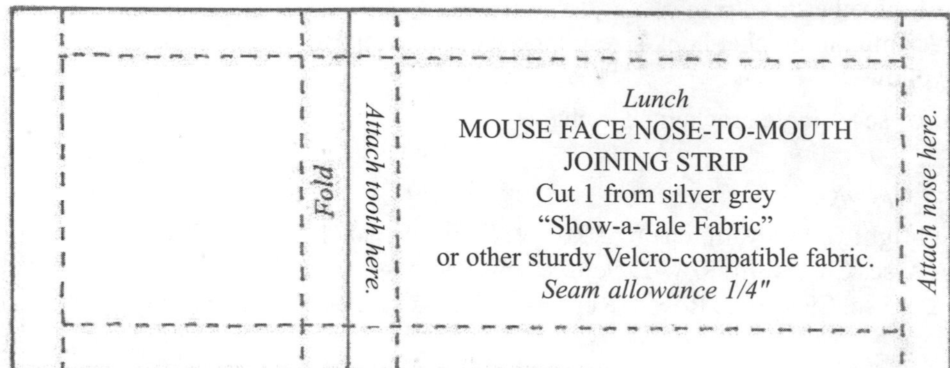

Photocopy this page at size 100%.

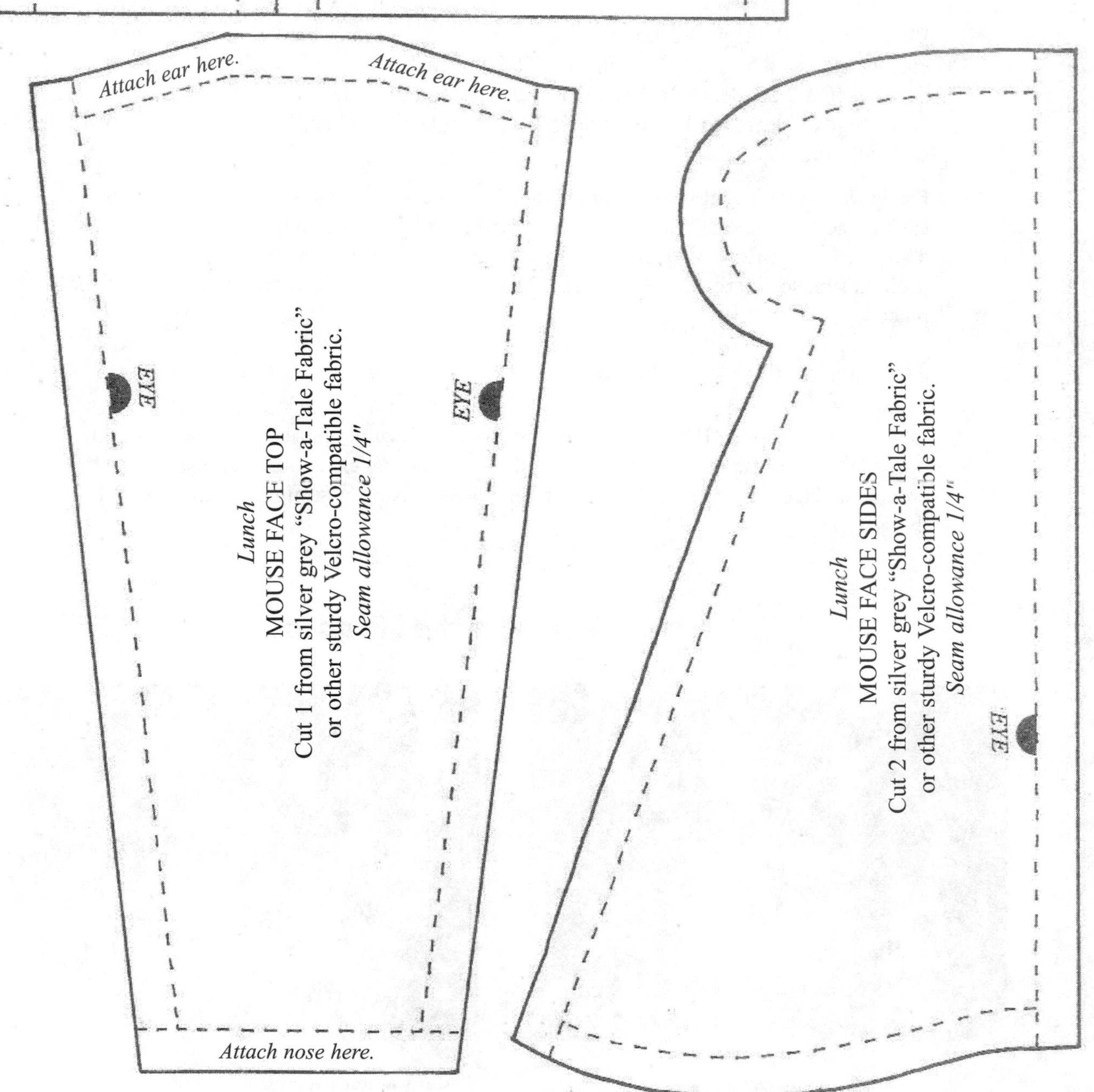

Photocopy this page at size 100%.

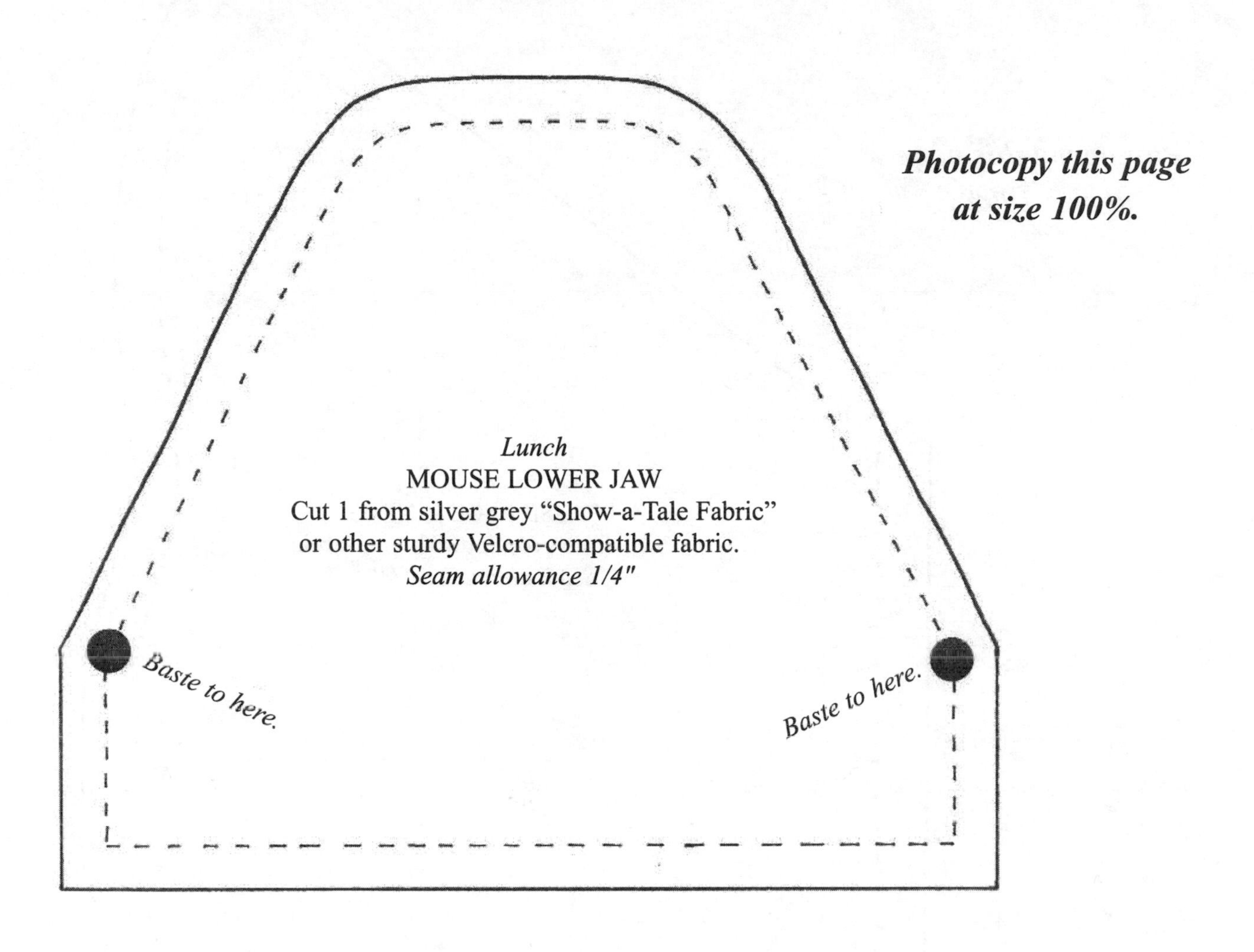

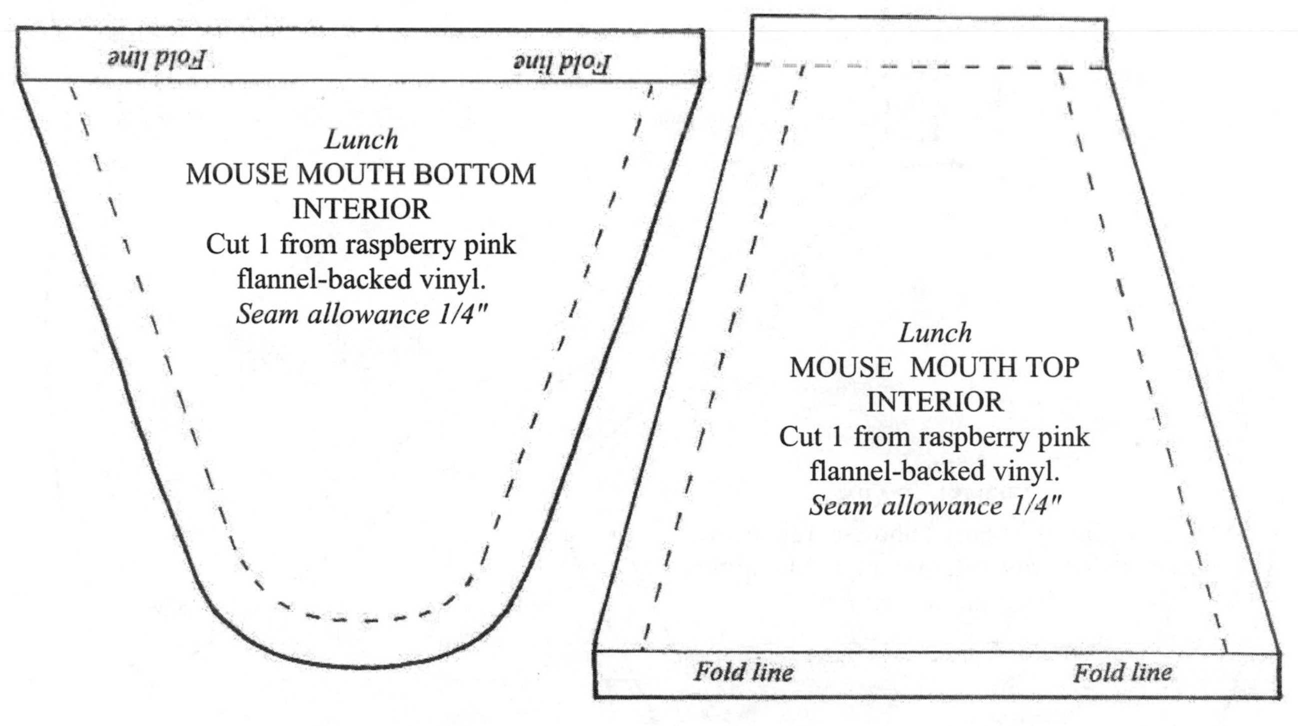

Photocopy this page at size 100%.

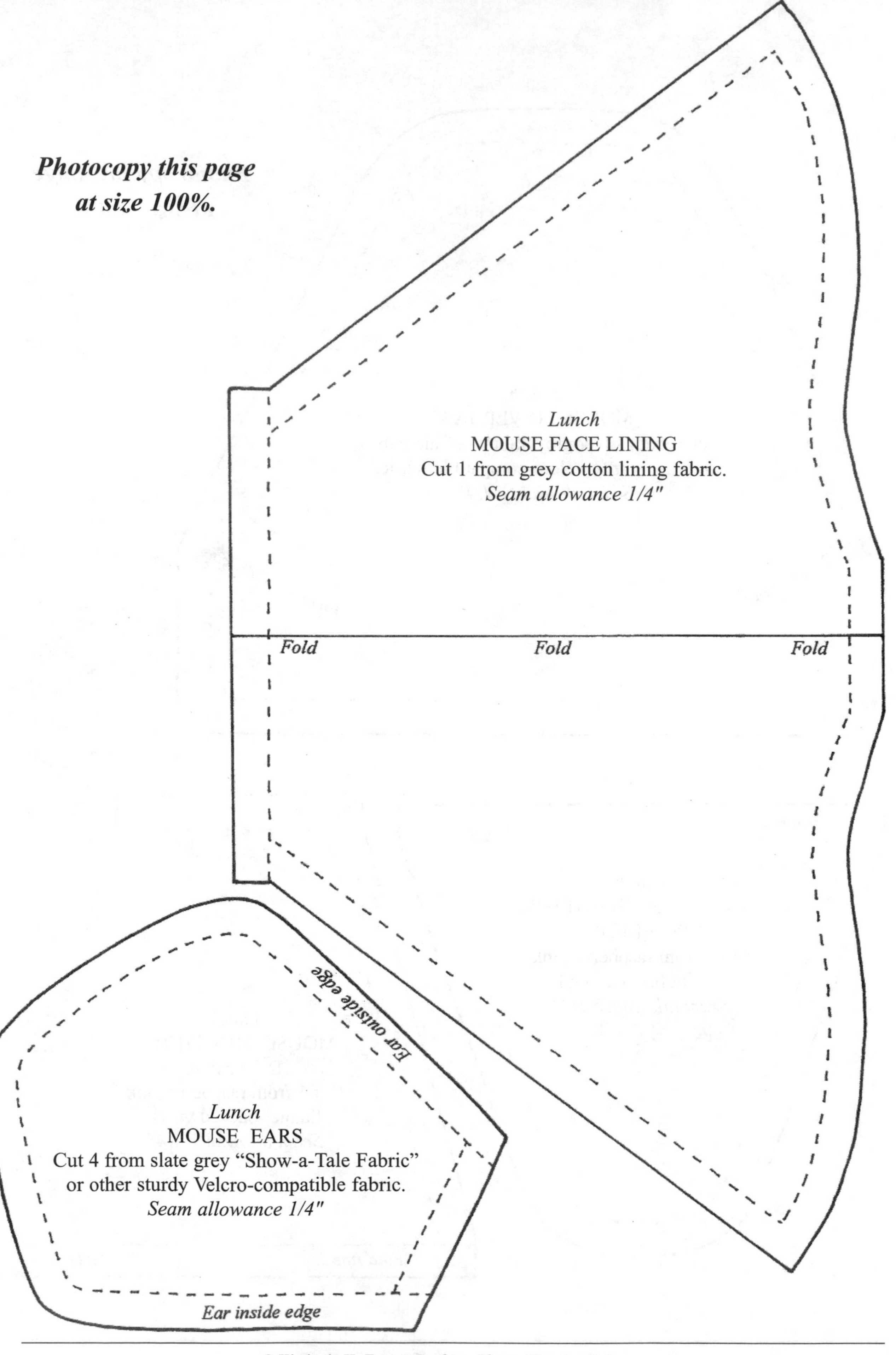

Photocopy this page at size 100%.

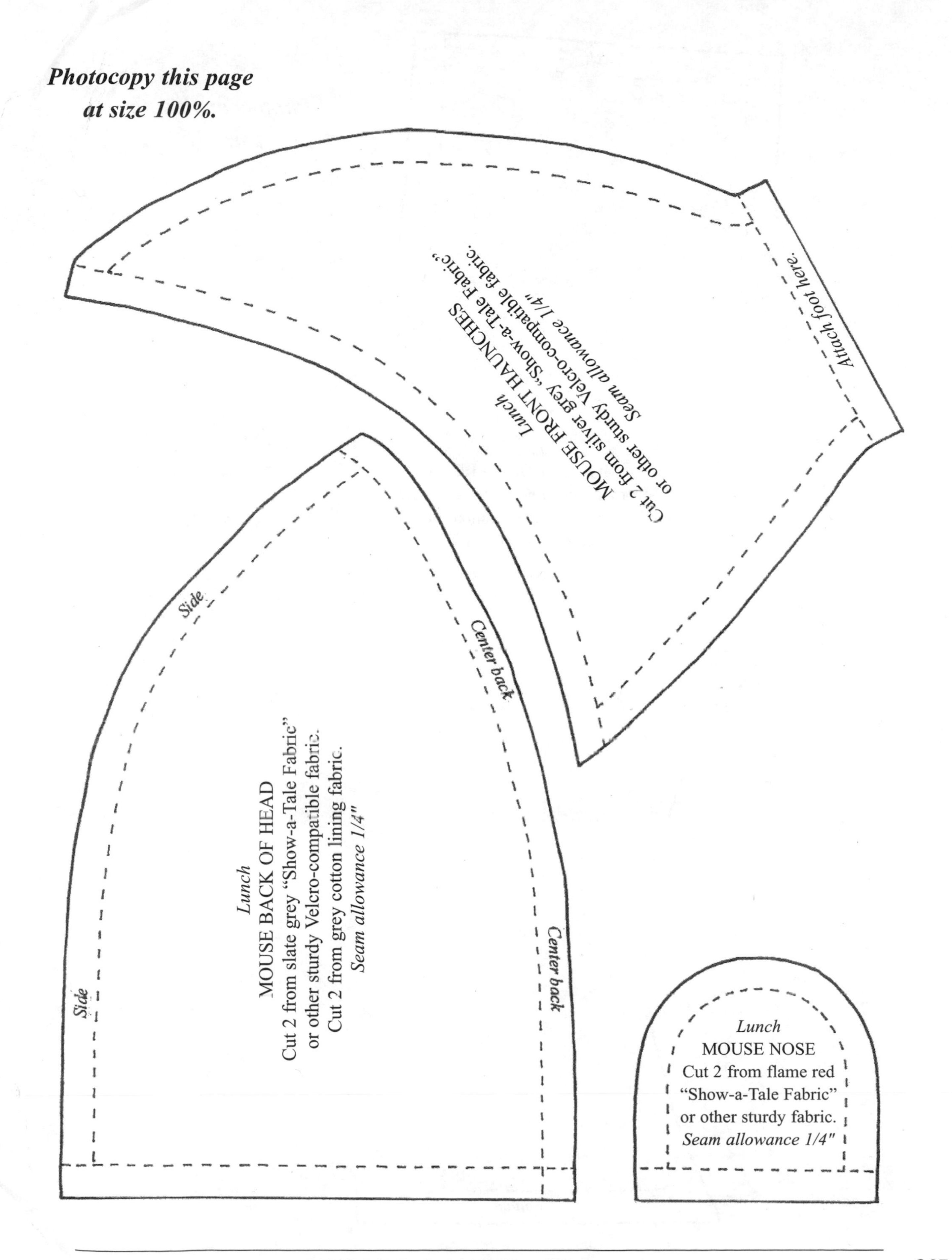

Photocopy this page at size 100%.

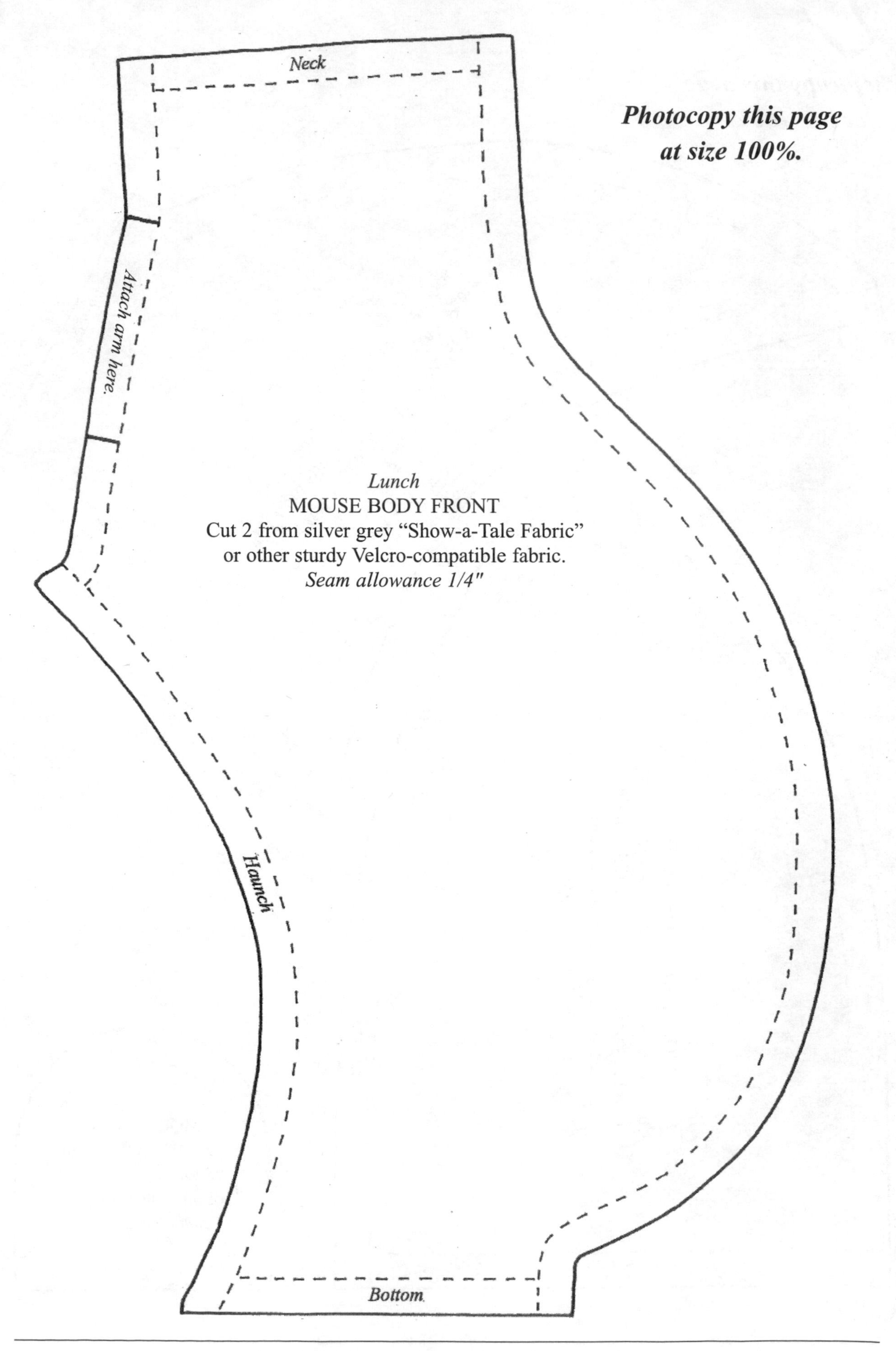

Photocopy this page at size 100%.

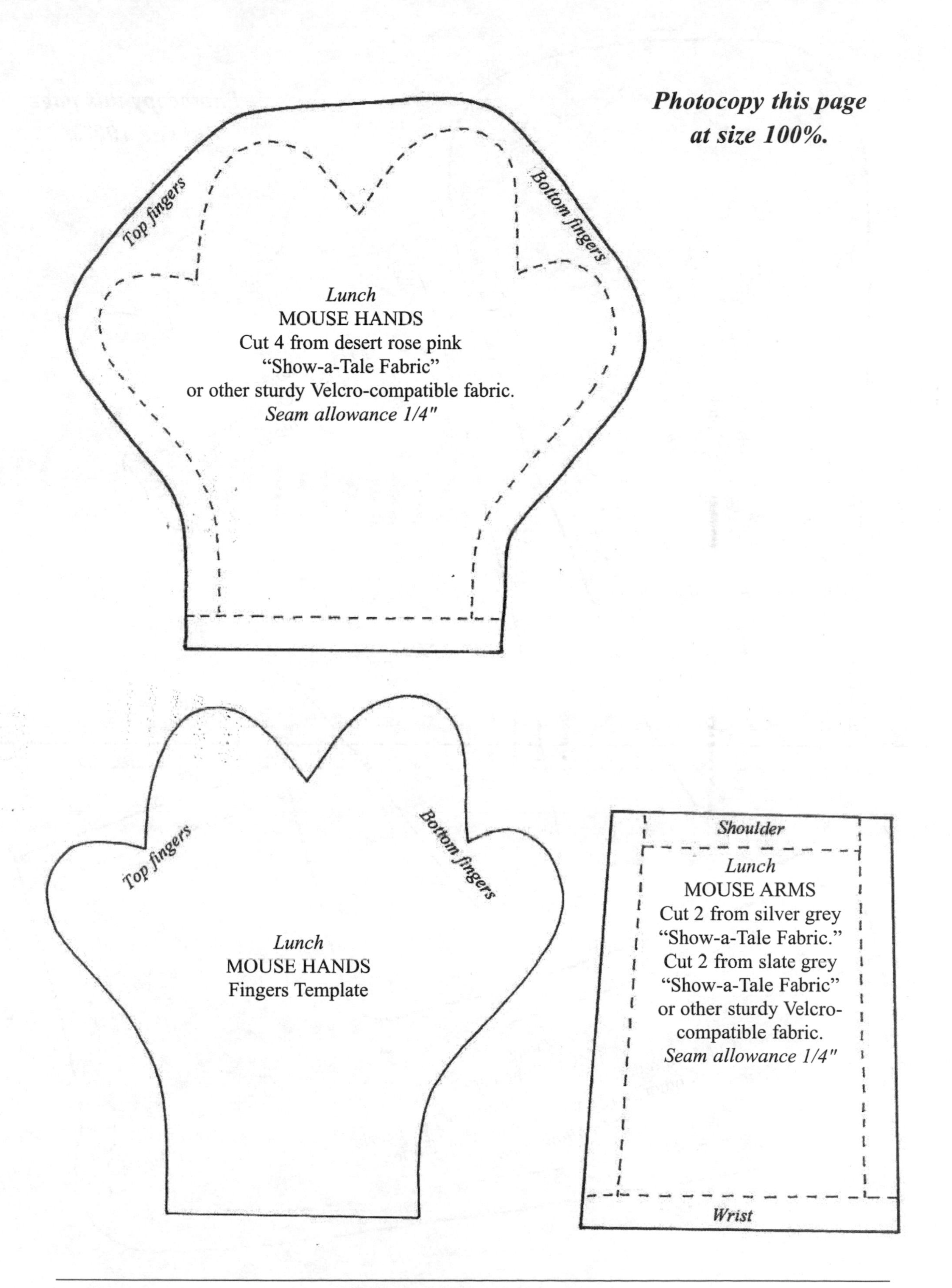

Photocopy this page at size 100%.

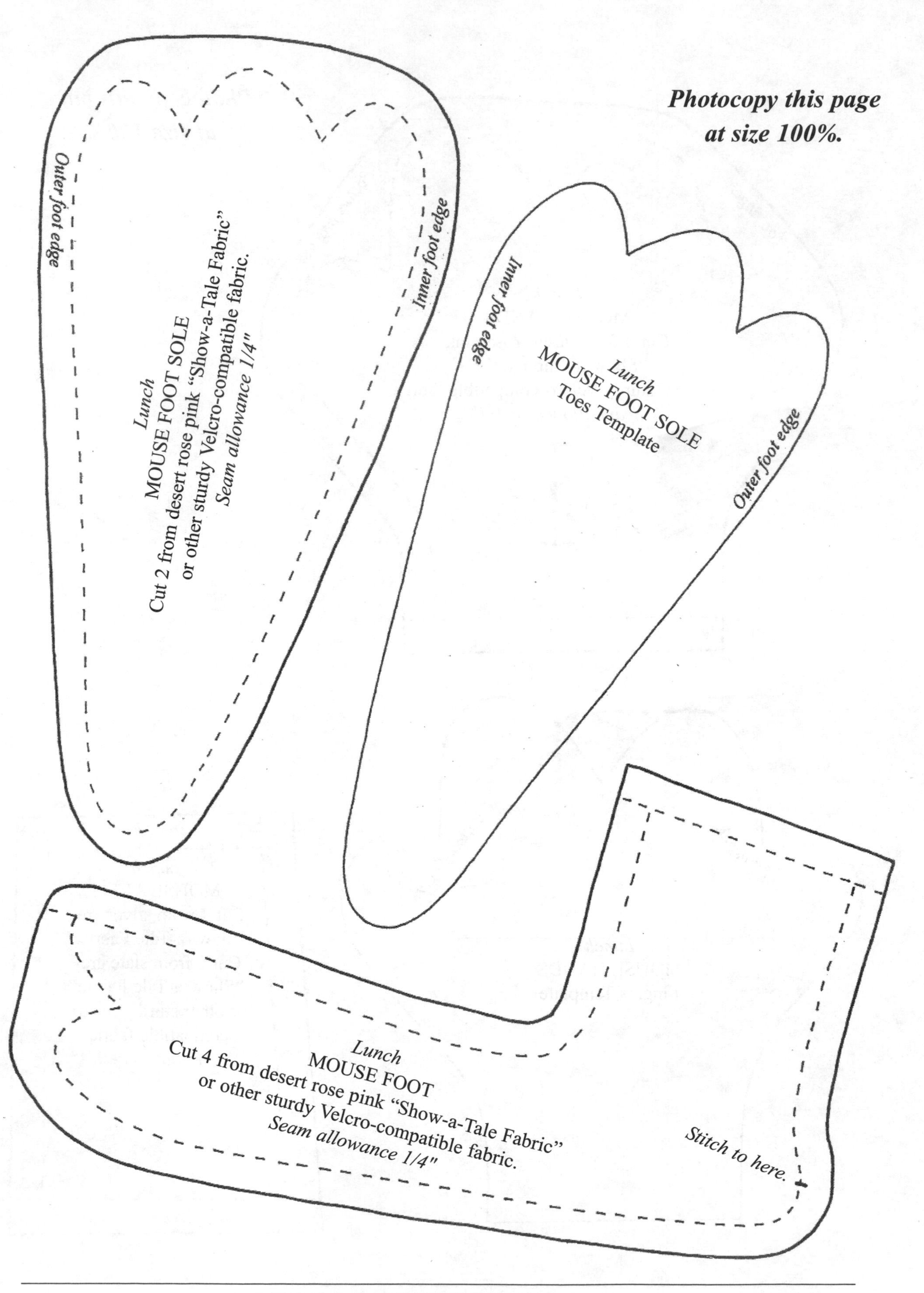

Photocopy this page at size 100%.

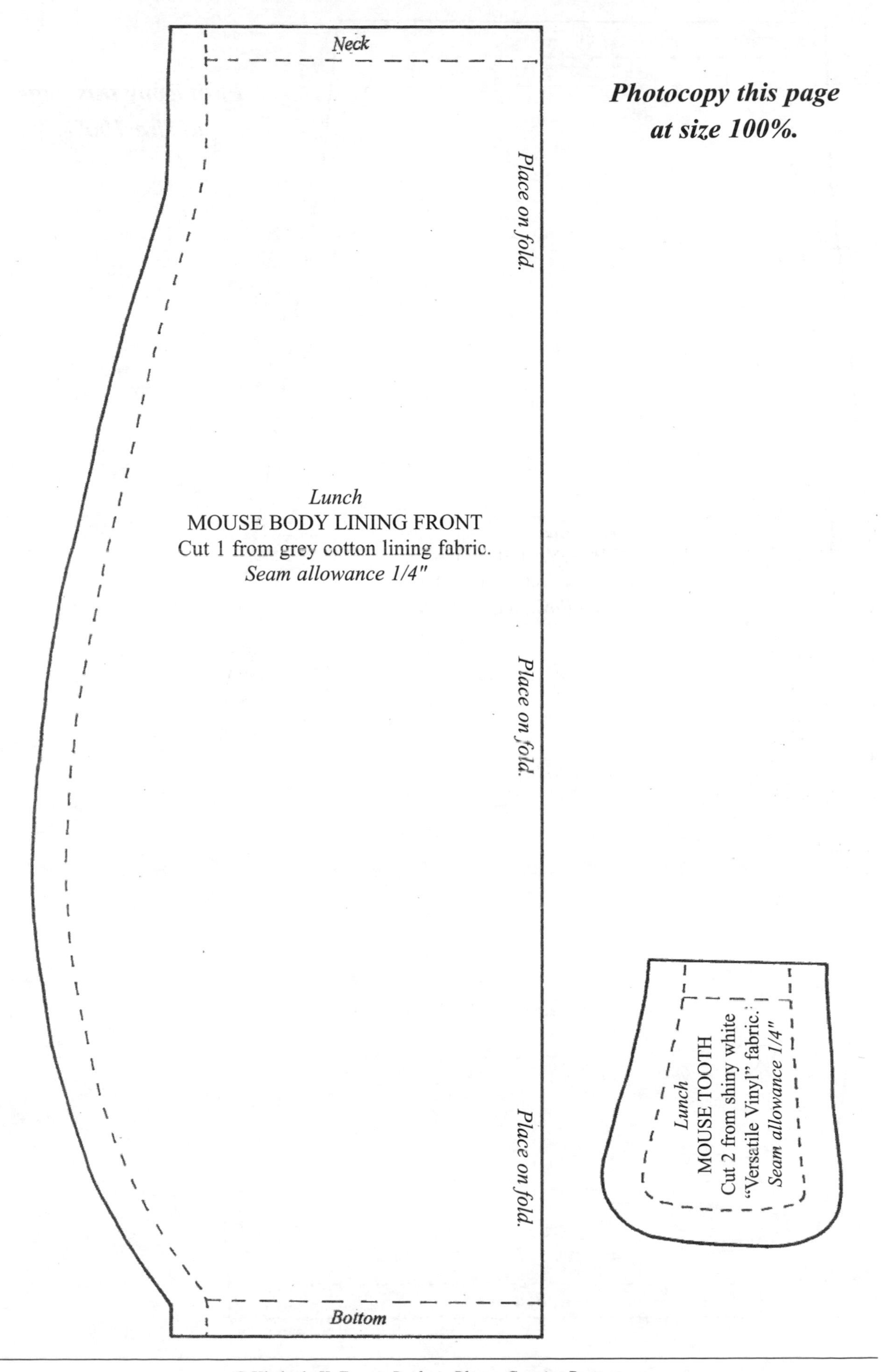

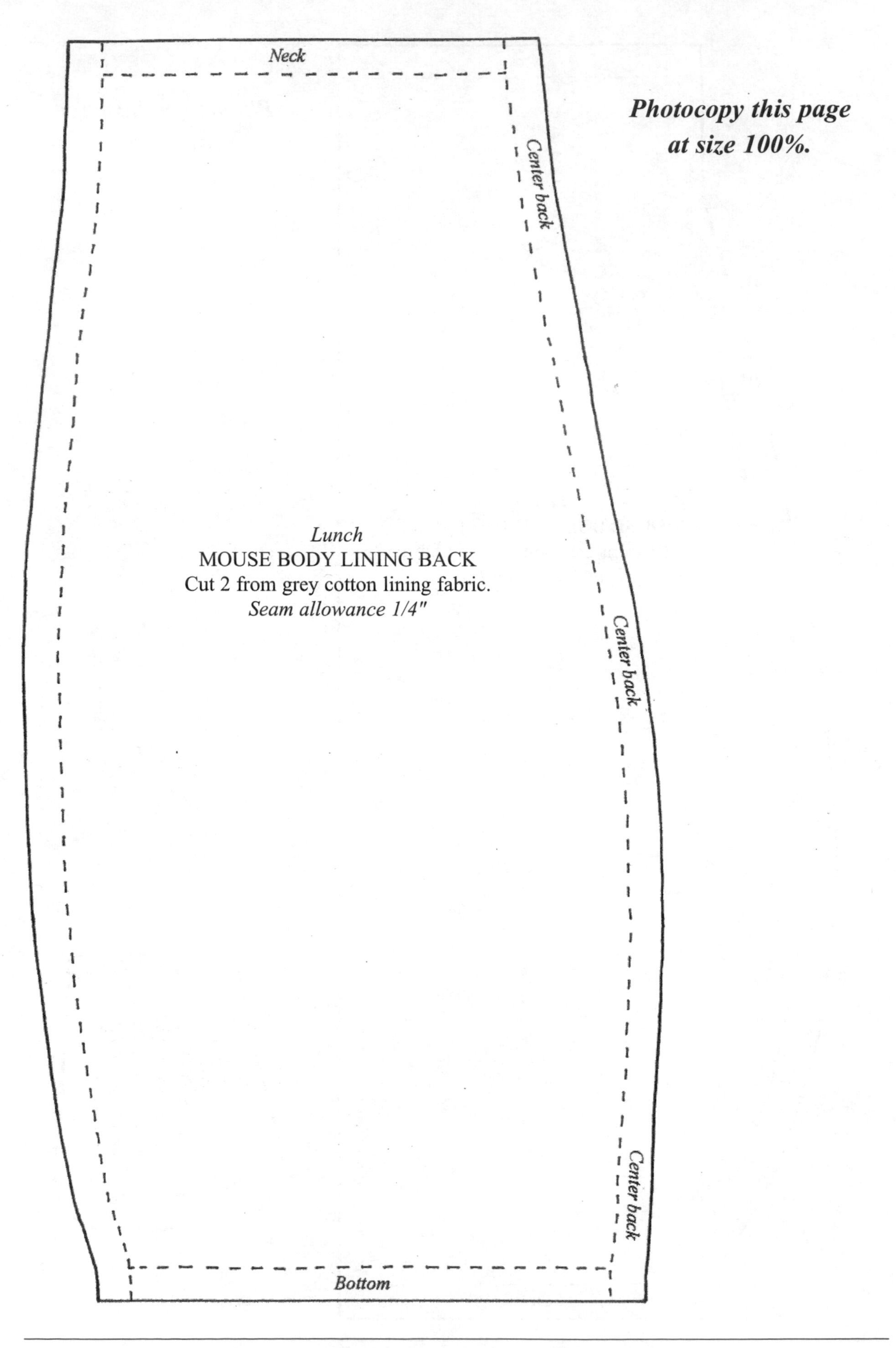

Photocopy this page at size 100%.

Photocopy this page at size 135%.

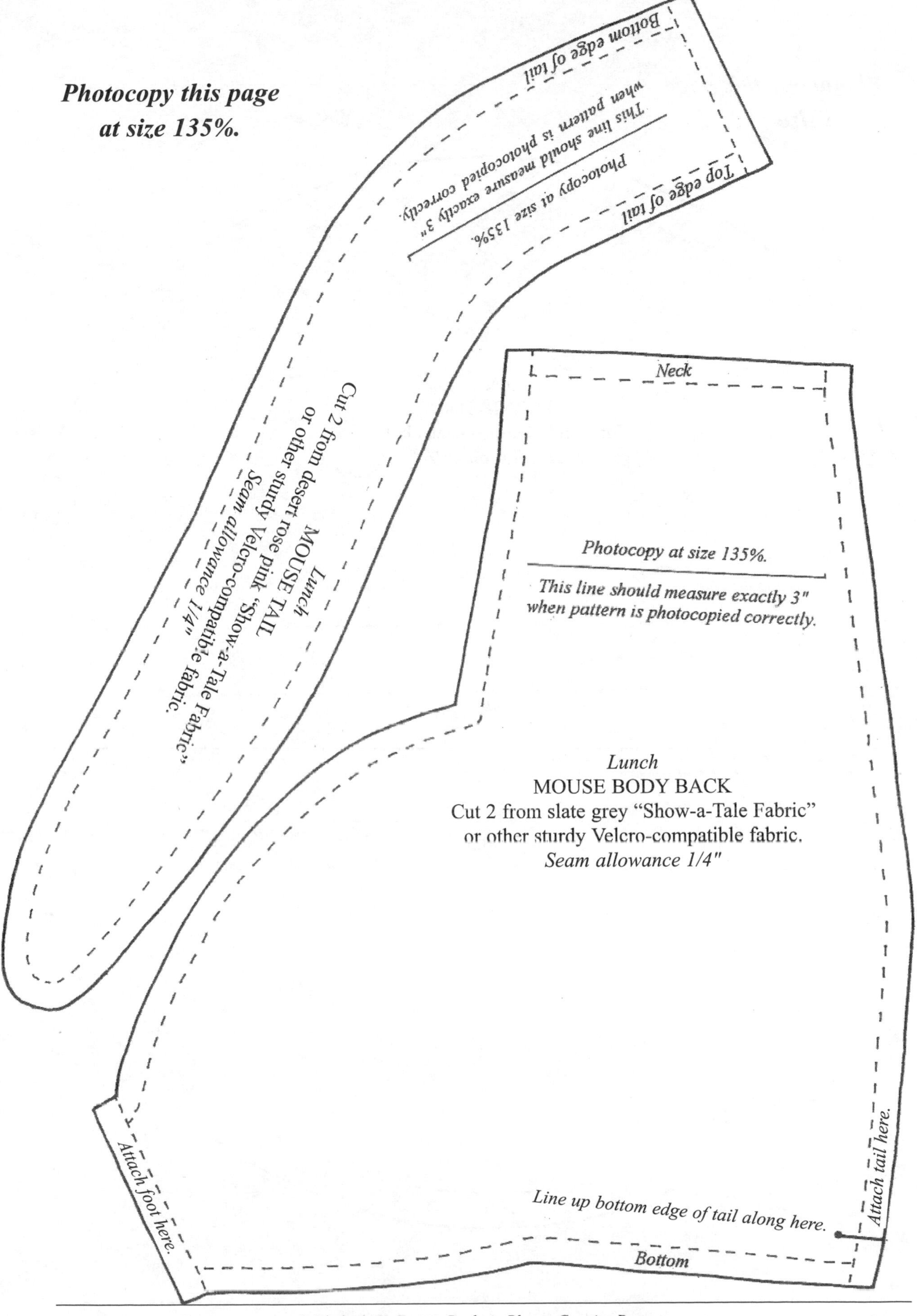

Photocopy this page at size 100%.

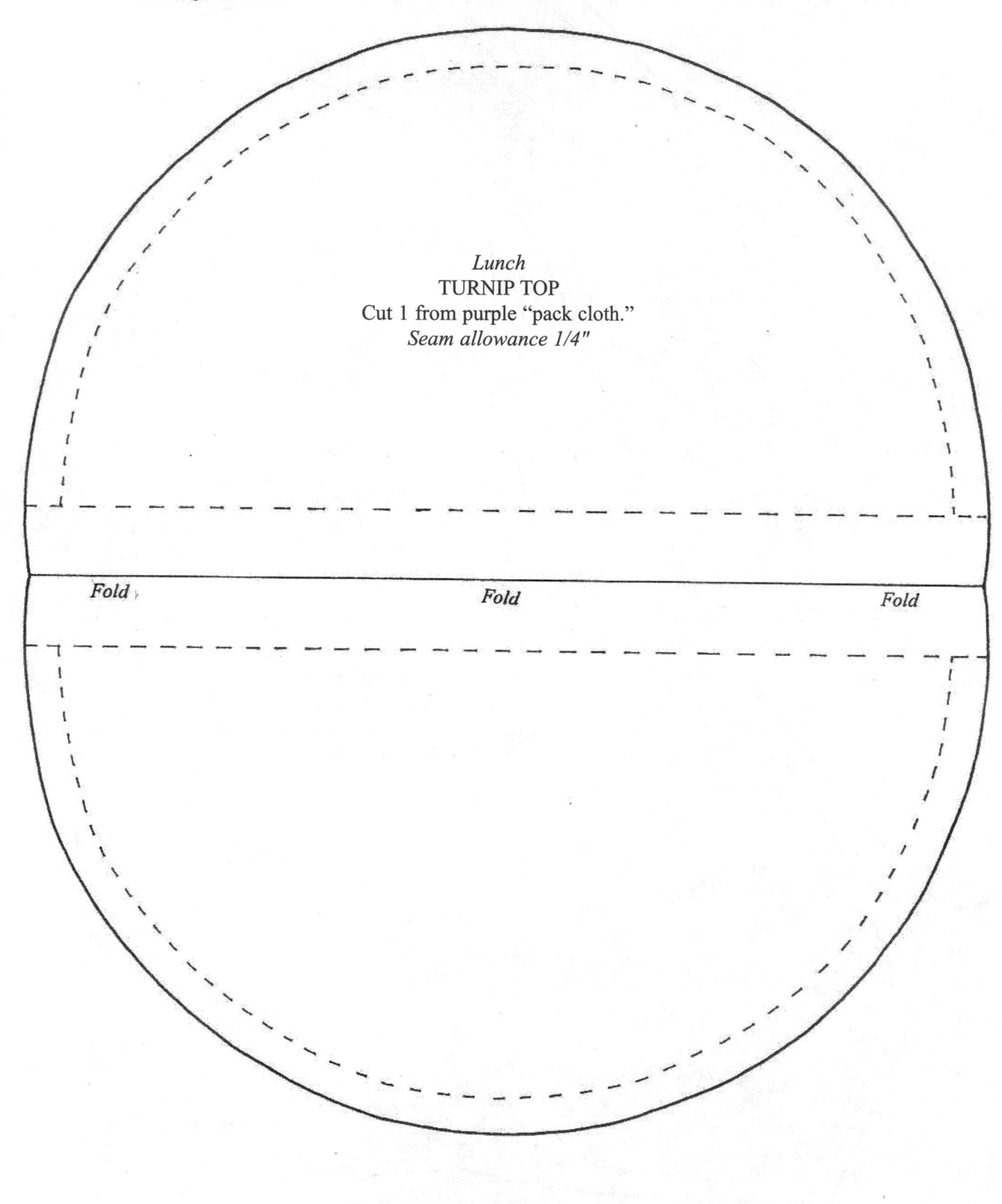

Photocopy this page at size 100%.

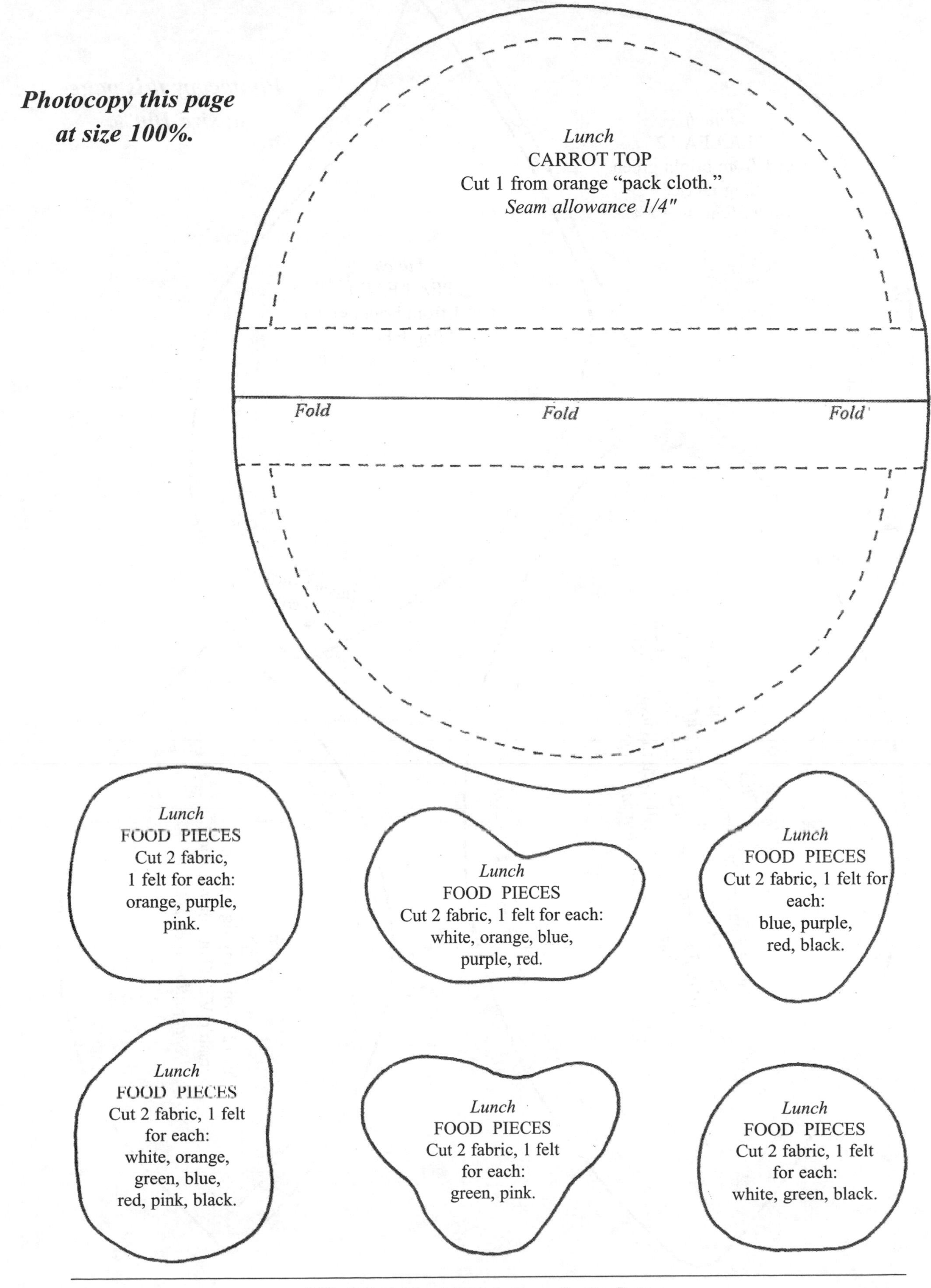

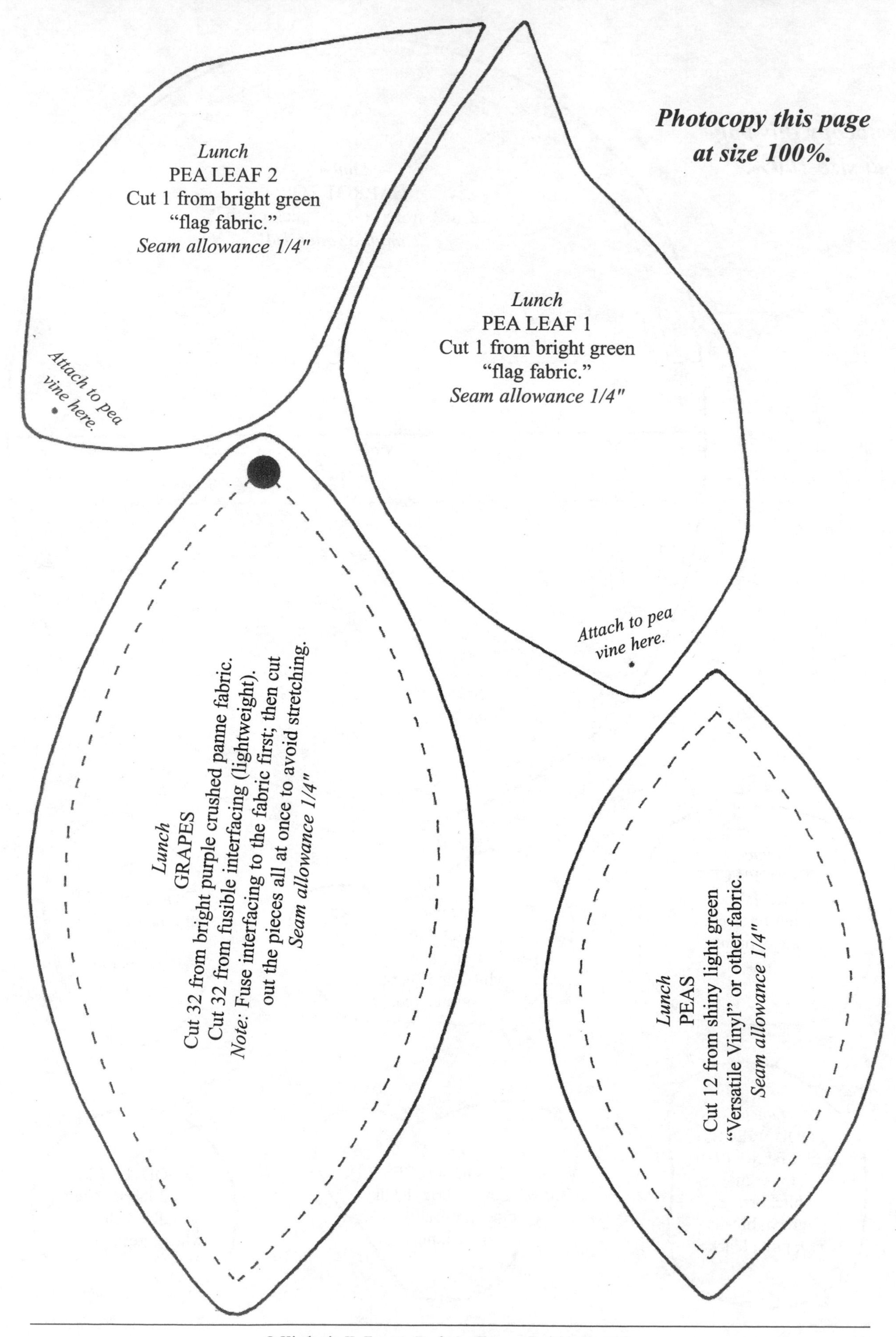
Photocopy this page
at size 100%.
Lunch
PEA LEAF 2
Cut 1 from bright green
"flag fabric."
Seam allowance 1/4"
Attach to pea
vine here.
Lunch
PEA LEAF 1
Cut 1 from bright green
"flag fabric."
Seam allowance 1/4"
Attach to pea
vine here.
Lunch
GRAPES
Cut 32 from bright purple crushed panne fabric.
Cut 32 from fusible interfacing (lightweight).
Note: Fuse interfacing to the fabric first; then cut
out the pieces all at once to avoid stretching.
Seam allowance 1/4"
Lunch
PEAS
Cut 12 from shiny light green
"Versatile Vinyl" or other fabric.
Seam allowance 1/4"

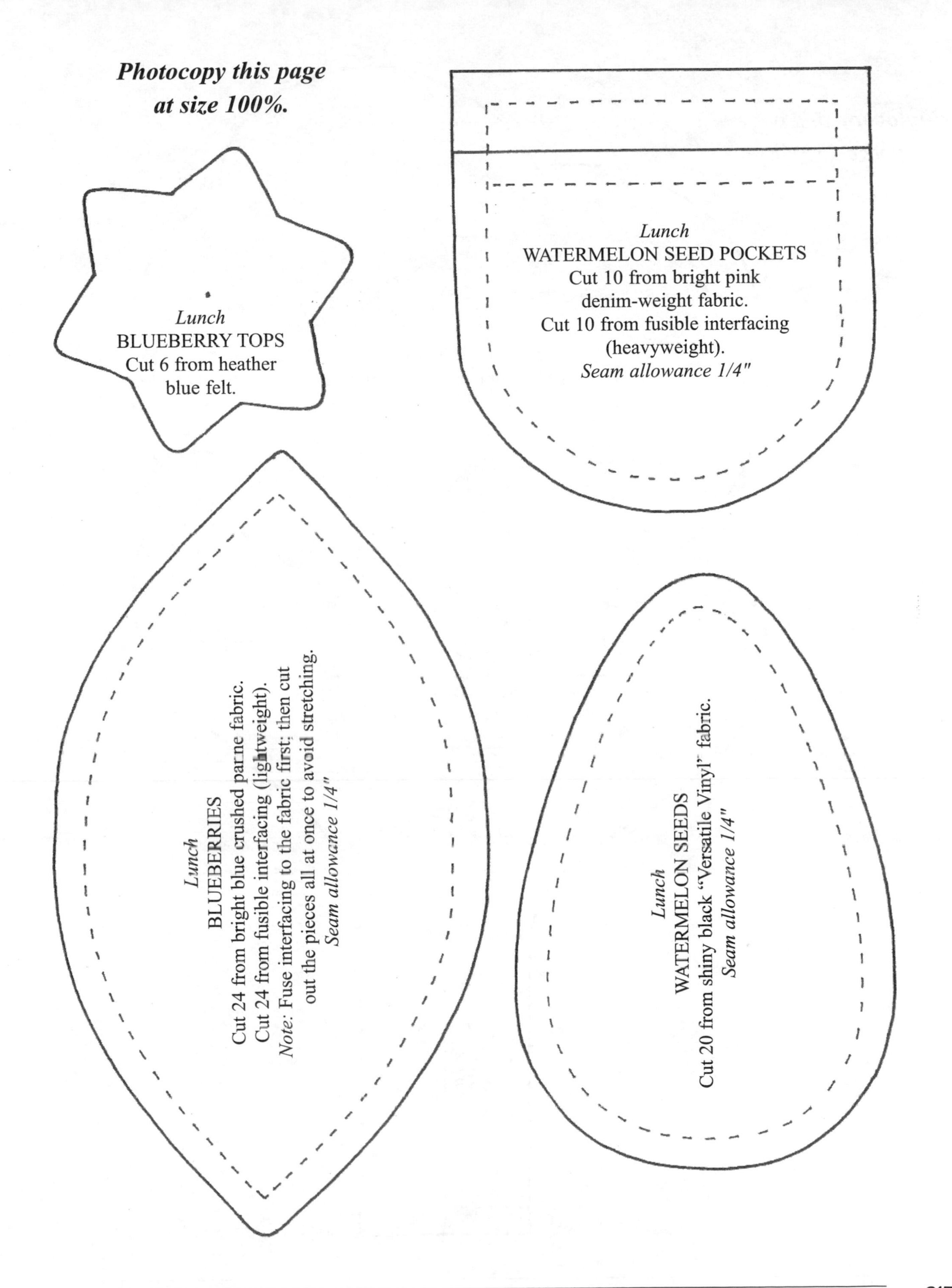

Photocopy this page
at size 100%.
Lunch
BLUEBERRY TOPS
Cut 6 from heather
blue felt.
Lunch
WATERMELON SEED POCKETS
Cut 10 from bright pink
denim-weight fabric.
Cut 10 from fusible interfacing
(heavyweight).
Seam allowance 1/4"
Lunch
BLUEBERRIES
Cut 24 from bright blue crushed panne fabric.
Cut 24 from fusible interfacing (lightweight).
Note: Fuse interfacing to the fabric first; then cut
out the pieces all at once to avoid stretching.
Seam allowance 1/4"
Lunch
WATERMELON SEEDS
Cut 20 from shiny black "Versatile Vinyl" fabric.
Seam allowance 1/4"

Photocopy this page at size 135%.

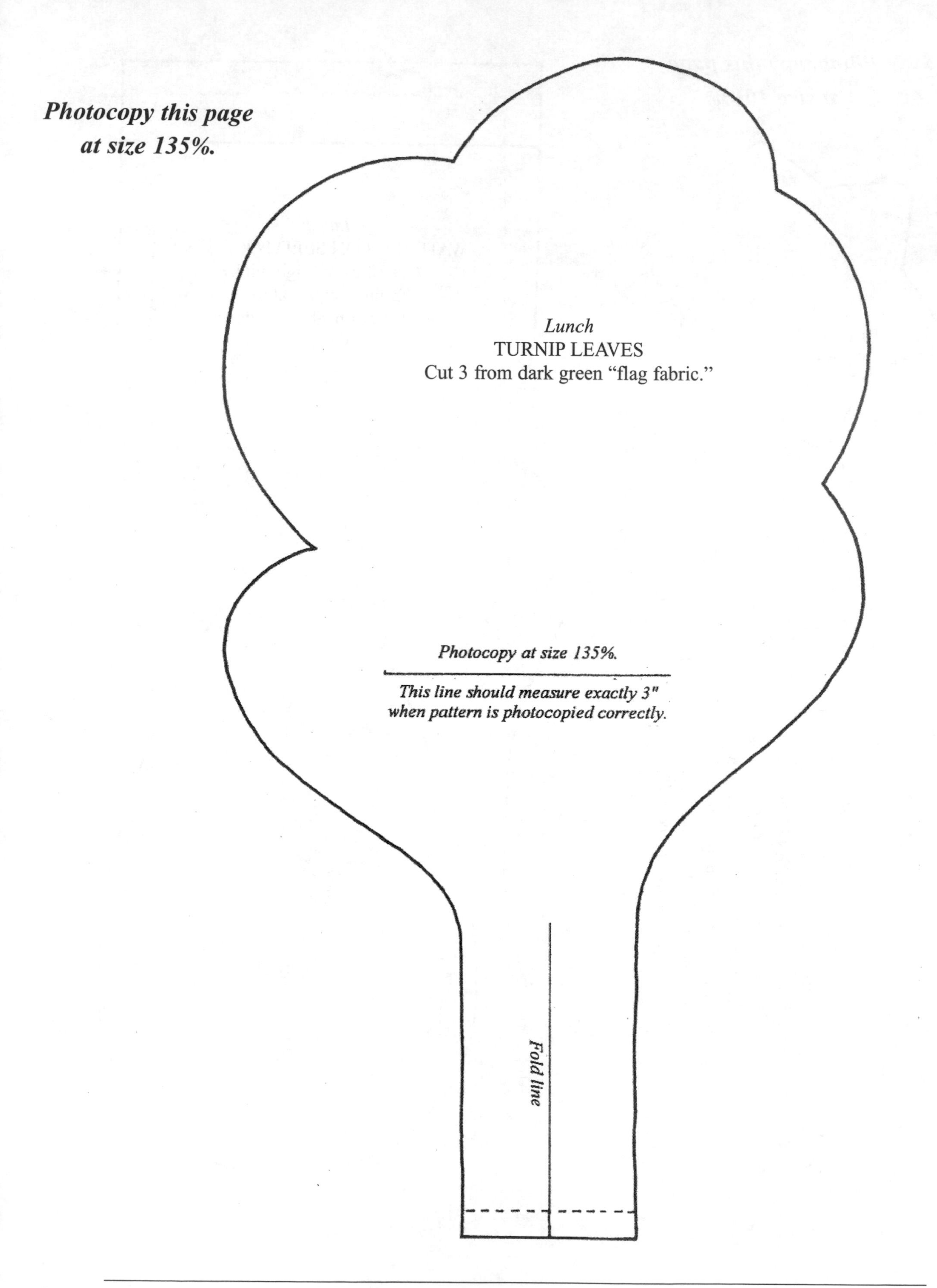

Photocopy this page at size 135%.

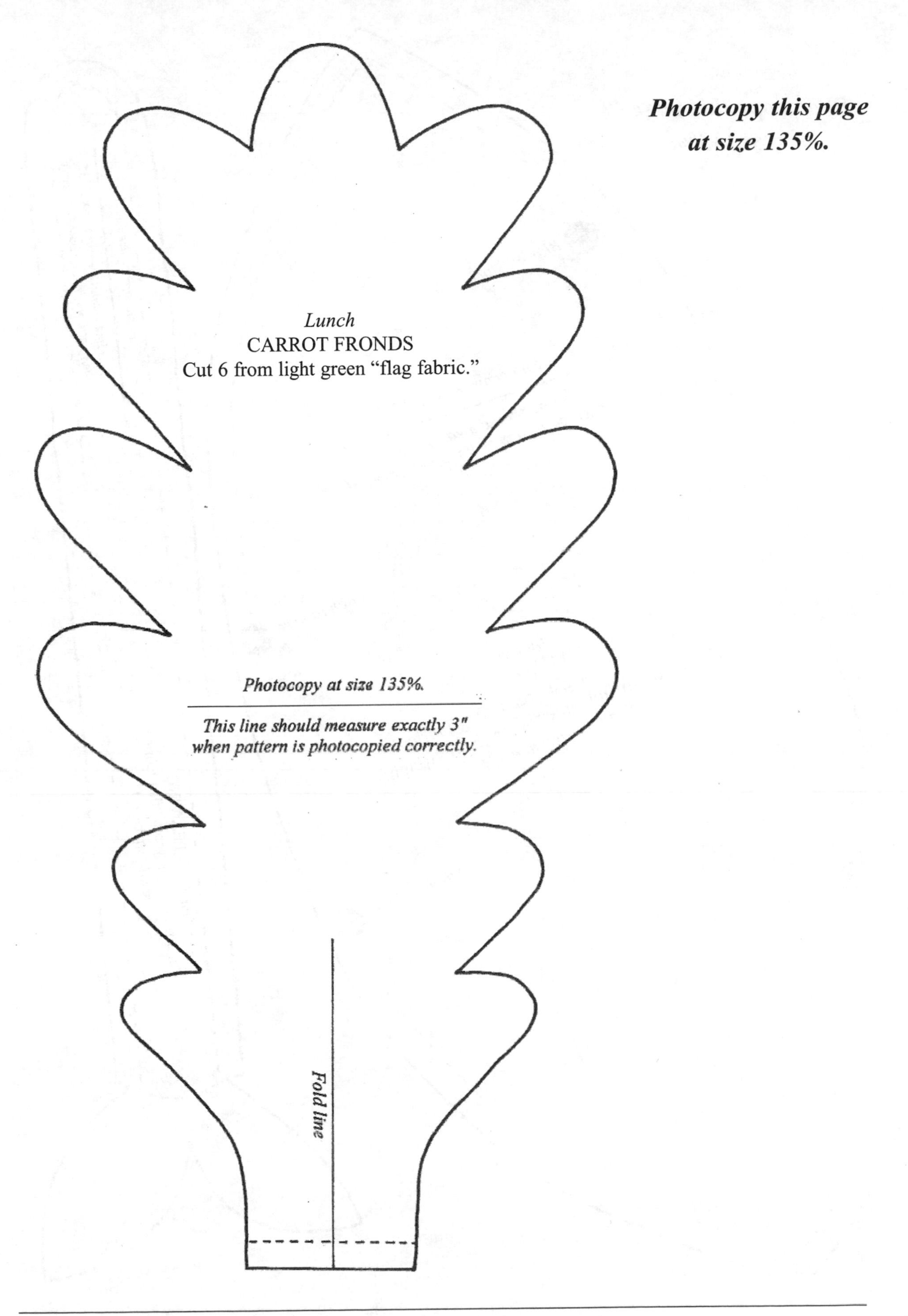

Photocopy this page at size 135%.

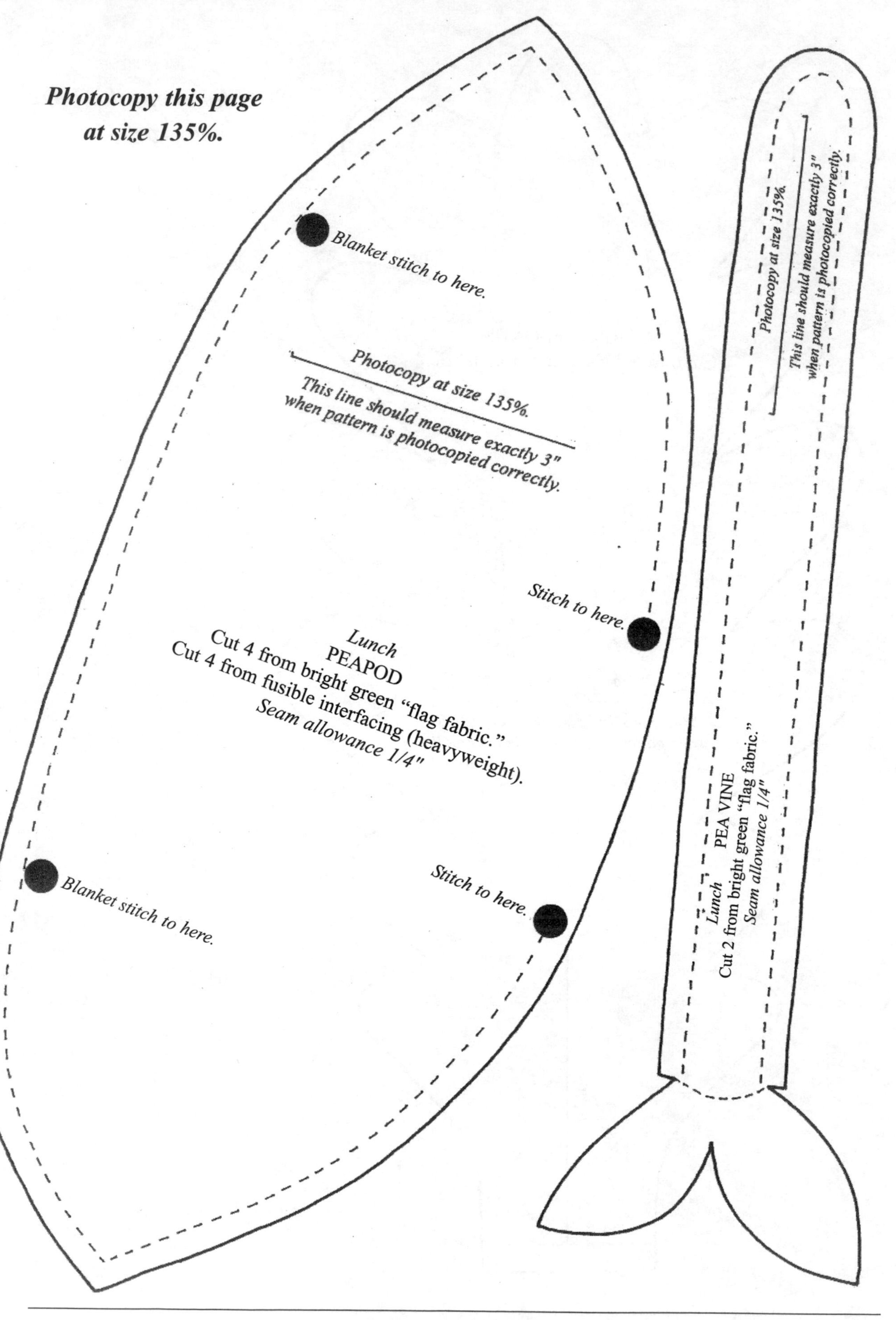

Photocopy this page at size 150%.

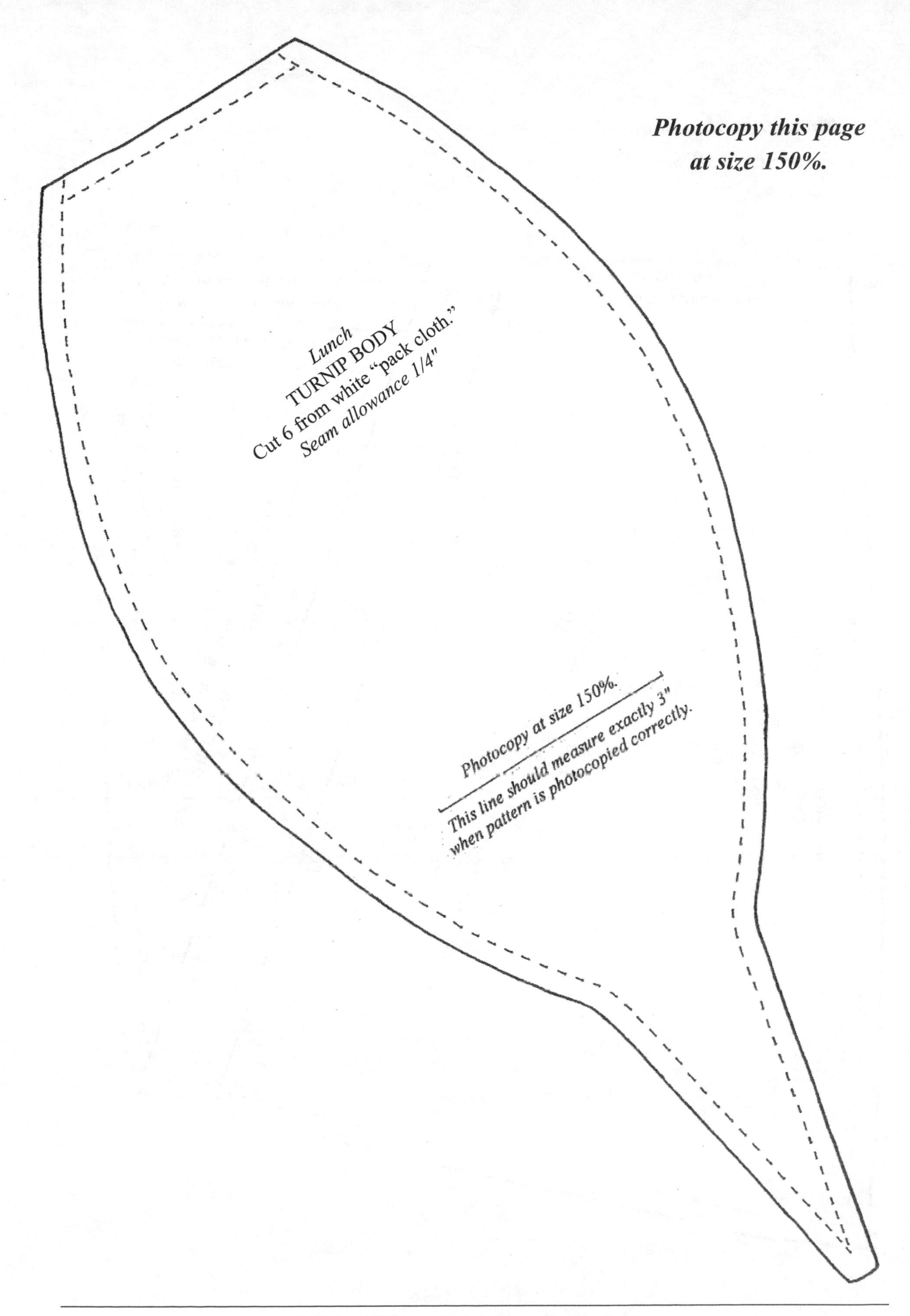

Photocopy this page at size 150%.

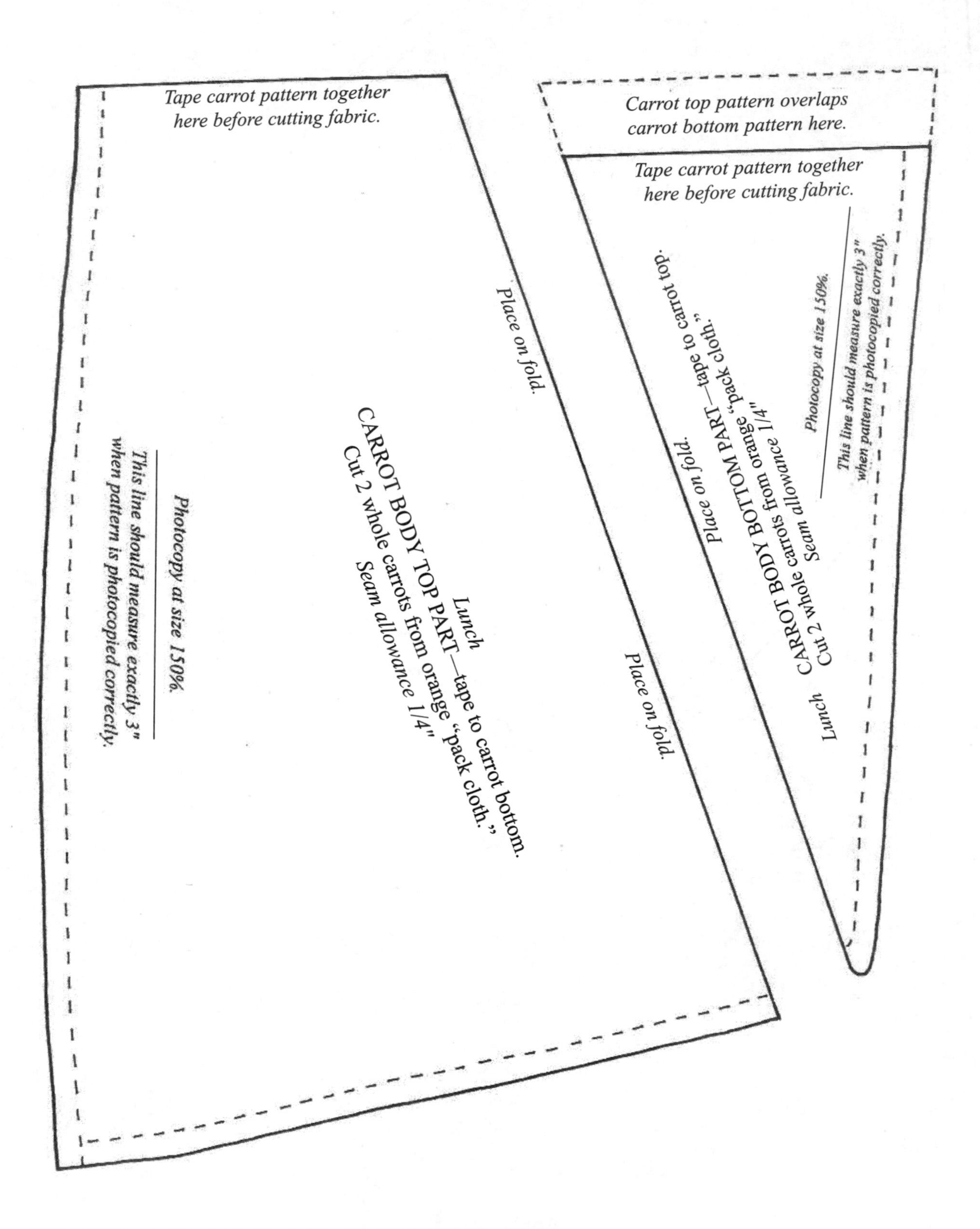

Photocopy this page at size 150%.

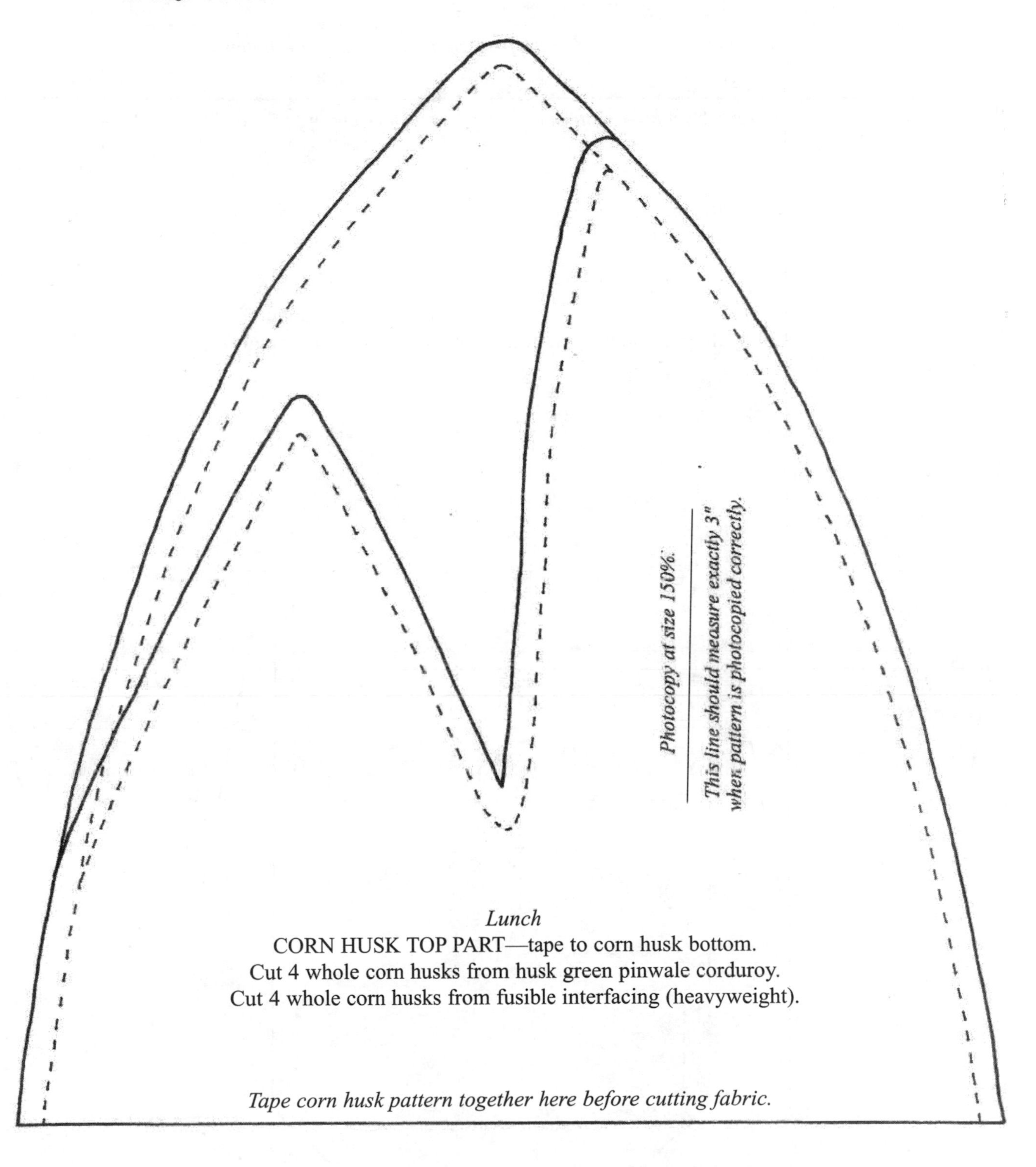

Photocopy this page at size 150%.

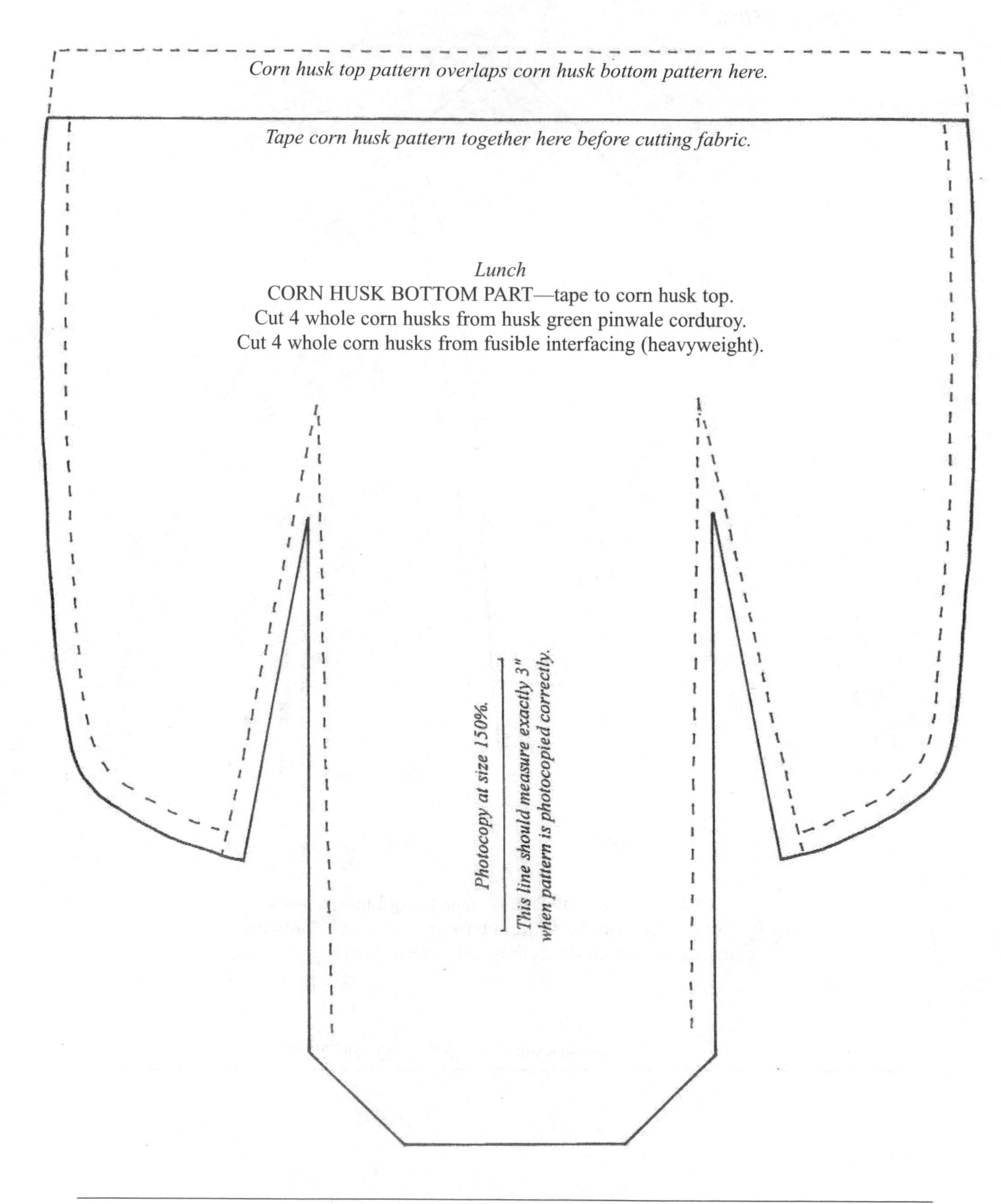

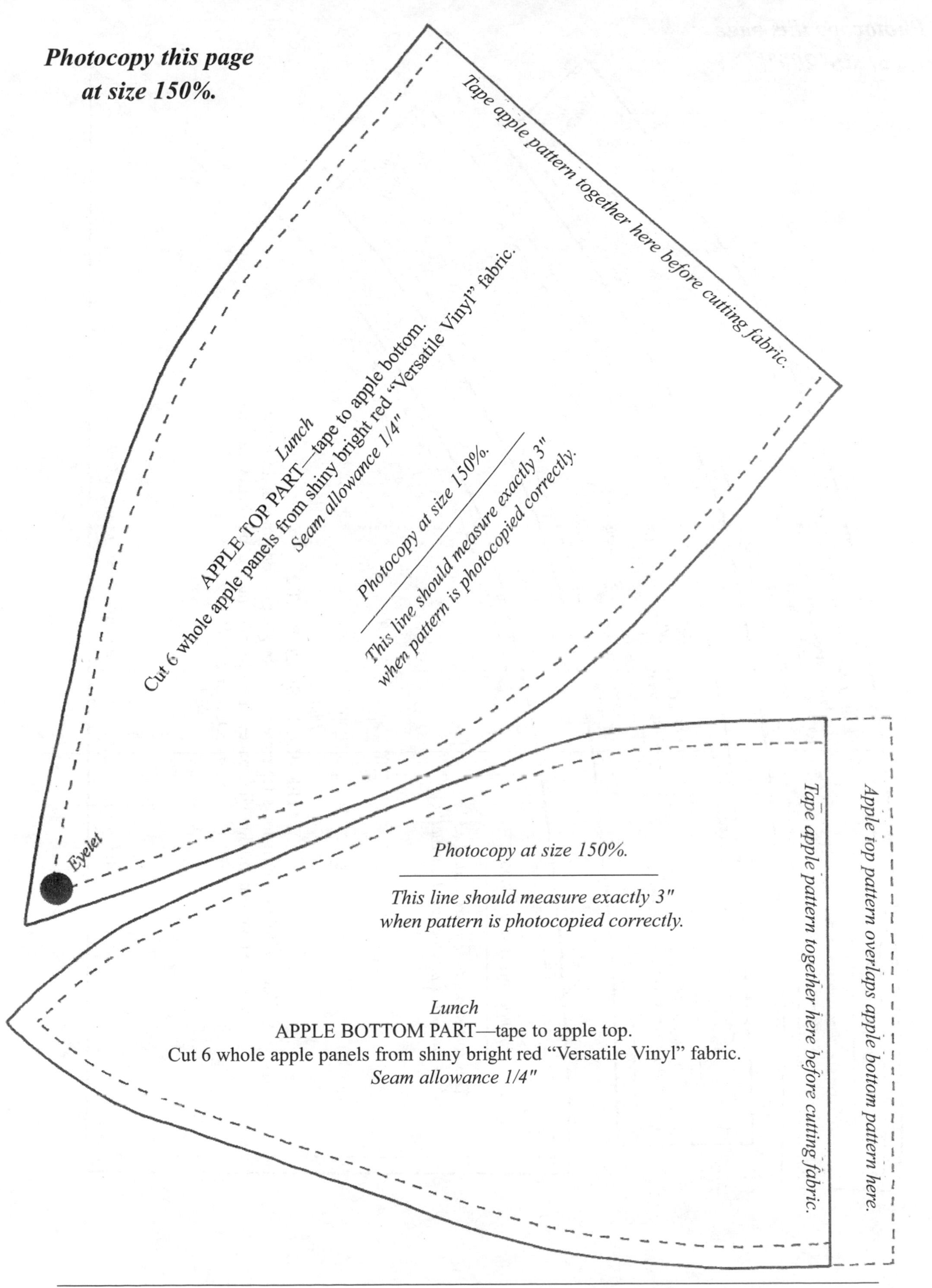
Photocopy this page
at size 150%.
Tape apple pattern together here before cutting fabric.
Lunch
APPLE TOP PART—tape to apple bottom.
Cut 6 whole apple panels from shiny bright red "Versatile Vinyl" fabric.
Seam allowance 1/4"
Photocopy at size 150%.
This line should measure exactly 3"
when pattern is photocopied correctly.
Eyelet
Photocopy at size 150%.
This line should measure exactly 3"
when pattern is photocopied correctly.
Lunch
APPLE BOTTOM PART—tape to apple top.
Cut 6 whole apple panels from shiny bright red "Versatile Vinyl" fabric.
Seam allowance 1/4"
Tape apple pattern together here before cutting fabric.
Apple top pattern overlaps apple bottom pattern here.

Photocopy this page at size 200%.

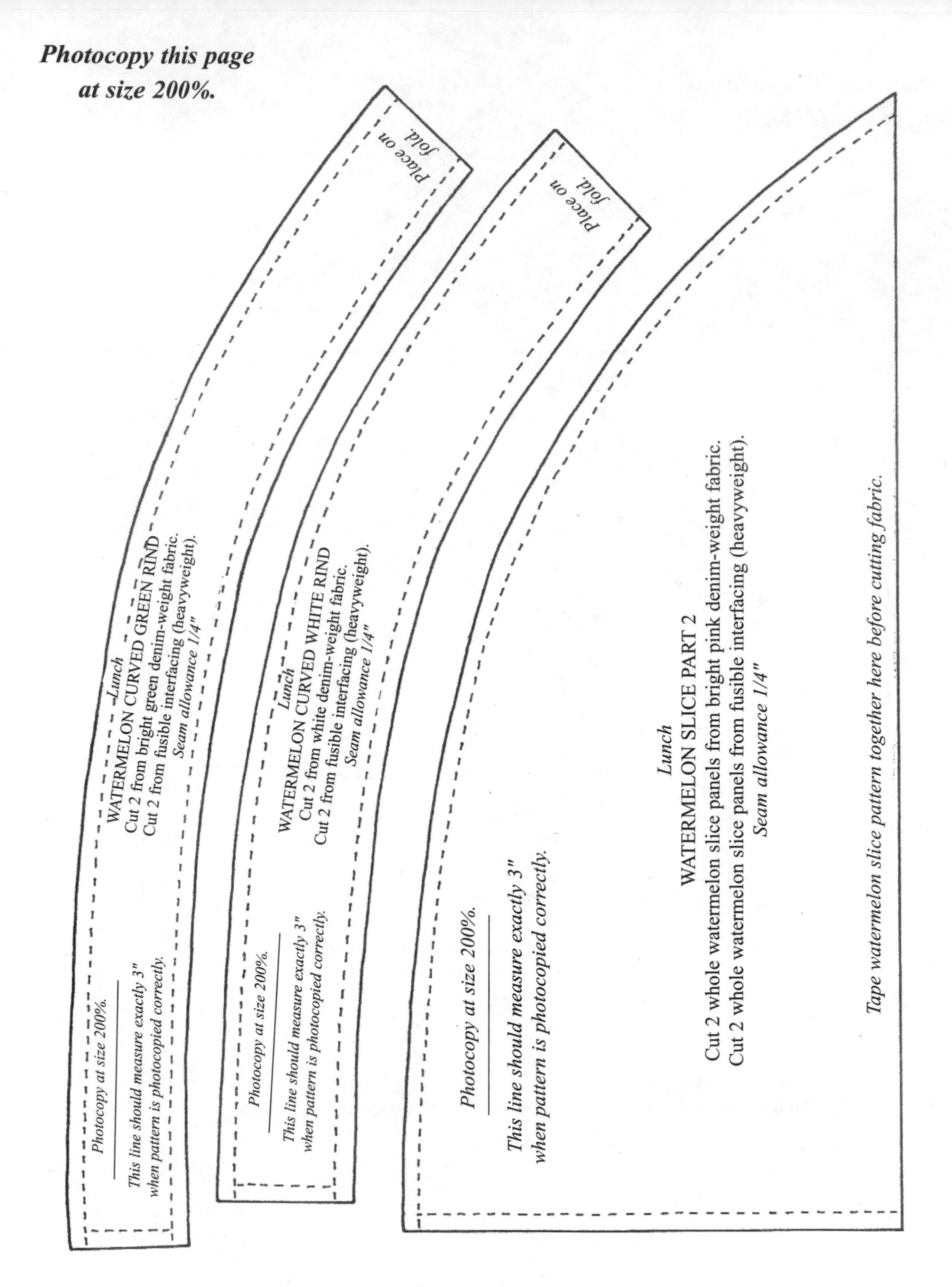

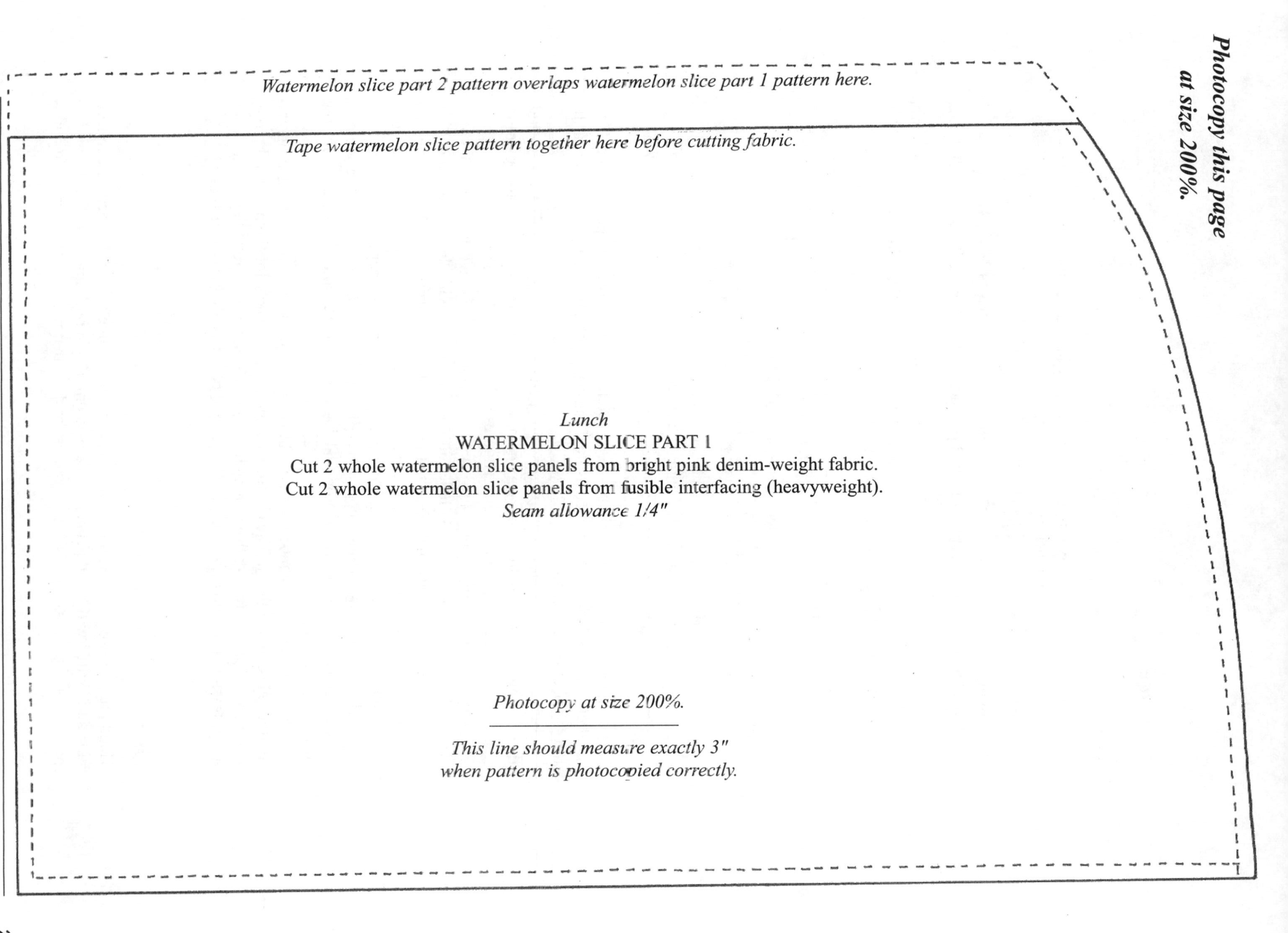

Photocopy this page
at size 200%.
Watermelon slice part 2 pattern overlaps watermelon slice part 1 pattern here.
Tape watermelon slice pattern together here before cutting fabric.
Lunch
WATERMELON SLICE PART 1
Cut 2 whole watermelon slice panels from bright pink denim-weight fabric.
Cut 2 whole watermelon slice panels from fusible interfacing (heavyweight).
Seam allowance 1/4"
Photocopy at size 200%.
This line should measure exactly 3"
when pattern is photocopied correctly.

Storage

You Will Need

1 sturdy, very large box (large enough to easily hold all of the *Lunch* props without crushing them)

2 copies of *Lunch* storage label

2 photocopies of the *Lunch* presentation notes/script (pages 169–74)

1 photocopy of puppet story finished product photos (figures 9-39 through 9-40)

Make two photocopies of the label provided below for the *Lunch* hand puppet prop and fill in the *date* and *name or initials* blanks. Cut out the labels and affix them securely to both ends of your storage container.

> ***Lunch***
>
> Denise Fleming (Holt, 1992)
>
> Prop created _______ by _________________
> DATE NAME OR INITIALS
>
> from patterns included in *Books in Bloom*
> by Kimberly Faurot (ALA, 2003)

The prop pieces for *Lunch* should be stored carefully to keep them in good shape. Place smaller or more delicate items such as the Mouse puppet, grapes, and pea pod near the top of the storage container.

Make two photocopies of the presentation notes/script (pages 169–74), and include them in the box along with the puppet and prop pieces. Also include a photocopy of the puppet story finished product photos (figures 9-39 through 9-40).

A professional storytelling copy of the original book *Lunch* by Denise Fleming (Holt, 1992) should either be included in the storage box with the prop or should be kept nearby in a professional "storytelling collection" so it may be shown when the prop is being presented. If you are unable to obtain a new copy of the book, investigate purchasing a used copy through one of the resources listed in chapter 10.

Make sure that the hand puppet storytelling pieces for *Lunch* by Denise Fleming are included on your storytelling props database or list (*see* chapter 2) as well as in your institution's inventory records.

Notify other staff members who might be able to include *Lunch* in their programming or classrooms that it is ready for use, and demonstrate it for them if at all possible. Make sure they realize that although the props look fairly sturdy, they are designed as professional resources, not as playthings, and could easily become damaged.

Summary

Hand puppets are a powerful tool. It is well worth the time it takes to become comfortable and skilled with hand puppetry as a medium. Begin building a small collection of puppets, and purchase or make accessories for them that will help them serve in multiple roles. Work toward using puppets to their full advantage in your classroom or library, incorporating them into your story programs and lesson plans. Use them to introduce an upcoming subject or story. "Interview" your puppets with a microphone on various topics, such as how they use addition and subtraction in their daily lives, or on the events that led up to the story you are about to share.

Present puppets yourself, and also encourage your students to do so. Puppets can enable children to experiment with alternate personalities and to address issues that they may be unable to manage directly. Provide sturdy puppets for the children in your classroom or library to enjoy on their own, and incorporate puppet making as art and craft projects for them to create.

As you explore the world of puppetry, it is important for you to both read about the art form and also to watch quality puppet performances whenever possible. You will be exposed to new ideas of things to create as well as to effective presentation techniques that will help you make your own performances come alive for your audiences.

10 Resources

Favorite Storytime Planners

Cobb, Jane. *I'm a Little Teapot! Presenting Preschool Storytime.* 2d ed. Vancouver, B.C.: Black Sheep Pr., 1996.

MacDonald, Margaret Read. *Bookplay: 101 Creative Themes to Share with Young Children.* North Haven, Conn.: Library Professional Pubns., 1995.

MacDonald, Margaret Read. *Booksharing: 101 Programs to Use with Preschoolers.* Hamden, Conn.: Library Professional Pubns., 1988.

Reid, Rob. *Family Storytime: Twenty-four Creative Programs for All Ages.* Chicago: American Library Assn., 1999.

Bibliography of Storybooks, Stories, and Poems Included or Mentioned in Books in Bloom

Allen, Pamela. *Who Sank the Boat?* New York: Coward-McCann, 1983.

Butler, Stephen. *The Mouse and the Apple.* New York: Morrow, 1994.

Ciardi, John. "I Wouldn't." In *Mice Are Nice,* compiled by Nancy Larrick. New York: Philomel Books, 1988.

Fleming, Denise. *Alphabet under Construction.* New York: Holt, 2002.

Fleming, Denise. *Lunch.* New York: Holt, 1992.

Gackenbach, Dick. *Poppy the Panda.* New York: Clarion, 1984.

Heine, Helme. *The Most Wonderful Egg in the World.* New York: Atheneum, 1983.

Krauss, Ruth. *The Carrot Seed.* New York: Harper, 1945.

Lionni, Leo. *A Color of His Own.* New York: Random, 1975.

Lionni, Leo. *Fish Is Fish.* New York: Random, 1970.

MacDonald, Margaret Read. "Witch's Brew." In *When the Lights Go Out: Twenty Scary Tales to Tell.* Bronx, N.Y.: Wilson, 1988.

Pinkwater, Daniel Manus. *The Big Orange Splot.* New York: Hastings, 1977.

Prelutsky, Jack. "A Frog, a Stick." In *A Pizza the Size of the Sun: Poems.* New York: Greenwillow, 1996.

Tolstoy, Alexei. *The Great Big Enormous Turnip.* Pictures by Helen Oxenbury. New York: Franklin, 1968.

Willard, Nancy. *The Nightgown of the Sullen Moon.* San Diego: HBJ, 1983.

Books for Further Professional Reading on the Topics and Media Covered in Books in Bloom

Baird, Bil. *The Art of the Puppet.* New York: Macmillan, 1965.

Baker, Augusta, and Ellin Greene. *Storytelling: Art and Technique.* 2d ed. New York: Bowker, 1987.

Bauer, Caroline Feller. *Caroline Feller Bauer's New Handbook for Storytellers: With Stories, Poems, Magic, and More.* Chicago: American Library Assn., 1993.

Bauer, Caroline Feller. *Leading Kids to Books through PUPPETS.* Chicago: American Library Assn., 1997.

Briggs, Diane. *101 Fingerplays: Stories and Songs to Use with Finger Puppets.* Chicago: American Library Assn., 1999.

Bruwelheide, Janis H. *The Copyright Primer for Librarians and Educators.* 2d ed. Chicago: American Library Assn., 1995.

Champlin, Connie. *Storytelling with Puppets.* 2d ed. Chicago: American Library Assn., 1998.

Crews, Kenneth D. *Copyright Essentials for Librarians and Educators.* Chicago: American Library Assn., 2000.

Currell, David. *Learning with Puppets.* Boston: Plays, 1980.

Engler, Larry, and Carol Fijan. *Making Puppets Come Alive: A Method of Learning and Teaching Hand Puppetry.* New York: Taplinger, 1973.

Flower, Cedric, and Alan Jon Fortney. *Puppets: Methods and Materials.* Worcester, Mass.: Davis, 1983.

Griffith, Christopher. *Puppet Cookbook: Recipes for Puppets from In the Heart of the Beast Puppet and Mask Theatre.* 2d ed. Minneapolis, Minn.: In the Heart of the Beast Puppet and Mask Theatre, 2000. (ISBN 0-9676776-0-2; In the Heart of the Beast Puppet and Mask Theatre, 1500 E. Lake Street, Minneapolis, MN 55407; 612.721.2535)

Hicks, Doris Lynn. *Flannelboard Classic Tales.* Chicago: American Library Assn., 1997.

Huck, Charlotte S. *Children's Literature in the Elementary School.* 7th ed. Dubuque, Iowa: McGraw-Hill, 2001.

Huff, Mary Jo. *Storytelling with Puppets, Props, and Playful Tales.* Palo Alto, Calif.: Monday Morning Books, 1998.

Hunt, Tamara, and Nancy Renfro. *Pocketful of Puppets: Mother Goose.* Austin, Tex.: Nancy Renfro Studios, 1982.

Hunt, Tamara, and Nancy Renfro. *Puppetry in Early Childhood Education.* Austin, Tex.: Nancy Renfro Studios, 1982.

Kelley, Robert P. *Paper Snowflakes Made Easy.* Mahwah, N.J.: Watermill Pr., 1990.

Koskey, Thomas Arthur. *How to Make and Use Flannel Boards: A Handbook for Teachers.* San Francisco: Fearon, 1961.

Lynch-Watson, Janet. *The Shadow Puppet Book.* New York: Sterling, 1980.

Minkel, Walter. *How to Do "The Three Bears" with Two Hands: Performing with Puppets.* Chicago: American Library Assn., 2000.

Painter, William M. *Story Hours with Puppets and Other Props.* Hamden, Conn.: Library Professional Pubns., 1990.

Pellowski, Anne. *The World of Storytelling.* Expanded and rev. ed. Bronx, N.Y.: Wilson, 1990.

Renfro, Nancy. *A Puppet Corner in Every Library.* Austin, Tex.: Nancy Renfro Studios, 1978.

Renfro, Nancy. *Puppets for Play Production.* New York: Funk & Wagnalls, 1969.

Renfro, Nancy, and Beverly Armstrong. *Make Amazing Puppets.* Santa Barbara, Calif.: Learning Works, 1979.

Roney, R. Craig. *The Story Performance Handbook.* Mahwah, N.J.: Lawrence Erlbaum Associates, 2001.

Sierra, Judy. *Fantastic Theater: Puppets and Plays for Young Performers and Young Audiences.* Bronx, N.Y.: Wilson, 1991.

Sierra, Judy. *The Flannel Board Storytelling Book.* Bronx, N.Y.: Wilson, 1987.

Sierra, Judy, and Robert Kaminski. *Multicultural Folktales: Stories to Tell Young Children.* Phoenix, Ariz.: Oryx Pr., 1991.

Simpson, Carol. *Copyright for Schools: A Practical Guide.* 3d ed. Worthington, Ohio: Linworth, 2001.

Talab, R. S. *Commonsense Copyright: A Guide for Educators and Librarians.* 2d ed. Jefferson, N.C.: McFarland, 1999.

VanSchuyver, Jan M. *Storytelling Made Easy with Puppets.* Phoenix, Ariz.: Oryx Pr., 1993.

Wilmes, Liz, and Dick Wilmes. *2's Experience Felt Board Fun.* Elgin, Ill.: Building Blocks, 1994.

Wilmes, Liz, and Dick Wilmes. *2's Experience Stories*. Elgin, Ill.: Building Blocks, 1999.

Wisniewski, David, and Donna Wisniewski. *Worlds of Shadow: Teaching with Shadow Puppetry*. Englewood, Colo.: Teacher Ideas Pr., 1997.

Internet Resources

Axtell Expressions, Inc.
www.axtell.com/manip.html
(manipulation tips for the beginning puppeteer)

Puppeteers of America
www.puppeteers.org

Puppetry Home Page
www.puppetry.info

Finding Out-of-Print or Used Books

www.abebooks.com

www.alibris.com

www.bibliofind.com

www.bookfinder.com

www.half.com

Sound Recordings

Educational Record Center
3233 Burnt Mill Drive, Suite 100
Wilmington, NC 28403-2698
888.372.4543 phone / 888.438.1637 fax
www.erckids.com

Kimbo Educational
P.O. Box 477 J
Long Branch, NJ 07740
800.631.2187 phone / 732.870.3340 fax
www.Kimboed.com
("Chicken Dance" on *All-Time Favorite Dances* sound recording)

Music for Little People
P.O. Box 1460
Redway, CA 95560-1460
707.923.3991 / 800.346.4445 phone
www.mflp.com

Hand Puppets and Finger Puppets

Axtell Expressions, Inc.
2889 Bunsen Avenue, Suite H
Ventura, CA 93003
805.642.7282 phone / 805.650.2139 fax
www.axtell.com

Folkmanis, Inc.
1219 Park Avenue
Emeryville, CA 94608
510.658.7677 phone / 510.654.7756 fax
www.folkmanis.com
(*see* website for distributor information)

Manhattan Toy
430 First Avenue N, Suite 500
Minneapolis, MN 55401
612.337.9600 / 800.541.1345 phone
612.341.4457 fax
www.manhattantoy.com
(*see* website or call for distributor information)

Playful Puppets, Inc.
11292 Landy Lane
Great Falls, VA 22066
703.430.4722 / 866.501.4931 phone
703.433.2411 fax
www.playfulpuppets.com
("Puppets That Swallow")

Puppet Safari
326 W. 11th Street
National City, CA 91950
619.477.1180 phone
www.puppetsafari.com

Ready-Made Storytelling Props and Miscellaneous

Book Props, LLC
1120 McVey Avenue
Lake Oswego, OR 97034
503.636.0330 / 800.636.5314 phone
503.636.8724 fax
www.bookprops.com

Childcraft Education Corp.
P.O. Box 3239
Lancaster, PA 17604
800.631.5652 phone / 888.532.4453 fax
www.childcraft.com

Kaplan Early Learning Company
1310 Lewisville-Clemmons Road
P.O. Box 609
Lewisville, NC 27023-0609
800.334.2014 phone / 800.452.7526 fax
www.kaplanco.com

Lakeshore Learning Materials
2695 E. Dominguez Street
Carson, CA 90810
800.421.5354 phone / 310.537.5403 fax
www.lakeshorelearning.com

Mister Anderson's Company
211 N. Perkins Boulevard
Burlington, WI 53105
262.767.0425 / 800.442.6555 phone
262.767.0862 fax
(many puppets and miscellaneous storytelling items; giant soft sculpture turnip and carrot; only sells tax-exempt, to schools and libraries)

Book Character Dolls and Toys

Crocodile Creek
2211 Roosevelt Road
Valparaiso, IN 46383
219.763.3234 / 800.230.8697 phone
219.476.9446 fax
www.crocodilecreek.com

MerryMakers Distribution, Inc.
6239 College Avenue, Suite 201
Oakland, CA 94618
510.596.9099 / 888.989.0454 phone
510.596.9033 fax
www.merrymakersinc.com

Cheap Novelty Items (Crowns and Miscellaneous Cool Stuff)

Kipp Brothers
P.O. Box 781080
Indianapolis, IN 46278
800.428.1153 phone / 800.832.5477 fax
www.kippbro.com
Showroom and warehouse:
9760 Mayflower Park Drive
Carmel, IN 46032

Oriental Trading Company, Inc.
P.O. Box 2308
Omaha, NE 68103-2308
800.228.2269 phone (orders)
800.228.0475 phone (customer service)
www.orientaltrading.com

Rhode Island Novelty
19 Industrial Lane
Johnston, RI 02919
800.528.5599 phone / 800.448.1775 fax
www.rinovelty.com

U.S. Toy Company, Inc.
13201 Arrington Road
Grandview, MO 64030-2886
800.255.6124 phone / 816.761.9295 fax
www.ustoy.com

Craft Supplies

Ben Franklin Crafts Home Office
800.992.9307 phone
www.benfranklinstores.com
Ben Franklin Crafts
2020 Weinbach Center Drive
Evansville, IN 47711
812.477.4602 phone
(provides mail-order service)

Crafts Direct
110 2nd Street S, Suite 101
Waite Park, MN 56387
320.654.0907 phone
www.craftsdirect.com
(provides mail-order service)

D C C (Decorator & Craft Corporation)
428 S. Zelta
Wichita, KS 67207
800.835.3013 phone / 316.685.7606 fax
(unpainted cardboard eggs, shaped boxes, and miscellaneous)

Schrock's International
110 Water Street
P.O. Box 538
Bolivar, OH 44612
330.874.3700 phone
800.426.4659 phone (orders only)
330.874.3773 fax
(wholesale prices; no returns)

Fabrics and Some Craft Supplies

Book Props, LLC
1120 McVey Avenue
Lake Oswego, OR 97034
503.636.0330 / 800.636.5314 phone
503.636.8724 fax
www.bookprops.com
("Show-a-Tale Fabric")

hancockfabrics.com
(website for Hancock Fabrics online)
3406 W. Main Street
Tupelo, MS 38801
www.hancockfabrics.com

joann.com
(website for Jo-Ann stores online)
800.525.4951 phone / 310.662.4401 fax
www.joann.com

Colored Acetate/Transparencies

The Art Mart
224 State Street
Madison, WI 53703
608.257.2249 phone/fax

Dick Blick Art Materials
P.O. Box 1267
Galesburg, IL 61402-1267
800.828.4548 phone / 800.621.8293 fax
www.dickblick.com

Graphic Products Corporation
1480 S. Wolf Road
Wheeling, IL 60090
708.537.9300 phone / 708.215.0111 fax
(self-adhesive gloss transparent Form-X film, Series 10000; also available from quality art stores)

Die-Cut Companies

Accu-Cut Systems
1035 E. Dodge Street
Fremont, NE 68025
402.721.4134 / 800.288.1670 phone
800.369.1332 fax
www.accucut.com

Ellison Educational Equipment, Inc.
25862 Commercentre Drive
Lake Forest, CA 92630-8804
949.598.8822 / 800.253.2238 phone
800.253.2240 fax
www.ellison.com

Flannel Boards and Velcro Boards

abc school supply
3312 N. Berkeley Lake Road
P.O. Box 100019
Duluth, GA 30096-9419
800.669.4222 phone / 800.933.2987 fax
www.abcschoolsupply.com

Demco
P.O. Box 7488
Madison, WI 53707-7488
800.356.1200 phone / 800.245.1329 fax
www.demco.com

Gaylord Bros.
P.O. Box 4901
Syracuse, NY 13221-4901
800.634.6307 phone / 800.272.3412 fax
www.gaylord.com

Highsmith, Inc.
W5527 State Road 106
P.O. Box 800
Fort Atkinson, WI 53538-0800
800.558.2110 phone / 800.835.2329 fax
www.highsmith.com

Kaplan Early Learning Company
1310 Lewisville-Clemmons Road
P.O. Box 609
Lewisville, NC 27023-0609
800.334.2014 phone / 800.452.7526 fax
www.kaplanco.com

Lakeshore Learning Materials
2695 E. Dominguez Street
Carson, CA 90810
800.421.5354 phone / 310.537.5403 fax
www.lakeshorelearning.com

The Library Store, Inc.
112 E. South Street
P.O. Box 964
Tremont, IL 61568
800.603.3536 phone / 800.320.7706 fax
www.thelibrarystore.com

General Library Supplies (Colored Corrugated Hinged-Lid Storage Boxes)

Demco
P.O. Box 7488
Madison, WI 53707-7488
800.356.1200 phone / 800.245.1329 fax
www.demco.com

Gaylord Bros.
P.O. Box 4901
Syracuse, NY 13221-4901
800.634.6307 phone / 800.272.3412 fax
www.gaylord.com

Highsmith, Inc.
W5527 State Road 106
P.O. Box 800
Fort Atkinson, WI 53538-0800
800.558.2110 phone / 800.835.2329 fax
www.highsmith.com

The Library Store, Inc.
112 E. South Street
P.O. Box 964
Tremont, IL 61568
800.603.3536 phone / 800.320.7706 fax
www.thelibrarystore.com

Overhead Projectors

abc school supply
3312 N. Berkeley Lake Road
P.O. Box 100019
Duluth, GA 30096-9419
800.669.4222 phone / 800.933.2987 fax
www.abcschoolsupply.com

Demco
P.O. Box 7488
Madison, WI 53707-7488
800.356.1200 phone / 800.245.1329 fax
www.demco.com

Gaylord Bros.
P.O. Box 4901
Syracuse, NY 13221-4901
800.634.6307 phone / 800.272.3412 fax
www.gaylord.com

Highsmith, Inc.
W5527 State Road 106
P.O. Box 800
Fort Atkinson, WI 53538-0800
800.558.2110 phone / 800.835.2329 fax
www.highsmith.com

Kaplan Early Learning Company
1310 Lewisville-Clemmons Road
P.O. Box 609
Lewisville, NC 27023-0609
800.334.2014 phone / 800.452.7526 fax
www.kaplanco.com

Lakeshore Learning Materials
2695 E. Dominguez Street
Carson, CA 90810
800.421.5354 phone / 310.537.5403 fax
www.lakeshorelearning.com

The Library Store, Inc.
112 E. South Street
P.O. Box 964
Tremont, IL 61568
800.603.3536 phone / 800.320.7706 fax
www.thelibrarystore.com

Kimberly K. Faurot has provided children's services in public libraries since 1991. A strong proponent of quality materials and services for children, she has created numerous visual storytelling pieces for use in library programming. Faurot has also designed several book character dolls for the MerryMakers, Inc. toy company. She earned a master's degree in library science from Indiana University.